SATHYA SAI SPEAKS

VOLUME XXVI

(Eleventh Volume in the New Series)

Discourses of
BHAGAVAN SRI SATHYA SAI BABA
delivered during 1993

PRASHAANTHI NILAYAM

SRI SATHYA SAI BOOKS & PUBLICATIONS TRUST
Prashaanthi Nilayam P.O. 515134,
Anantapur District, Andhra Pradesh, INDIA
Grams: BOOKTRUST   STD: O8555   ISD: 91-8555
Phone: 87375, 87236, Fax: 91-8555-87236 & 87390

International Standard Book No. 81 - 7208 - 217 - 7
81 - 7208 - 118 - 9 (SET)

Published by
The Convenor,
Sri Sathya Sai Books & Publications Trust
Prashaanthi Nilayam, India, Pin Code 515 134
Phone : 87375, 87236   Fax : 91-8555-87236 & 87390

Typeset   by : **Sharptech Graphics, Mumbai.**

Price : Rs. **49/–**

Printed by: **Vipla Printers Pvt. Ltd.**, Nallakunta,
Hyderabad - 500 044. Phone: 7636242

Publisher's Note

SATHYA SAI SPEAKS series is, according to late Prof. N. Kasthuri, the original translator and compiler, "a fragrant boquet of flowers that never fade or falter." These discourses were delivered by Svaami out of profound compassion towards seekers of Truth during the last few decades. The discourses delivered after 1982 are printed for the first time, which have not been published in book form so far. Volume XVI, covering the year 1983 is the first in the new series. Further new volumes are being added, one Volume for each year, covering the discourses delivered from 1983.

The retention of *Sanskrith* words on page after page, without their English equivalents in most cases, was causing great confusion to readers, especially foreigners, who were not familiar with *Sanskrith*. An attempt has been made to aid easy reading by replacing *Sanskrith* words with English equivalents wherever they do not affect Baba's original expression. *Sanskrith* words have been retained wherever it was felt necessary to preserve the essence of the original expression of Baba and where the English equivalents may not do full justice to the text in the particular context. However, in all such places, the English equivalents have been given along with *Sanskrith* words. Some very commonly understood *Sanskrith* words or such words which are repeated too often are retained without English meanings to retain the original flavour of Baba's discourses. Furthermore, a more phonetic English spelling of *Sanskrith* words has been used to facilitate better pronunciation of *Sanskrith* words written in the English script as favoured by Bhagavaan.

A Glossary has been added in all the editions to provide comprehensive and detailed explanation of the more important *Sanskrith* words for the benefit of lay readers who may be interested in *Vedhic* religion and philosophy. It is hoped that this will be of great help to devotees to understand more clearly the topics of Baba's discourses covering a wide spectrum of *Vedhic* philosophy.

The volumes of Baba's discourses are being brought out in a larger format, Demy Octavo size, so that they can be companion books with other publications in private libraries. Computerised typesetting using a larger size of type, a more readable type face and better line spacing have been adopted for more comfortable reading of books, especially by elder readers. Very long paragraphs have been split into shorter paragraphs and suitable sub-headings have been added in every page, to relieve the monotony on the eye and to make reading a pleasure.

Better quality paper, improved binding, dust cover with new designs and foil printing and plastic cover have been adopted for these volumes for better preservation and durable shelf-life of the volumes.

It is hoped that the revised and enlarged volumes of "Sathya Sai Speaks" Series upto Volume XV and fresh ones from Volume XVI onwards, will be of great benefit to earnest seekers in spiritual realm.

Our sincere thanks to Sri V. S. Krishnamurty who compiled the discourses, to Sri G. V. Subba Rao, who edited them and to Smt. Sandya Verma, Creative Director, Fountainhead Communications (P) Ltd., Chennai, for designing the title cover. They are born, as it were, to serve the Sathya Sai fraternity.

Convenor
Sri Sathya Sai Books and Publications Trust
Prashaanthi Nilayam (India).

Contents

CHAPTER 1

Purity—the path to Divinity

The Lord of the Universe permeates the entire Cosmos
Remaining invisible in the visible Universe,
The Cosmos Consciousness illumines everything
Like the thread that runs through a necklace of gems.

THE phenomenal world that is perceived by us is called *Vishvam* (the cosmos). This Cosmos is *Kaaryam* (action or effect). Every action is preceded by a cause. This cause is God. Hence, God and the Cosmos are related as Cause and Effect. The relationship is inter-dependent and inseparable.

Vishvam means that which has emerged from the Divine with many limbs. *Vish + Vam* means that which is pervaded exceptionally. Another meaning for *Vishvam* ь *Vaayu* (air). Air is all-pervading. *"Vishnuh Vishvasvaruupah"* (The Cosmos is the embodiment of Vishnu). Vishnu also means all-pervasive.

There is no specific proof for the Divine. Hence, He is called *Aprameya* (Immeasurable). For such an Infinite being Time is the proof and Time is the basis. God is adored as *"Samvathsaraaya Namah."* *"Samvathsara"* means *Daivasvaruupam* (the form of the Divine). The mere passage of 365 days does not amount to *Samvathsara*. *Samvathsara* refers to one who is the *Kaalaathmah* (Time-Spirit). Spirit means *Brahman* (the Supreme Absolute). The *Brahman* Principle refers to the *Chaithanyam* (consciousness), that is omnipresent. *Brahman* has no specific form. It is present in all human beings as Consciousness.

God is the Consumer of Time itself

For man to recognise the *Brahman*, he has to comprehend the nature of that which transcends Time. Time is consuming the body. God is the Consumer of Time itself. Hence, the *Vedhas* have declared that *"Kaala-Kaalaprapannaanaam, Kaalah kim karishyathi"* (Time is powerless against those who have taken refuge in the Over-Lord of Time).

Man's joys and sorrows, happiness or misery are not dependent on Time. They are based on man's actions. Time has no relations or friends. Time is not subordinate to anyone. All are subject to Time. Hence, if one has to realise the Divine, who is the Lord of Time, one has to carry out His injunctions. God looks with love only at such a person.

In this context, the Geetha has described the traits of the devotee who is dear to the Lord:

> *Anapekshah shuchir-Dakshah*
> *Udhaaseeno Gathavyathah*

Sarvaarambha parithyaagee
Yo madbhaktah sa me priyah

(That devotee is dear to me who is free from desire, who is pure in body and mind, who is resolute, unconcerned, free from sorrow and has renounced all sense of doership).

True meaning of "desireless" actions

Anapekshah: In this world, man, with his body, senses and mind cannot be free from desires. But how is he to become *Anapeksha* (free from expectation)? When he performs actions, regarding himself, as the doer, the actions become fetters that bind him. All actions which are performed with the feeling that they are intended as offerings to please the Divine, do not lead to bondage. They become *Anapeksha* (desireless actions). One has to recognise that it is the Divine principle in all beings which is getting all actions done through human beings as instruments. As long as man regards himself as *karthruthva* (the doer) and *bhokthruthva* (enjoyer) he cannot escape from the consequences of his actions.

When a man regards a certain piece of land as his, the crops grown on it will belong to him. The *Geetha* teaches that when actions are done as offerings to God, they become "desireless" actions. Man has taken birth to perform his duties and not to enjoy power or assert his rights. When one's duty is performed, the right comes of its own accord. Men today fight for their "rights" and forget their duties. Hence discharge of duty comes first. It is through duty that man realises God.

Inner purity is vital for all aspirants

Shuchih: This refers to purity. It is not enough if the body is clean. Inner purity is essential. The latter, in fact, is more essential than the former. For the proper enjoyment of all things, purity of mind is essential. Whatever sacred acts you may do in the external world, if you have no purity of mind and heart, all of them are valueless. The food cooked in an untinned vessel will be spoilt even if all the ingredients are good. Likewise, in the vessel of the heart, the inside must be purified by *Prema* (love). Then, all that one consumes will be wholesome. Hence, purity is vital for all aspirants; without it, all man's actions get tainted. Actions done with an impure heart can only produce undesirable results.

Whatever good results you want to secure in the external world, inner purity is the basis.

Dakshah: This refers to the determination that is needed to accomplish anything. One must have the fortitude and resoluteness to achieve one's purpose, whatever might be the obstacles in the way. To accomplish any sacred task one has to possess this determination. *Daksha* signifies this quality of unwavering determination in the devotee.

Udhaaseenah: One who is unaffected by whatever happens. This means that one should be totally free from selfishness. He must consider the performance of his duties as the sole purpose of his existence. The human body is the result of past actions. Man is bound to the world by his actions. The body is the primary requisite for the performance of *Dharma* (right action). Indifferent to fame or blame, not seeking power or position, one should perform one's duties selflessly. Do not be swayed by any consideration other than your duty. Whether it be in a political organisation or in regard to a personal matter, or in relation to national issues, you should act according to the dictates of your conscience, without any other concern. One can become a courageous leader only if he performs his duties in this spirit. All actions must be done in a spirit of service. Only one who serves is fit to become a leader. The man who seeks a position, can he be pure-hearted? No. Forgetting power and position, concentrating only on one's duties, men should engage themselves in action. This is the true import of *Udhaaseenah.*

Act in the present to get rid of mental anguish

Gathavyathah: Vyathah refers to anguish in the mind. Falling a prey to mental anguish, man is totally confused. Man has a tendency to brood over the past. Of what use it is to worry about what has happened? Nor should one worry about the future which is unknown and uncertain. Bear in mind only the present. This is the way to get rid of mental anguish— *Gathavyathah.* The present is the product of the past and the parent of the future. When you act properly in the present, the future will take care of itself. Do what is appropriate for the present moment. If there are no expectations, there will be no disappointments.

Sarvaarambha-parithyaagee: This means do not give room for ostentation in any of your undertakings. The world today is immersed in ostentation and egoism. What does it matter whether the world praises you or decries you? For instance, why should a devotee show off his devotion to earn the approbation of others? His devotion must be for pleasing the Lord and not for earning the approval of the world. In the spiritual path, what matters is the inner joy you experience. That is the key to self-satisfaction. *Sarvaarambha parithyaagee* means one who is prepared to relinquish all his possessions and acquisitions including wealth, knowledge and strength.

Thus, it is only the devotee who has these six qualities that is dear to the lord. It is such a devotee whom the Lord loves.

Man is ruined by six enemies—lust, anger, delusion, greed, pride and envy. Equally man is redeemed by the six qualities mentioned in the above mentioned Geetha *shloka*.

Without cultivating these qualities, without cherishing such pure feelings, what is the use of immersing one's self in so-called devotion? It is only a hallucination, which cannot lead man to the experience of the Divine.

True devotee is one who practises what he has learnt

If you are true devotees, examine for yourselves how long you have been listening to Svaami's discourses? Years have gone by. To what extent have you gone spiritually? How far have you put into practice Svaami's teachings? What is the use of merely listening? Is it not all a waste? You are listening, but not putting the teachings into practice. Hunger can be appeased only when the cooked food is eaten. Only the devotee who practises what he has learnt is a true devotee.

Your practices are different from precepts. You are leading selfish and self-centred lives. Such a life is led by birds and beasts. Even these exhibit selflessness often. Man alone leads a totally selfish existence. It is a shame to call such persons as devotees. One must strive at least to practise one or two of the teachings. This calls for *Thrikarana shuddhi*— purity in thought, word and deed. Without such triple purity, man ceases to be human.

Today, human values have given place to demonic tendencies. Animality has become dominant. The Divine has been forgotten. Consequently, all spiritual exercises are filled with ostentation.

What is needed is sincerity. One should not do anything for the sake of earning other's approbation. If one acts with sincerity, he will be duly respected. But if one merely preaches and does not practise, he will be ignored. How can such a person expect to win the grace of the Lord?

Self-interest cannot be totally given up, but there should be a limit to it. Everything in the world, including the body, organs like the eyes and other things are governed by strict adherence to limits. When the limits are exceeded disease sets in and the consequences may be serious.

The mortal man and the Immortal Divine

Among youth today, there is no regard for the limits to be observed in any sphere. Whether it be eating or sleeping or wandering about, they indulge in excesses in the name of freedom. What is real freedom? It is *Aathma Jnaana* (knowledge of the Spirit), *Aathma Nigraham* (self-control) and *Aatmaanandam* (Bliss of the Spirit) which constitute real freedom. Man is mortal and the Divine is immortal. In the mortal human being, there is the immortal Divine Spirit. In the field of the heart, there is a *Kalpatharu* (wish-fulfilling tree). The tree is surrounded by bushes and briars. When these are removed, the tree will be visible. This wish-fulfilling tree is within each person, but it is encompassed by the bad qualities in man. When these qualities are eliminaced, the celestial tree will be recognised. This is the *saadhana* that each one has to perform. This is not the quest for something new. It is to experience what is yours. The entire cosmos is within you. The Universe is permeated by *Brahman*. One should be lucky to get this experience.

How to experience the *Aathma?*

How is the *Aathma* experienced? It is the consciousness that is experienced in the interval between one *sankalpa* (thought) and another.

This may be illustrated by an example. Once, a man holding a time-piece in his hand and listening to the endless tick-tick of the second-hand, asked the time-piece whether it has any rest at all. The time-piece announced: "You simpleton! I have all the rest I need. It is the interval between one tick and another!" The "rest" is given by the "Rest watch." "Watch" means "look out." Seeing the watch, you have to look at the "rest" indicated by it. This is the way lessons are learnt in their spiritual journey.

When you want to swim across a river, you push the water ahead of you, behind you so that you may move forward. Today, people do not make this effort. They remain stagnant, going through the same experiences all the time. With the result, that they do not comprehend higher ideas.

For instance, there is the example of the ocean. All kinds of rivers flow into the ocean. It absorbs all the waters, but its level hardly rises and all the water that comes in becomes saltish. What happens to the water that rises from the sea as vapour and cloud? It is pure and sweet. The clouds, when they produce thunder, proudly declare that by going up from the sea, they have achieved eminence as well as purity. Moreover, the clouds come down as rain and nourish the crops on earth. Can all the waters of the ocean nourish a farm? No. Only the transformation of the sea-water into vapour and clouds can serve this purpose.

If one wishes to go up spiritually, one has to get away from the low level. Only then, will it be possible for a person to engage himself in service to others.

Unity is supremely important

It is not time that is responsible for all the chaos and violence in the nation and for all the difficulties experienced by the people. Men's thoughts are responsible for all these. These thoughts are filled with selfishness. It is because of these selfish and self-centred people that the nation is suffering from so many troubles.

As long as self-interest prevails there can be no unity. Without unity you cannot experience happiness. Therefore, unity is all important. With the strength derived from unity, you can accomplish anything. The weakness of the nation is due to growing discord between man and man. Unity is supremely important. This calls for the shedding of selfishness to some extent.

The years are passing endlessly. It is now 1992 years since the birth of Christ. After nearly 2000 years what is it the people have learnt? What ideals are they upholding? People are celebrating the advent of the New year, but what are they doing to improve their conduct? This is what matters. Without it the celebrations are meaningless.

Act according to your conscience

Jesus taught many good lessons. Allah gave many high teachings. Raama and Krishna taught many good lessons. What have people gained from all this? How far have they tried to put this into practice? There are numerous persons who read the Bhagavath Geetha everyday. There are persons propagating the Geetha in every street. Preachers have multiplied but the number of those practising the precepts is dwindling.

People talk about what Svaami has been saying. How many are practising what Svaami says even to the slightest extent? No. What, then, is the use of all this? Whether it is Svaami's teachings or the instructions given by elders, whatever is good you should put into practice. You must act according to whatever your conscience tells is good. This is the way to honour the great ones. Not to practise their teaching is to disrespect them.

Joy is not derived from the mere advent of a New Year. All people want to know whether the New Year will bring better progress and improvement in the general condition. Having regard to time, place and circumstances, some good and bad things may occur. If, however, people desire an improvement in the state of affairs they have to change their attitude. It will be helpful if the time factor is favourable for change. This month, January, is not quite promising. January 1st starts on *Ashtami,* the eighth day after the New Moon. The end of the month January 31st will also be an *Ashtami.* All kinds of difficulties are likely during the month.

The New Year appears to have started on an *Ashtami,* which is considered inauspicious but this should not cause any apprehension among the people. With purity of heart, anything can be accomplished. Even the course of destiny can be changed by human will power.

Only the Divine has a free Will

Some students today talk about free Will. Only the Divine has free Will. Man is endowed with a Will but not a free Will. When the Divine free Will moves, the human Will also operates. There are a myriad leaves in a tree but not a leaf will move in the absence of wind. The leaves have no free Will but they have a Will which can be swayed when a breeze blows. In the tree of life human beings are like leaves. When the Divine Will blows the human Will begins to move.

Thus, there is need for the coming together of Divine Will and the human Will. Then, there will be a blossoming of human nature. Man can never achieve anything by his own efforts. There is something which a man accomplishes without much effort on his part. There are other things which he is unable to accomplish even with his best efforts. What is the reason? It is on account of the play of the Divine Will.

How the Divine operates may be known from two examples from every one's experience. The heart beats and the lungs breathe without any conscious human effort. These are the results of the operation of laws of nature according to the Divine Will. There is Nature on one side and human effort on the other. The two should function in unison. When there is such unity you have purity. That purity leads to divinity. These are not three different things but three stages in the process of a tender fruit achieving ripeness.

Bhaarath's foremost need today is unity. When the nation is in peril all parties should come together. There is no room here for ideological or partisan interests. All should regard themselves as the children of Bhaarath. All should have the nation's interest in their forefront. When this view prevails the nation's welfare is assured.

Help ever, Hurt never

Students! Regard every second as a new year and act on that basis. You need not wait for the passing of twelve months to embark on any enterprise. Transform yourselves every moment. Get rid of the bad old ideas; that will herald the birth of the new year. Take part in service activities to sanctify your lives. Adhere to righteous conduct. Live upto the motto: Help ever, Hurt never. This is the essence of the message of Vyaasa's eighteen puranas.

In rendering service you must have total dedication. For instance when you have to attend on a patient you should not leave the patient for the sake of having Svaami's *dharshan.* Your first duty is to look after the patient. Your devotion will be mere show if you leave the patient in the lurch and go for Svaami's *dharshan*. Duty is God. Work is Worship. Some nurses are behaving in this manner. They imagine that they are filled with devotion but this is not devotion. This is hurt, not help. This is not proper. God will not be pleased with this kind of "devotion." You must be by the side of the patient when he is in pain. This is real service to Svaami. But this does not happen. When delivery cases have to be attended to, instead of looking after them, people come to Svaami. This is not right at all.

In our old hospital some nurses used to behave in this manner. They are not good devotees at all. They are merely putting on the cloak of devotion. Duty comes first. Divine grace will come according to your desserts. Devotion may be there, but duty should be the first concern.

This applies to students also. They have to attend to their duties first. If duties are neglected, any pretence of devotion is merely a show. It is even a form of deception.

See the Divine in every patient

A patient should be regarded as Naaraayana Himself. You may come to Svaami in your free time. I have been saying these things for many years. But how many are acting up to them? Very few. In this manner, they are not only neglecting their duties but also acting against the directive of Svaami.

Hence, you should see the Divine in every patient and render service in the feeling that God is the Indweller in all beings. This will promote your spiritual progress. When you regard yourselves as devotees of Svaami, you have to bring glory to Svaami's name. If you behave in a wrong way, you are betraying Svaami.

God alone is the Master and so follow Him

All the world's problems today are due to selfishness. Individuals are concerned about the welfare of themselves and their families and do not care what happens to the rest of the world. It should be realised that the welfare of the individual is related to the welfare of society, the nation and the world. Students must develop a broad outlook. Selfishness and narrowness of outlook are more prevalent among the educated than among the villagers and tribal folk. The evil practices prevailing in big cities are not to be found even in jungles. Yudhishthira learnt that the educated man who had bad qualities was truly blind. Educated persons should develop discrimination, humility and a right sense of values. Students should try to enquire into the cause of the world's problems, seek remedies for them and live in unity.

If you carry out the injunctions of the Divine, all will be well with you. Every one is selfish in this world. God alone is selfless. He alone has the authority to confer joy even on selfish persons. He alone is the Master. Follow the Master.

Discourse on 1.1.1993 at Prashaanthi Nilayam.

CHAPTER 2

Sanctify sports and games

The advent of the Sankraanthi festival is greeted
by farmers who have brought home their harvest,
singing with joy.

THIS sacred and auspicious Makara Sankraanthi
is a divine occasion for people to transform their
lives so that they may experience the divinity, the
grandeur and greatness of human birth.

Whatever possessions and luxuries one may have,
They will not confer peace of mind.
Only when Godly feelings are developed,
Man will realise peace and bliss.

In this mundane world, what people regard
ordinarily as *jnaana* (knowledge) is not proper *jnaana*
at all. *Aathmajnaana* (knowledge of the Self) alone is

true knowledge. *Aathma* and *Jnaana* are synonymous. *Jnaana* is fundamental. It cannot be got through thought or sense perceptions. All that is acquired as knowledge about the things of the world is not *jnaana*. *Jnaana* is that which remains after the mind is stilled.

Students! Remember that wealth lost can be regained, health lost can be recovered, but time lost is lost forever. Hence, do not waste time. Time is God. Sanctify the time given to you by worthy deeds, experience bliss and share it with others.

Commercialisation of sport has lowered its value

Sports and Arts are intended to give pleasure. But the commercialisation of sports and music has lowered their value, together with the decline in human values. There should be no room for hatred or jealousy in games and sports. Our Institute students should engage themselves in sports for health and enjoyment. The participation of students coming from different regions and different backgrounds in games should be conducive to the promotion of unity. Even games should be regarded as sacred. Thereby, the participants become holy.

Students! Uphold your human status by developing firm faith in the Divine. Men act on faith in a hundred trivial things in daily life but why don't they have firm faith in the *Vedhic* dictum that they are one with the Divine—*Tath Thvam Asi* (Thou art That)? Because immersed in sensual pleasures, they are oblivious to their real potency and state.

In worldly matters, every action has a subject, object and predicate, as in the statement: "Raama killed a dog." But this rule does not apply to the actions of the Divine. He is the doer, He is the deed and He is the object of action (*Kartha, Karma* and *Kaarana*). No one is competent to enquire into the actions of the Divine. One cannot know how the Divine is directing his actions in relation to his past. Each one should carry out his self-examination himself. Students should continue spiritual exercises together with academic studies.

Regard yourselves as instruments of the Divine

Men should realise that they are entitled only to carry out their duties without concern for the fruits thereof. Duties come first. The results will come in due course. Men should realise how so many vital things are happening without any conscious efforts on their part. Their breathing, the functioning of their hearts and digestive organs are taking place naturally without any effort on their part. Even the time and manner of one's death are dependent on the Will of the Divine. However, man should regard himself as an instrument of the Divine. This was the advice Krishna gave to Arjuna. After Arjuna has exhausted all his questions to Krishna and got the answers from Krishna, his final decision was: *"Karishye vachanam thava"* (I shall abide by what you say).

Priding himself on his talents and powers, man ruins himself. He does not realise that all his powers come form God. But it is in his power to ruin himself by the misuse of his talents.

No one can know the origin of anything. For example, there is a green gram seed. Who can trace its genealogy? But one can recognise its future. The moment it is placed in the mouth and munched, that will be its end. Its origin is not known, but its end is in our hands. This is the reason why man is enjoined to concern himself about his end. Do not worry about rebirth because that is not in your power. Strive only to ensure that your end is pure and sacred. That calls for *saadhana* (spiritual practice). Many imagine that the quest for God is *saadhana*. There is no need to search for God. When the God is all-pervading, inside and outside, where is the need to search for Him? The only *saadhana* one has to practise is to get rid of the *Anaathma bhaava* (identification of the self with the body). *Anaathma* is that which is impermanent. When you give up the impermanent, you realise what is permanent and eternal.

Man today foolishly seeks to enjoy all things indiscriminately. This is wrong. One must enjoy what is good and wholesome and eschew what is bad and unwholesome. In spiritual. terms, this means that one should give up the impermanent physical objects and realise the *Aathma* that is permanent. This alone is true *saadhana*—not various forms of worship and meditation, which are not genuinely concentrated on God.

Combine studies with elevating actions

All acts should be performed in spirit of dedication, realizing that God is omnipresent. Then bliss will be experienced.

Students should combine normal studies with the refinement of their way of living through *Samskaaras* (elevating actions). This refinement cannot be got from teachers or books, but only by one's daily conduct.

Some students refrain from taking part in sports and games on the pretext that they are not interested in winning prizes. This is not genuine detachment, but only a form of laziness. Participation in sports and games is necessary for your health and recreation.

Our Institute students are doubtless filled with devotion and faith. But together with these, they should cultivate humility and discipline. Their bhaviour should be exemplary. When Svaaami's car is going, students run beside it faster than the car. This is a bad example to others. During *bhajan* sessions students are eager to sit as near as Svaami as possible. But in their eagerness they rush forward and fall upon each other in a manner which may cause serious collisions. Is this a good example for others? No. Students should set a good example even in small matters like these.

Students have abundant love for Svaami but this is exhibited in unseemly ways. There should be restraint in doing anything.

Life is a game! Play it!

Students think that sports events are confined to a few days in January. On the contrary, they should regard life itself as one continuous game. Life is a game! Play it! Treat the play as an ideal. Thereby you will be adhering to your ideals wherever you go.

Understand the true meaning of discipline. It is not something that should be observed only when you are in the hostel. Discipline must accompany you like your shadow. After leaving College, when you get employed, then also you should observe discipline. Discipline is the life-breath of man. It is like the spine for the human body.

Moreover, students should take care to avoid undue risk in their physical feats. You may desire to please Svaami to the maximum extent. But if you sustain injuries, will it give joy to Svaami? Your safety is important. All the spectators should feel happy. Your displays should be attractive without being unduly hazardous. You may perform thrilling feats. But do not give room for anxiety to others. Svaami is concerned about your welfare. Whatever you do, it should be pleasing and enjoyable. Where there is devotion and earnestness, nothing serious may happen, thanks to the grace of Bhagavaan.

Devotion earns the grace of God

One student fell from a height with the head downwards. Doctors felt that it was a serious case and that the boy should be sent to Hyderabad. But I declared that it was nothing serious and that all would be well with him. The boy is full of devotion for Svaami. Without any bandage or treatment, he was all-right. (Svaami summoned the student to come on stage. The entire audience cheered as the student came walking to Svaami). Look at this boy. The doctors said that his entire leg has sustained a fracture. How did he come here after the severe fall? His devotion and faith helped him to overcome the effects of the fall.

Hence, if devotion and earnestness are present, even great dangers can be averted. Dangers may come from any cause. But even mountains of danger can be removed by the grace of God. But that does not mean you may take any risk. You should be cautious. Moreover, when some hazardous exercises are performed, there should be safety measures to meet any untoward contingencies. Soft mattresses should be kept on the ground. Such precautions should be taken by the organisers of the sports events.

Cars for hostels presented by Svaami

The students from the Brindhaavan Campus put up a good show. They spent money from their own pockets to go to several places and arrange for attractive programmes. They suffered form lack of adequate facilities. Our Prashaanthi Nilayam students, despite the nearness of the old hospital, have oftentimes need to go to the speciality hospital by taxi or auto-rickshaw.

You have witnessed the superb performance of the Primary School children. Not even the grown-ups reached the level of their excellence. All their programmes were designed by themselves without any outside help. This is an amazing achievement. Their displays were done with ease and were thoroughly enjoyable. Likewise, the performance of the girl students from Ananthapur was splendid. Even they desired to perform some hazardous feats. They showed great presence of mind in their exercises. No accidents occurred. Their only concern was to please Svaami and win His approbation.

All the students from all the three campuses are full of devotion to Svaami. To meet the needs of the four Institutions in regard to transport facilities during emergencies. I am presenting cars to each of the three Institute campuses—Brindhaavan, Prashaanthi Nilayam and Ananthapur—and one for the Primary School. In view of the high cost of petrol, they are being given diesel-driven cars. Students, however, should use the vehicles carefully. The Wardens and Principals must see to this.

The cars should not be entrusted to juveniles. I am handing over the keys of the cars to the Wardens of the Brindhaavan Campus, the Prashaanthi Nilayam Campus and the Primary School. The key of the car for the Ananthapur hostel has already been given.

I bless you all that you should continue to give joy to your parents and others by your performances in the future and acquit yourselves well in every way.

Discourse in the Puurnachandhra
Auditorium on 14-1-1993.

Hate breeds fear; hate is the seedbed of anxiety, sacndal and falsehood. It drains your mind of peace. You may have light without oil, fire without smoke, breeze without a bearer fanning you, a chillness in the air of your room in the sizzling heat of summer— but, unless you are at peace with yourselves and with those around you, your pulse will be quick and your blood will be racing in rage and rancour. Love alone can alleviate anxiety and allay fear.

—BABA

CHAPTER 3

The predicament of man today

The influence of the Western style of life
and the alien language has eroded
The glorious culture and righteous conduct
of the people of Bhaarath.
It is high time Bhaaratheeyas woke up
and made efforts to restore the
Wisdom and Culture of their motherland
to its ancient glory.

THE primary requisites for ensuring the safety, security and peace of this great country are tolerance, understanding and unity amongst its people. The feeling that the same Divine Aathma is residing in all beings should be cultivated so that wisdom, social justice and real sense of freedom can prevail. The entire humanity should be considered as one brotherhood on the   basis of Universal Love. Then only the objective of human birth can be fulfilled. The feeling of oneness is essential for enjoying bliss based on realisation of divinity in everyone.

In ancient times, the   Rishis enjoyed fullness of human life. They experienced this bliss of Universal Love within them and conveyed it to all   mankind. They propounded the Premathathva (doctrine of Love) which is the means to know one's Inner Reality.

Today, there is no security or safety for the people in the country and there is disorder all over the world. Hatred and anger are rampant among the people. Under these circumstances, the only path they have to follow is the Path of Love.

Man has become a slave to selfishness

With the rapid growth of industrial development in the West, humanness has deteriorated. Because of this, man has moved away from his true inner self. Though man has advanced considerably in the field of Science and Technology and has reached higher levels in the development of secular and physical knowledge, he has strayed far away from spiritual and moral goals. Everyone is indulging in selfish pursuits only. In fact, man has become a slave to selfishness.

Because of the scientific and technological advancement man is attaching importance to the physical body, taking it to be the real self, and spends his time in catering to the needs and comforts of the body. He is using the body as a toy and plays with it in a mechanical way. The body is functioning through the power of Prajna Shakthi (Integral Awareness) which

is directing the functions through the *Spandana Shakthi*
or *Praana Shakthi* (Pulsatory life force).

The triple forces through which man functions

Man is functioning by the combination of three
forces: Radiation, Vibration and Materiality. The body
is just matter only. It is called *Prakrithi*. *Praana Shakthi*
makes it vibrant. This vibration is directed by the
Prajna Shakthi which is consciousness (awareness).
Thus man's life is a combination of consciousness,
vital force and matter. Without realising this fact, man
is always keen on looking after the body alone, with
the wrong conception that the body is all powerful.

All of you know that America (U.S.A) is
considered to be a land of plenty where there is no
dearth of food. So the people eat well and enjoy
material pleasures. They consume excessive food and
lead a life of luxury. But we find that there are more
deaths owing to heart diseases in that country, than
in other countries.

Sweden is very affluent country in Europe and
the government is also providing all possible comforts
and looks after the people well. In spite of such
prosperity, there are more suicide cases in this country
than anywhere else and the number of divorce cases
are plenty. What is the cause for this? It is not lack
of any physical or material facilities but lack of
spiritual outlook that is responsible for such a
situation. It is because they identify themselves with
the body, which is perishable and impermanent,
and are ignorant about their Real Inner Self which
is the permanent and eternal entity. They lead an
artificial life.

The power of Gaayathri manthra

In Bhaarath, from ancient times, through the sacred *Gaayathri manthra*, spiritual awareness has been developed. The *manthra "Om Bhur Bhuvas Suvah"* represents the three basic principles of the godliness in every one. *Bhu* means matter. *Bhuvah* is the *Praana Shakthi* (the vibrant principle). *Suvah* is the *Prajna Shakthi* (awareness). These three constituent forces—radiation, vibration and material energy—activate the human being. But man is not able to realise this fact.

In the mythology of Bhaarath, Naaradha is a sage well known as *Thriloka Sanchaari* (to constantly travel in the three worlds). Naaradha represents the life principle. The three worlds are *Bhur, Bhuvas, Suvah* meaning material energy, life force and latent *Aathma Shakthi* (spiritual energy).

Man is not making efforts to understand the relationship between *Prakrithi* (phenomenal world) and *Jeevathma* (man) and *Paramaathma* (Supreme Spirit). These are very intimately inter-related to one another. They are not disparate. The relationship between *Paramaathma* and *Prakrithi*—God and Nature—is the same as that between mother and child. The relationship between man and society is the same as that between the honey-bee and the flower. Just as the child is fed by mother's milk, as the honey-bee is fed by the honey in a flower, man must enjoy the gifts of Nature. From time immemorial man has been plagued by negative ideas. There is a legendary tale in which one greedy man killed the goose that laid golden eggs thinking that he can extract all the eggs from it in one lump. Such acts of folly are committed freely by scientists today by exploiting Nature's gifts beyond all limits, creating disastrous imbalance resulting in natural calamities such as earthquakes, spelling danger to humanity. We cannot blame science for this. Those who apply the scientific discoveries without discrimination are to be blamed for this. They fail to consider with deep deliberation the effects of excessive depletion of the natural resources.

Do not trigger the negative aspect of Nature

Man has to consider himself as a limb of the society and help in the welfare of society, just as the organs of one's body are used for one's well-being. Again society is a limb of *Prakrithi* (Nature) and *Prakrithi* is a limb of *Paramaathma* (Supreme Lord). Thus there is close relationship between man and God. Nature is more progressive than man, and to protect Nature, man has to exploit it within limits. When man tampers with Nature recklessly, it reacts adversely and trouble arises. In order to protect Nature, man has to practise ceiling on desires. He should not trigger the negative aspect of Nature.

In this respect, scientists have no concern for the harmful effects that may accrue to society by their inventions. They don't care for the welfare of the mankind and go on making use of intelligence to produce their weapons of destruction.

Care should be exercised in providing comforts as excessive comforts may spoil man's mind and cause misery instead of happiness. *"Na Shreyo Niyamam Vinaa"* (Nothing good can be achieved without certain restraints). Because of the advancement of technology and provision of excessive comforts, life has become mechanical and spirituality has declined. Science fragments everything to pieces while spirituality builds up unity in diversity. Today man is not making efforts to cultivate the feeling of oneness among humanity.

Intimate relationship of man, God and Nature

To quote an example you have the ozone layer in the atmosphere which protects the people on earth from the evil effects of solar radiation. Because of the advance of technology, several factories have sprung up causing emission of harmful gases in the atmosphere as a result of which the ozone layer has become thinner and if this goes on unchecked it may have disatrous consequences. The scientists are trying to stop the break up of the ozone layer but they are unable to find a remedy.

The actual cause for this situation is that more carbon-dioxide is let into the atmosphere, which normally is absorbed by the plants and trees which can assimilate the gas and supply oxygen by the natural process of photosynthesis. But, because there is de-forestation to an alarming extent, the extent of carbon-dioxide in the atmosphere has considerably increased. Therefore, the remedy for this situation is intensive afforestation, growing more tress everywhere and protecting the existing trees without destroying them for other purposes. Thus the relationship of man, Nature and God is very intimate which scientists may not be able to realise.

You have to enquire into everything thoroughly. *Dharma* is a word that has originated in Bhaarath and is misinterpreted often. The attitudes of the Westerners and our countrymen differ widely. In the

West, they are more keen on the rights of the individual. Immediately on birth, the child acquires a right. Father, mother, society and government each has a right. The worker has a right, the ruler has a right. While in the West, they were more concerned about rights the people of Bhaarath had been laying stress on *Dharma* or the duty of everyone.

The concept of *Dharma* is peculiar to Bhaarath

The word *Dharma* is peculiar to Bhaarath and no language other than Sanskrith has it in its vocabulary, nor any country for that matter. It is interpreted by some as 'Righteousness' and by yet others as 'reason', etc. *Dharma* is *Dharma* only. No other word can give the same meaning. *"Dharmo Rakshathi Rakshithaha"* (*Dharma* protects those who protect it). That which controls and encompasses everything is *Dharma*. There is a lot of difference between *Dharma* and religion. *Dharma* is like an ocean. Religion is just like a small lake.

Religion is related to the individual while Culture is "fundamental order." They use the terms 'Mohammedan culture,' 'Hindu culture,' 'Christian culture' and fight against one another. In reality, there is no difference between one Religion and another. There is no difference between man and man as God is in the form of love in everyone. So it is not correct to fight on the basis of religious differences. All belong to the human race. When one understands this truth one can comprehend *Dharma*.

"Karmanyeva Adhikaarasthe Maa Paleshu" says the Geetha. You have the right to perform your duty only. You have no right to demand the fruits of your

action. No one has got any right other than doing his duty. He has the responsibility to discharge his duty. But, today people are clamouring for rights and don't want to discharge duties. The result will always be there whether you ask for it or not. Right and Responsibility are like two wings of a bird which make it fly or like the two wheels of a vehicle which facilitate a person to ride on it. How long can you drive with a single wheel? How can a bird fly high with one wing?

If you discharge your duty with responsibility result will take care of itself. This is what everyone should clearly understand today. If everyone does his duty well there will be no trouble in the world. It is because people claim rights without doing their duty there is chaos and confusion. Man is immersed in self-conflict because he is keen on exercising his right without discharging his responsibility.

The body is given to man for helping others

Man should realise his reality. The body is given to him for performing his duty. What kind of duty? *"Paropakaaraartham Idam Shareeram"* (This body is given for helping others). So your duty is to help others. But people don't cherish this broad outlook.

Today there is terrible conflict and misery and disorder in the country because such a broad outlook is not there and people are narrow minded. They should discard this narrow selfish feelings and practise expansion of love. You should cultivate the feeling that all human beings belong to one family. The divinity in all beings is one.

Constant Integrated Awareness

Bulbs are many but current is one,
Jewels are many but Gold is one,
Beings are many but Breath is one,
Nations are many but Earth is one.

People should develop broad feelings on the above lines. Then only humanity will prosper. There is divinity in every one which one should sincerely try to realise. It is not enough only to propagate the theory. There are a large number of people who propagate and preach but those who practise are rare. Many speak one thing and act differently. There should be harmony in thought, word and deed. This is the unity of head, heart and hand. But, now-a-days people think in one way, speak in another and do yet another thing. This is why the *Prajna Shakthi* (power of conscience), *Praana Shakthi* (life force) and material force are diverted in different directions. Matter, life force and conscience should be unified.

One should be careful about conscience which will always spell the truth. It will never lead you on the wrong path. *Vedhas* call this *"Prajnaanam Brahma."* It is present equally in body, mind, intellect and Inner Instruments. This is Constant Integrated Awareness. No one is making efforts to realise the latent Divine Power in him. In the world today, people care only for material things. Selfishness is on the increase. 'Right' is born out of selfishness and ends in conflict. *Dharma* is born from *Prema* (love) and merges in *Aathma* (spirituality). Therefore one should discard 'rights' and take up 'responsibility' born out of love. Such an individual only will lead a true life.

Divinity within is responsible for the functioning of all organs of the body. That divinity is the *Prajna Shakthi*, the life force and also the *Chaithanya* (Awareness). This awareness is in everyone. It is *Brahman*. "The One is in all beings." This is a *sutra* (aphorism). *Sutra* means also a thread. When you make a garland of flowers, the thread keeping them in position is only one though flowers are many. They may be in different stages of bloom and change every day, but the thread is the same today and tomorrow. Similarly the *Chaithanya* (consciousness) is the same while one is a child or boy, or adult or in old age. Though the description of the person changes as boy; man, grand father etc., the *Chaithanya* inside is changeless. There is no distinction of woman or man too. Changes are in the body and not in *Aathma* which is changeless. It exists in all brilliance at all times. There is beauty in it. We should understand the principle of beauty.

Service to humanity is beauty

For the hand, charity lends beauty. For speech, it is truth that lends beauty. For ears, wisdom lends beauty. What more beauty do you need than these? For life, service to humanity is beauty. In Kannada there is a wise saying that houses make a village beautiful, flowers make the branch of the tree beautiful, moon beautifies the sky, waves beautify the Ocean and character makes a person beautiful.

Every man has intelligence. When you put it to skillful use it is serving well. But actually man is misusing knowledge. This is termed as technology which is in fact 'Trick'nology. Because of this man is not having peace. An individual utters falsehood to please another person. He may think that he is deceiving the other. But he is deceiving himself. One should not act against the dictates of his conscience. Conscience is *Chith*, awareness is *Sath*. Both combine and give *Aanandha*. They are like syrup got by mixing sugar and water *(Sath + Chith)*. The syrup is *Aanandha*. I and you should combine to say 'we'. Many don't understand this properly and say "I and you are one." This is not correct. "I and you are We" is the correct statement. "We and We are One." I am in you and you are in me and so we are one. This is a combination of *Aathma* and *Aathma* and not matter to matter. The bond between matter and matter is the life force. Life is sustained by the infinite force of *Prajna Shakthi*. *Prajna* is the source and *Praana* is propelled by this. Even if there is life unless the *Prajna Shakthi* is there this can't work. Human life is therefore, the combination of three: *Prajna, Praana* and Matter. Man is ignorant of this truth and concerns himself only with the body which is matter only.

Unity leads to purity and divinity

Ancient *Rishis* called these three as *Bhurh, Bhuvah* and *Suvah*. When you realise this unity in everyone— child, boy or old people—how can you hate any body? When one develops this principle of unity there will be peace. The 'divide and rule' policy is driving the society to destruction in the political field. In the spiritual field unity must be the basis. It leads to purity and divinity.

Embodiments of Divine Love! Spirituality is not mere worship, *japa* or *dhyaana*. These may be good activities but they don't constitute spirituality. The driving away of animal qualities and proceeding from the human to the divine is real spirituality. There are human, divine and animal traits in every one. You should get rid of the animal nature and develop divine quality.

What is *Saadhana?* It is doing good deeds with this body. These good works are God's work too. The essence of the eighteen *Puraanas* of Vyaasa is condensed by him as "Help ever; Hurt never." This is true devotion. While doing worship and meditation on one side if you hurt others can it be real *saadhana?*

God is love; love is God

One may get angry. He should not plunge into action immediately. If he does so his hasty action will be fraught with undesirable consequences. "Haste makes waste; waste makes worry." He should think whether it is right or wrong before plunging into action to hurt the other man towards whom he is angry. Slowly as his temper comes down he will change his mind and desist from hasty action. This is the practical way of controlling oneself in daily life. This is the way of life which is called culture. You should engage in such thoughtful action as will serve the cause of society and foster goodwill and unity. You should foster good thoughts. This is real *Saadhana.*

God is Love; Love is God (Bhagavaan sang the song *Prem Eeshvar Hai; Eeshvar Prem Hai*). Love is one. It is not good to cause hurt to others. The world is a globe. You know that the balance has to be maintained to keep it stable. We utilise the natural resources without any limit and create imbalance.

I have been visiting Madras for the past 45 years. Now I see that there is traffic even at 2.00 a.m. as it used to be in Bombay. There is more carbon dioxide smoke released. There are factories and industries everywhere. So there is more pollution of the air and diseases are on the increase. All these are dangerous offshoots of technological progress.

Love all and Serve all

One can serve God only through *Shrama* and *Prema*, (effort with love). The best way to serve God is to Love all and serve all.

There was an old lady in Mathura. She used to take blankets in the darkest hour of the night and distribute them to poor people who were shivering in cold. One day she was bending her head and serving the poor. A few youths gathered there and asked her "Oh! Lady! while you are doing such selfless work why are you bending your head and walking?" She replied: "God has given so much of wealth to the people with so many hands. But I am able to serve the people only with my two hands. Is it not a thing about which I should feel ashamed?"

We are not prepared to share with others and are only ready to receive whatever we can get. This is one way traffic. "There is no chance of immortality without doing sacrifice" say the *Vedhas*. You should sacrifice and share what you have with others. Then only you may have peace. You should make others happy. You must do the *Saadhana* of Sacrifice. You should provide help to other devotees. Charity is the beauty for hands and not decoration with bangles.

The Mind is like a key to the lock of the heart. If you turn it towards God you get liberation; if you turn it towards the world you get into bondage. You should develop the feeling "Lokaas Samasthaas Sukhino Bhavanthu." You should aspire for world unity. Out of unity you get purity and from purity comes divinity. Now there is only community and enmity, which has to be eliminated.

Prema is the binding factor to unite all humanity together. Therefore, cultivate Prema or Universal Love.

Discourse in the Kaamaraj Memorial hall,
Theynaampet, Madras, on 21-1-1993.

The Mahaabhaaratha and Raamaayana which are the most precious jewels of India are like vast oceans. If we look at these oceans one side, we will have only a limited view but if we climb up a hill and have a look at them, we get a fuller view and a better understanding of them. What we have to do is to delve into them and try to explore and understand the treasures contained in these big oceans.

—BABA

CHAPTER 4

Integral approach to human ailments

One whose heart is filled with compassion,
Whose words spell truth,
And who works for the welfare of others
Will never suffer from difficulties
Or diseases even in the Kali age.

IN THIS wide world, everyone aspires for long life, prosperity and health. A healthy body is essential if one has to achieve the four goals of human life, namely, *Dharma* (righteousness), *Artha* (wealth), *Kaama* (desire) and *Moksha* (liberation). Science and technology have made great strides in contributing to the progress of human society. But man has deteriorated morally and spiritually.

Among the four *Vedhas,* the *Atharvana Vedha* is the one that has given the science relating to longevity, known as Ayurvedha. Ayurvedha transcends time and space and is valid for all places, at all times. It relates to the spirit, mind and the body and has an integrated approach. The Allopathic system came much later. It is based on an objective, external approach while Ayurvedha is subjective. Both have to be coordinated for better results. Since Ayurvedha is subjective it is more efficacious than the Allopathic system. There is a superior artistic sense in Ayurvedha.

Doctors have to realise the distinction between subjective and objective approaches. The latter has an external outlook while the former has an inner view. The object is a reflection of the subject. Without realising this relationship between Ayurvedha and Allopathy, doctors are wasting their time in arguments.

Basic difference between Ayurvedha and Allopathy

Ayurvedha affirms that purity of mind is more essential for one's health while Allopathic doctors do not consider the mind as so important. They give importance to the eradication of disease-causing germs and consider this as the only means to cure diseases. This does not take into account the role of the mind and the Spirit in the eradication of disease. Allopathy is based on external knowledge and experimentation, while Ayurvedha is based on inner knowledge and experience. There is gulf of difference between experiment and experience. Because of the difference between the subjective and objective approaches, in course of time, Allopathy resorted to the use of antibiotics to deal with various diseases. The antibiotics act powerfully and yield quick results in curing a disease. But, in the process of curing a disease they give rise to adverse side-effects.

The role of the mind in causing sickness

Allopathic doctors experiment only with matter. They do not take the inner consciousness (Self) into account. In spite of the prodigious technological developments in the world, man is not able to enjoy peace. Peace cannot be achieved by knowledge of the physical. Peace should come from inner feeling or the Spirit within. It is only when the body, the mind and the Spirit are in harmony that peace will prevail. Medical science should recognise the role of the mind in causing sickness. Good health confers mental peace. Mental worry impairs physical health. Ayurvedha, therefore, lays emphasis on mental peace and aims at the elimination of the root cause of disease.

There are three basic factors which are responsible for health or disease in the human body according to Ayurvedha. They are *vaatha* (vital air), *piththa* (bile) and *shleshma* (phlegm). *Vaatha* accounts for 36 diseases, *piththa* accounts for 98 and *shleshma* for 96 diseases. These three factors are essential for the human body but they should be in proper balance without exceeding their respective limits. When they are in balance, there will be no disease. Moderation is the golden rule for good health.

For the treatment of disease arising out of *vaatha*, *piththa* and *shleshma*, gingely oil, ghee and honey respectively are prescribed as remedies. These should be taken in moderation. The body is a gift of God and cannot be made by doctors. The human heart beats 1,03,000 times a day. The blood circulation in the body is computed to cover 1,68,000 miles per day. Man breathes 21,600 times and consumes 438 cubic feet of air every day. These are based on Divine Will and are regarded as a Law of Nature.

God is the preceptor of *Prakrithi* (Nature). The body is unclean in many ways and is subject to various diseases. But in such an inherently unattractive abode dwells the most valuable divinity. Man should always act in harmony with Nature, which is reflection of Divinity.

Heart troubles are caused by hurry, worry and curry

What is the cause of heart ailments? Many doctors say that they are due to smoking, consumption of fatty foods, overeating and other habits. The relationship between food and habits should be properly understood. We should see that proper balance is maintained between the physical body and inner feelings (Spirit). Modern man is continuously in a hurry. Hurry causes worry which affects the physical health. The main cause of heart troubles may be said to be hurry, worry and curry. Curry means fatty foods. Many doctors have made investigations in this field but the results have not been made known widely. Heart diseases are found to be more rampant among non-vegetarians while vegetarians are not prone to heart ailments to the same extent. This is because of higher percentage of fats in non-vegetarian food which increases the cholesterol in the blood. Worry causes high blood pressure and hurry causes diabetes. Both of them are like twins, one acting on the heart inside and the other externally on the blood.

Every one should know how to control these causes. Some people do not do any physical exercises and lead a sedentary life. My advice to office-goers and students is that it is good for them to commute by cycle at least 5 or 6 kilometers a day. This cycling exercise is very useful not only for maintaining health but also for reducing the expenditure incurred on automobiles. Another advantage is the avoidance of accidents. Moreover, it serves to reduce atmospheric pollution caused by the release of harmful fumes from automobiles. The carbon-dioxide smoke form motor vehicles and factories is already polluting the air in cities and is affecting the ozone layer above the earth.

Purifying the environment is the primary task

The primary task is to purify the environment which is affected by pollution of air, water and food. All the five elements are affected by pollution. People should, therefore, try to reduce the use of automobiles and control the emission of harmful industrial effluents.

In the ancient times, sages and scientists commended the Ayurvedhic system of treatment as it was considered a natural system for curing disease. Trees play a vital role in helping mankind to receive oxygen from the atmosphere while they absorb the carbon dioxide exhaled by human beings. Hence, the ancients favoured the growing of trees to control atmospheric pollution. But nowadays trees are cut down indiscriminately and pollution is on the increase. The relationship between man and trees is indicated by the term "Vanaspathi" (herbs) employed in Ayurvedha.

Man is leading an artificial life today. One should understand that he is not merely the body but a combination of body, mind and Spirit. In the *Gaayathri mantra*, "*Om Bhur Bhuvas Suvah*" is the first line. In this *Bhu* refers to matter, that is the body, *Bhuvah* refers to the *Praana Shakthi* (Life Principle) which animates the body, and *Suvah* refers to *Prajna Shakthi* (Awareness or Conscience) which acts through radiation. Hence man is made up of *Prajna* (awareness), *Praana* (the vital force) and the body (the material substance). The doctors should not consider only the body (matter), but should take into consideration the *Praana* (Life Force) and *Prajna Shakthi* (Integrated Awareness). *Prajna Shakthi* is the radiation energy that promotes wisdom. Vibration is the expression of the *Praana* (Vital Force). In every action, there is a vibration which is in between the consciousness and the physical body. We should see that the mind is not influenced by any external 'force' but by the internal 'source,' which is *Prajna* or integrated awareness.

Doctors' duty to ensure healthy life for all

Esteemed Doctors! You must strive to ensure long and healthy life for the people. In my view a godly life is more important than mere longevity. What is the use of a selfish person leading a long life without rendering service to society? Only those who serve the society and the nation should have a long life. The essence of the Eighteen *Puraanas* of Vyaasa was given by him in the motto: Help ever, hurt never.

It is true that doctors generally work with devotion and dedication. It will be better if they develop more

devotion towards God instead of being concerned
with earning money. Obviously money is needed to
carry on worldly life but there should be a limit to
the acquisition of money. The use of money should
be properly regulated. When one does not observe
restraint in daily life, he is a prey to disease. The
body is governed by limits and controls. The
temperature should be 98.4° F—neither more nor
less, the blood pressure should be 80-120. Any increase
or decrease spells illness. Doctors should not compete
with one another in earning huge sums and acquiring
more and more possessions. They should render free
service to the needy and the poor. The spirit of
sacrifice is the hallmark of true education. Money
earned should be usefully spent in a spirit of sacrifice.

Health and human values

There should be a harmonious blend of religion,
philosophy and art for man to live healthily in the
world. In this context religion means the religion of
love. This is the only religion in the world. There
is only one caste, the caste of humanity. One should
cultivate human values for healthy living. This calls
for harmony in thought, word and deed. When you
cultivate this harmony you will be free from desires
and fears. As selfishness is rampant in the field of
medical science and other branches of sciences, the
world is rocked by many hazards and calamities.

Doctors should educate laymen about the various
reasons for heart ailments. Whenever people think
of heart disease, the prospect of an operation looms
large before them as a bugbear. As far as possible
you should avoid surgery and try to cure the patients

by drugs. Doctors should treat operation as a last resort. As the word operation creates fear in all types of people, whether rich or poor, high or low, you should help them to develop self-confidence and remove the cause of fear.

What the Super-Speciality hospital signifies

Divine members of the medical fraternity! It is not my intention to extol the excellence of our Hospital here. I wish to highlight the fact that the people in these areas used to be mortally afraid of heart disease because there was no facility for high-grade medical or surgical treatment and they had to take the patients to far off places entailing enormous expense. But, from 22nd November 1991, when the Super-Speciality Hospital started functioning, even kids entered the hospital smilingly without any sense of fear. Their courage and faith ensure successful treatment. This is the only hospital where you can see patients, doctors, nurses, technicians and paramedical staff with smiling faces. Even the relatives accompanying the patients are all smiles. Wherever you move in the hospital, you can see smiling and cheerful workers doing their duty with devotion and dedication.

How has this happiness come to the people who go to the hospital for treatment of dreaded diseases? Happiness arises out of union with God. Because there is lack of faith in God elsewhere, there is grief. But in our hospital there is full faith in Divinity. Most people who have all physical comforts do not have inner peace. We get peace only from within us. If one acts in consonance with one's conscience one gets peace. A spirit of sacrifice is essential for securing peace.

This hospital is not Svaami's. It belongs to all
of you. This hospital was established with the noble
aim of serving suffering humanity. Besides excellent
equipment of the highest quality, we have here the
most modern facilities for medical and surgical
treatment and, above all, a team of dedicated doctors
and other staff who render selfless service with a
smile. The construction of the hospital was completed
in an incredibly short period of five months. The
construction of a hospital of this magnitude might have
taken even ten years if the Government had taken up
the work. When I announced on 23rd November 1990,
that this hospital will function from 22nd November
1991, many eyebrows were raised, doubting the
possibility of the date being kept up. But it became
an accomplished fact as willed by Svaami.

Devotion and selfless service of doctors

Dr. Venugopal came from Delhi to conduct the
operations on 22nd November, 1991. Ever since he took
up the work; it has been a saga of success. It has not
been mentioned in the public before that he is a doctor
in government service working in the All-India Institute
of Medical Sciences. He used to start from Delhi on a
Saturday, arrive here and perform operations on Sunday
and return to Delhi for work on Monday. He has not
taken any remuneration for his work and has defrayed
even the travelling expense himself. I am mentioning
these facts only to highlight his devotion and sense
of selfless service. His entire team is of the same type.
They are very happy to have the opportunity to serve
here. Their purity of heart and selfless service have
helped the hospital to achieve such splendid results.

Most of the nurses and technicians are our college students. They were sent to Delhi for technical training in the operation of highly sophisticated equipment. They have often been working smilingly from 6 a.m. to 12 midnight. They serve here only out of devotion to Svaami and not for money.

To cite an example of the spirit of dedication of the staff, yesterday while Svaami was returning from the hospital, nurses who had done hard and strenuous work for more than three days were found walking on the road and on enquiry it was learnt that their bus broke down and they decided to trek the long distance back to the *Mandhir* on foot. Svaami asked them to wait there and arranged for a relief bus to pick them up. The relationship between Svaami and devotees is heart to heart based on love.

A word of advice to the doctors

Not a single paise is collected from patients for anything, right from diagnostic tests to surgery and after-care. Even nutritious food is supplied free to the patents. In the beginning, the innocent and simple village folk did not know how to use the hospital beds. Some of them slept under the cot saying in utter simplicity that they were not worthy enough to sleep on such expensive beds. Patients do not show any sign of worry in this hospital.

I wish to give a word of advice to the doctors. While you are examining the patients you should have smiling faces and talk to the patients sweetly. If you check the pulse with a grim face the patients may collapse fearing that there is something radically wrong. Some patients even dread the very sight of a doctor when he approaches to examine. This is not good. Doctors should infuse courage in the patents and speak soothingly radiating compassion and love. The kind approach of the doctor will have greater healing effect on the patients than the medicine itself. Doctors must instill courage in the patients. Svaami wants more hospitals to render free treatment to the poor. Doctors should cooperate and work with unity.

Aim at a disease-free human society

It is only by sense control and steadfastness that one can lead a happy and healthy life. Along with control of the mind, one should control the temper and avoid tension. Prevention of disease should be the goal. We should aim at a human society free from diseases. It will be a happy day when a hospital gets no patients at all.

All of you have assembled here to discuss and exchange your knowledge and experience in the field of medical science, particularly relating to treatment of cardiac and cardio-vascular cases. I wish you should discuss freely and find solution to problems and render service to the people.

Discourse to an international gathering of Cardiac specialists present at a symposium held in the Auditorium of the Shri Sathya Sai Institute of Higher Learning, Prashaanthi Nilayam, on 6-2-1993.

CHAPTER 5

Doctors, patients and society

Charity is the ornament for the hand.
Truth is the adornment for the tongue.
The scriptures are the ornaments for the ears.
Of what avail are other ornaments?

*E*MBODIMENTS of the Divine Practioners of Modern Medicine! It is *dhaanam* (charity) that lends adornment to the hand. Only Truth lends beauty to speech. The scriptures serve to adorn the ears. Man needs no more beautiful ornaments than these. The glory of Divinity consists in sanctifying human existence by these ornaments.

The human body is a thing of marvellous beauty. men cannot easily comprehend the secret of God's creation. No one can explain how the eyes have acquired the power of seeing this phenomenal world.

The beauty of all the organs in the human body is a secret of creation. Doctors try to find out how each sense organ and how each limb functions. No one tries to find out why they are functioning in this manner. This secret can be grasped only through the *Aathmik* or Divine Principle.

Human life is based on six constituents in the *Panchabhuuthas* (five basic elements) and the *Aathma*. To recognise this fact, three paths have to be pursued. One is to recognise within one's self the presence of Nature and the Divine. A second path is to recognise in God the cosmic creation and one's self. The third path is to see in Nature the presence of God and one's self. It is only when knowledge is acquired by these three paths that *Aathma Jnaana* (Knowledge of the Self) arises. This three-fold path is termed *Prajna* (Integrated Awareness). Every man should try to understand this three-fold path. This can be done at all times in all places. It has universal application. It has permanent validity everywhere. But, man gets involved in what is impermanent and ever-changing.

Treat the patient; not the disease

There are in the world today highly intelligent and experienced doctors of great renown. They are, however, concerned only with the cure of diseases and not the redemption of the patient. It is more important to cure the mental condition of the patient than to relieve his physical illness. Doctors treat the disease and not the patient.

During the past two days, the doctors have been discussing how to cure diseases. They have presented statistics as to the number of cases handled, the number of cures effected and the incidence of mortality. The doctors have had some doubts about how all diseases are cured in our Sathya Sai Hospital. How does this happen? There is a good answer for this doubt. In regard to any action, if it is done with a pure heart and good intentions, it is bound to be successful. Man today regards self-interest as a way of life. This has become the philosophy of the modern world. But, we should consider *thyaaga* (sacrifice) alone as the true philosophy for the world. When you approach the patient in a spirit of sacrifice, the patient's feelings get purified.

Vibrations of light around the body

Our body is surrounded by Divine vibrations. If you look at the thumb, there are vibrations of light around it. Few attempt to recognise this phenomenon. The body is surrounded by vibrations of light. When these vibrations of light from one person meet another's, several good things happen.

There are two important organs for man. One is the heart and the other is the hand. The head is preoccupied with enquiring into mundane phenomena. It is concerned with the external. Its focus is on objects outside. The heart looks at what is within. The concern with the external has been termed *Pravritthi Maarga* (the path of externals). All man's actions today, including the knowledge he acquires and the wealth he gets, are all related to the *Pravritthi Maarga*. The six vices of *Kaama* (lust), *Krodha* (anger), *Moha* (infatuation), *Lobha* (greed), *Madha* (pride) and *Maathsarya* (jealousy) are related to the *Pravritthi*

Maarga. These undergo constant changes. Because the body is associated with these qualities, it is also subject to change.

But the heart remains unchanging. It is associated with the *Nivritthi Maarga* (the Inward path). What are the qualities associated with the heart? Truth, compassion, love, forbearance, sympathy and sacrifice. These human qualities emanate from the heart. So, in human life, the head and the heart play crucial roles. These two are kept in balance by the hand. Thus, the heart, the head and the hand are the three H's which are important in studying the human predicament.

Close nexus between the mind and *praana*

What are the causes of diseases of the heart? All diseases are a reflection of *Pravritthi*, the disposition of the mind. Hence, in worldly matters, man should follow the right path. In this context, two elements among the five basic elements are important. "*Bhikshaannam Dheharakshaartham, Vasthram Seetha nivaraaranam*" (Food is essential for protecting the body; raiment is necessary for protection against cold). Associated with food is water. These two occupy pride of place in human life.

Life is the subtle form of the water consumed by man. The mind is the subtle form of the food taken by man. Hence a close nexus should be established between the mind and *Praana* (life force). As is the food, so is the head. Man's thoughts, desires and aspirations are related to the kind of food he consumes. For instance, you may discern from practical experience how food affects the mind. The cyclic process which starts with the formation of clouds and ends in the harvest of grain, determines the kind of food one can have.

Heat (or fire) is the basis of this process. This fire is present within man as *Jatharaagni,* the digestive fire, which accounts for the conversion of the food consumed by man into various forms of energy. This fire has to be in proper balance. When the balance is upset, you have illness. The state of man's body depends on the maintenance of this balance. Man's entire life depends on preserving this balance. When is the balance upset? When there is no mental steadiness. Men today develop all kinds of intellectual abilities, but they have not learnt how to keep the mind steady. When serenity of mind is achieved, there will be no disease. Illness will not approach you at all.

Importance of food in maintaining health

There should be some regulations with regard to food. Many doctors emphasize the value of proteins and recommend meat, eggs, etc. But proteins got in this form serve only to build the body, but do considerable harm to the mind. Doctors are primarily concerned with the gross physical body. They pay little attention to the subtle form of the mental make-up. Most of the diseases that are prevalent in the world today are related to the mind. Mental illness seem to outnumber physical ailments. The *Vedhaantha* has declared that the mind is the cause of man's bondage or liberation. This means that the mind has to be used properly and turned godwards. Equally the mind is responsible for health or sickness.

In this context, food is all important. Proteins are present in milk, curds and vegetables as much as in meat. If, in the matter of diet, the doctors give the right prescription, diseases can be averted.

Prevention is better than cure

In my view, instead of treating people after the onset of illness, it is better to ensure that they do not fall ill at all. Both doctors and the authorities should educate enceinte women about pre-natal care of children in the womb. It is distressing to find that new-born babes suffer from congenital heart diseases. Dr. Iyer showed the picture of a smiling child that had grown up after a heart operation shortly after birth. While one rejoices at such a sight, it is frightening to think of the operation that had to be done on a ten day old infant. In the case of congenital heart diseases, neither the parents nor the child can be happy. Nor can society be happy with such a situation. Something must be done to prevent heart troubles developing during pregnancy. There are medicines for preventing congenital heart ailments. For instance, if the mother is given various vitamins, the child's heart can be strengthened. The mother should be taught all about pre-natal care and given the necessary medicines. Pregnant women should be periodically checked in the hospital. It is better to take all preventive measures before the birth of a child than to carry the burden of bringing up a weak and crippled child all his life.

Doctors alone cannot impart this message to all women. They can only advise those who come to them. But doctors can bring home to the authorities their responsibility in the area of preventive measures. What is the use of spending crores on curative measures without promoting health? It is a waste of money. There are many hazards in the use of anti- biotics in the treatment of certain diseases like tuberculosis and the use of pesticides in agriculture.

Doctors should be grateful to the society

Doctors should realise what they owe to society, which has preserved and imparted to them their knowledge of the medical sciences. Medical knowledge has been enriched by the contributions of dedicated investigators over centuries. Doctors should be grateful to society for all the knowledge and skills they have acquired from the dedicated labours of others. They should realize their deep indebtedness to society for all they have received from it. Only then, they will use their knowledge and skills in the right way.

People today think in terms of only their personal interests. They should develop a social conscious- ness, realising what all they owe to society. Men today have become so utterly selfish that they behave in inhuman ways. They do not make proper use of their talents and resources in the service of their fellowmen.

Doctors are embodiments of the Divine. As such, it is their duty to see that people do not shed tears of grief. They may doubt how far this is possible. Do as much as lies within your power. What happens thereafter need not bother you. Treat Duty as God and Work as Worship. If you carry on your work in this spirit, the world will be a happier place for all.

I have to give a word of advice to the doctors present here. There is a tendency to specialize in the treatment of heart diseases which has gone to absurd lengths. I would advise the doctors to treat the heart as a whole and not fragment every part of it for specialised treatment. Specialisation has grown to alarming proportions in the world today. Doctors should be "generalists," who know how to treat different ailments of a patient.

The heart teaches an important lesson to man. It appears to beat tirelessly without stopping. But, in fact, it is able to rest in brief intervals between one beat and another. The heart teaches you how to take rest even while at work. I often tell the students that "change of work is rest." This is the way the heart functions when it pumps the blood from one chamber to the other.

Lessons from the human cell

Few can realise the limitless potentialities of each cell in the human body. It is one of the great secrets of creation. The cells teach man the lesson of *thyaaga* (sacrifice). For the progress of human life, sacrifice is essential. The scripture declares that immortality can be attained only through sacrifice. Immortality means the removal of immorality. The various cells in the body account for the performance of various functions by the senses and other limbs of the body. The power of the cells comes from the Divine. No one can explain it. Modern scientists term it as a "law of Nature." But wherefrom has this "law" emerged? There should be some one who lays down the law? For every product, like this silver tumbler, there is a maker. Silver is God's creation. The tumbler has been made by a goldsmith. It has not come as a ready-made tumbler. You have on the earth water and clay. They are God's creation. By mixing them both, the potter makes pots out of them. The creator for the pot is the potter. God is the Creator for the five elements—space, air, fire, water and earth. No one else can create these elements. But man makes use of these natural elements for making objects for his enjoyment. One man produces an aeroplane for flying. Another makes a parachute for safety if something happens to the plane. Scientists should be concerned with producing things that ensure safety.

How the Divine works

In this connection, I should like to tell you something whether you believe it or not. I do not have any worry. When I embarked on the construction of such a big hospital (the Super Speciality Hospital), Joga Rao used to say: "We are drawing up such gigantic plans. We don't have enough money. How are we going to construct this hospital?" He was highly apprehensive. I told him: "What we are undertaking is good work for the welfare of others. There is no selfishness in Me. We are doing everything for the well-being of the world. Do not give room for these depressing thoughts. It is bound to come up. Have this confidence."

When does such confidence arise? When you know you are engaged in a good cause. There is a difference between an optimist and a pessimist when they view a glass half-full of water. The optimist is glad that the tumbler is half-full, while the pessimist is sorry that the tumbler is half-empty. You should not give way to pessimism. You must feel content with whatever you have. With contentment, anything can be achieved.

Medical education should lay stress on quality

The plight of doctors (in India) deserves sympathy. Many of them have to spend large sums to get seats in medical colleges and to complete their education. The doctor is worried how to recover the money that has been spent on his education. Something must be done to solve this problem. For instance, no one should be admitted in a medical college merely because he is able to pay a large capitation fee (of lakhs). Only those who have the talents and aptitude for medical studies should be admitted. Such students will immensely benefit from medical education and will be of use to society. Today you must have either plenty of money or influential backing to get into a medical college. Students who get admitted this way take even twelve years to complete the five year medical course. Of what use are such men? The stress should be on quality and not quantity in the sphere of medical studies.

In earlier years, medical students used to work hard spending even 18 hours a day. Without such hard work, no one would get his degree. Alas! today things are otherwise. Students pass without much study. Such ill-educated doctors are a calamity to the nation. Not all doctors are of this kind. There are quite a few competent doctors.

It is the duty of the medical profession to rectify this situation. They should contact the authorities to bring about reforms. Only then will the nation progress.

We do not need many hospitals. Patients can be treated easily. In my view, there is no need for you to worry about money and resources. Treat your patients with love: Duty is God. This love should be mutual give and take. You may charge fees for your services, but do it with love. This is the right course for you. When you render service in this spirit, you will be successful in all cases. When you treat the patient with love, you will win the patient's love. Hence, your motto should be: "Start the day with love, fill the day with love and end the day with love." This is the way to God.

Our American doctor, who addressed the valedictory session, said that doctors should speak sweetly to patients. Whatever you do should be filled with love. A patient feels reassured when he sees the smiling face of a doctor.

Tribute to participants of Medical Conference

Embodiments of Divine Love! You have come from long distances, undergoing many strains. Conferences and symposia of all kinds are held all over the world all the time. But none of the decisions arrived at these gathering are implemented. Our Symposium is different. You have all come in a spirit of dedication. The decisions taken here should be implemented. You came here to learn from others as well as to share your experiences with others. You should return all the better for your visit. You should feel encouraged by your experiences here. Elated by this experience, you should be able to achieve many things. Return to your countries with joy in your hearts. You have had edifying experiences. It is fortunate that highly experienced doctors have been able to participate in this Symposium. They have also visited our Hospital and given many useful suggestions for enlarging its usefulness in the years ahead. We shall try to give effect to these suggestions. We are making plans for developing the Urology and Neurology wings. Please convey your experience and suggestions from time to time and encourage our doctors to do better. We wish that you should also make occasional visits to our Institute and Hospital. You are always welcome. Do not have any hesitation. This is your Hospital! Not mine. You are my property. Do not wait for invitations from here. There can be no objection to your coming to your own home.

Highly experienced professional men have come here. No conference could have taken place in such a peaceful atmosphere as here with such pure hearted participants. In most conferences there are heated debates. Here everything was peaceful and calm. It was a sacred exercise. As Dr. Somaraju said, we have here a temple, where proper prayers should be offered. What should be this prayer? It is: All patients should get well. *"Lokaassamasthaas Sukhino Bhavanthu!"* (Let all people be happy).

I conclude my discourse with the benediction that in the years to come all people should lead healthy and ideal lives.

Address to the Valedictory session of the Cardiac Speciality Symposium on 7-2-1993.

CHAPTER 6

Secure God's grace by *Shraddha* and *Vishvaasa*

Why does sun rise and set in the sky regularly every
day?
Why do the stars that shine so peacefully in the sky
at night hide themselves during the day?
Why does the wind that blows tirelessly protect living
beings?
Why do the murmuring brooks flow ceaselessly?
Why are there among the myriad human beings
In the world differences of race, religion, caste and
wealth?

Who is the Lord of all this?
Who is their Controller?
Come forward, all ye, to learn to carry out His commands!

Isaanah sarva vidhyaanaam
Iswaras-sarvabhoothaanaam
Brahmaadhipathih Sadaa Shivoham.

THE entire creation is the cosmic dance of the Lord. It is a marvellous and incomparable dance. It is an enchanting scene to behold.

In this world, birth and death, happiness and sorrow follow each other in ceaseless succession. However, Sumathi, an exemplar of chastity, could stay the sun from rising to prevent the death of her husband. In order to restore her husband to life, Saavithri confronted successfully the lord of Death. Such extraordinary power is given only to human beings.

Dharma and *adharma* are prevalent in creation

In this creation, both *Dharma* (Righteousness) and *Adharma* (unrighteousness) are prevalent. At one time righteousness is predominant. At another time unrighteousness reigns. Only a man filled with devotion can attain the triune embodiment of the Divine—*Sathyam, Shivam, Sundaram* (Truth, Auspiciousness and Beauty).

When confronted with his final destiny man becomes a prey to many fears and doubts. The moment Kamsa heard that the child that would be born to his cousin Devaki would prove his slayer, he wanted immediately to kill her. Vasudeva saved his wife's life by promising to hand over to Kamsa every child born to Devaki. To kill or to save a life, the power vests in man alone.

Every human being is a fragment of the Divine. Only when a man discharges his duties will his life find fulfilment. Duty is man's primary obligation. If a man is endowed with wealth and possessions, he has a duty to enjoy them. But to covet or seize other people's wealth is a crime. Wealth is not confined to money or gold or other possessions. All the knowledge and skills acquired by a person also constitute his wealth. Even health is wealth. The power to think is also wealth. Physical strength and mental abilities are also wealth. The time at one's command is also his wealth.

Hence, it is man's primary duty to utilise his time and every other form of wealth in the right manner. Unfortunately, today man wastes the time, wealth and talents of others. This is *Adharma*—opposed to righteousness.

Dharma implies right use of one's time

Oftentimes, I advise the students not to indulge in excessive talking for the reason that it is a gross abuse of the time available to them. Moreover, by excessive talk with another person, he is robbing the latter of his time. This is also wrong.

Dharma implies the right use of one's time and resources. *Adharma* is the abuse of one's time and wealth and depriving others of their wealth.

Every person has a mind of his own in which thoughts arise based on his *Ichcha-Shakthi* (will power). One person favours adoration of Raama. Another prefers Shiva. A third one enjoys worshipping Krishna. A fourth is inspired by contemplation of Jesus. Another is musing over the thought of Allah. All these are based on individual preferences.

But, in the minds of all persons, in whatever country or region, whatever form one wishes to adore, whatever deity one wants to worship, whatever name one likes to chant, two things are essential. *Vishvaasam* (faith) and *Shraddha* (earnestness). Without earnestness, even the most trivial act cannot be performed well. Without *Shraddha* nothing can be accomplished.

"*Shraddhaavaan labhaathe Jnaanam,*" says the Geetha. Only the earnest seeker can acquire knowledge of the Divine. However intelligent one may be, without earnestness he will achieve nothing. A man with earnestness can convert a small burning cinder into a huge bonfire.

Shraddha and Vishvaasa represent Shakthi and Shiva

Shraddha (earnestness) is the means to the realisation of the Divine. What does *Shraddha* signify? It signifies *Dhaiva-Shakthi* (Divine power). *Shraddha* is called *Bhavaani*. It refers to a goddess, to *Shakthi* (Divine energy) or *Prakrithi* (Nature).

Next comes *Vishvaasam* (faith). What is faith? It symbolises *Eeshvarathvam* (the Divine Principle). Through *Shraddha* (earnestness) *Ichcha shakthi, Kriyaa-shakthi* and *Jnaana-shakthi* (will power, the power of action, and the power of wisdom) are manifested. The essence of these three potencies is *Eeshvarathva* (Divinity). They constitute the power of *Vishvaasam* (faith).

Thus, *Shraddha* and *Vishvaasam* represent Paarvathi and Parameshvara. Humanness represents the combination of Shakthi (or Nature) and Shiva. These two are not disparate. Just as fire and the power to burn go together, these two go together. Sugar and sweetness are similarly interrelated. There is no sugar without sweetness. Where there is sweetness there is sugar. Likewise *Shraddha* and *Vishvaasam* are symbiotically related to each other. Hence these should be regarded as present in man in the form of Shiva and Shakthi.

The whole of *Prakrithi* (nature) is *Ardhnaari-svaruupam* (the feminine half of the Divine couple). Any man who has no *Shraddha* and *Vishvaasa* is verily a corpse.

Although both *Shraddha* (as God) and *Vishvaasa* (as Nature) are present in man, by ignoring God (lacking earnestness) man wastes his life. Earnestness and faith together constitute spirituality. Without these, all spiritual exercises have no value.

Dedicate all actions to God

How is man to realise the presence of Shiva and Shakthi in Him? It is by doing all actions as a dedication to the Divine. *"Mathkarmakrith, Math-paramah, Madh-bhakthah,"* declares the Geetha (Whatever actions you do, dedicate them to me. Consider me as your Supreme Lord. Be devoted to Me). This is the message of the Lord in the Geetha. This is the right way to worship the *Saakaara* (attributeful Lord). This kind of worship promotes devotion.

Only a land that is properly ploughed, weeded, manured and sown with good seeds will yield a rich harvest. Likewise, after the field of the heart has been cleared of the weeds of bad thoughts and qualities, fertilised by good feelings and virtues, and the pure seed of *Prema* (Love) is sown, the sacred crop of *Jnaana* (wisdom) can be enjoyed.

Based on this, two paths have been laid down in the spiritual field: *Vidhvamsaka* and *Vidhaayaka* (the destructive and the constructive paths). *Vidhvamsaka* path refers to the clearing of a field of bushes, thorns and the like before it is got ready for cultivation. *Vidhaayaka* path refers to the planting of good seeds in the form of good qualities which will yield a harvest of joy. Hence everyone's heart has to be filled in the right way by *Shraddha* and *Vishvaasa.*

It is not enough for a devotee to claim that he loves the Lord. He must find out whether the Lord loves him. You must see whether God showers His grace on you. Only then, your devotion becomes meaningful.

In all his actions, man should not be concerned only with self-interest. He must find out whether his actions are approved by his conscience. Just as the Divine is always blissful, the devotee should be a *Santhushtah* (ever-blissful). But in the present times, men have no contentment or sense of joy. They are racked by doubts and apprehensions. How can such persons ever experience divine bliss? It has been said that one who is vacillating is merely a living creature, but one who is firm and unwavering is divine.

Treat God as a friend

God has the appellation *Suhrith* (a good hearted friend). In every human relationship, there is an element of selfishness in the display of affection. God alone showers His love with no trace of selfishness. Man fails to understand this sacred, Divine Love principle. I would like to illustrate what it means to have God as friend from the example of the Pandavas whom Krishna was all in all. When Arjuna returned to Hasthinaapura from Dhvaaraka after the passing of Krishna, he could not bear to answer his

mother Kunthi's question as to what had happened
to Krishna. With tears in his eyes, he said that
Krishna, who had been their charioteer, their coun-
cellor, their preceptor, friend, lord and everything else,
had left the world. There can be no greater thing
than to have God as one's *Suhrith* (friend).

Our aim should be to dwell in the Lord

Another appellation of God is *Nivaasah* (the
Supreme Abode). Our aim should be to dwell in the
Lord. This cosmos is the abode of the Lord. We
are living in this cosmos. We are not separate from
it. But the sacred feeling that we are living in the
abode of the Lord should be cherishable by everyone.
Such sacred feelings do not arise in man because of
the barriers created by *raaga, bhaya* and *dhvesha*
(attachment, fear and hatred). Attachment is the
feeling that one develops when he considers that
something other than himself can give him satisfaction and joy. This sense of separateness should go.
The consciousness that the same constituents are
present in one and all should be realised. Then, there
will be no room for differentiation and alienation.
The sense of oneness will be experienced.

Where there is attachment, there is *dhvesha*
(hatred), which is a reflection of *raaga*. Fear is born
out of attachment—the fear of losing what one has.
Attachment and fear breed hatred. These three lead
man to stray from his adherence to *Shraddha* and
Vishvaasa. Hence, these three have to be brought under
control.

To realise the Divinity within man, everyone has
to turn his vision inward. All that is perceived in

the external world is subject to changes. Man cannot derive happiness from an unchanging world. He desires change. But the change He should seek is a divine change, not changes in the mundane world. he should seek to know the truth about himself. Ignorant about his true self, man today is harried by fears. As long as the fear remains, God will elude him. He has to develop faith in the Divinity (Shiva) within him, to get rid of this fear and acquire the *Brahmabalam* (strength of the Divine).

Difference between *raathri* and Shivaraathri

Every night is marked by darkness. But tonight it is Shivaraathri. What is the difference between *raathri* (night) and Shivaraathri? For the man who has recognised his divinity, every night is Shivaraathri. For the man immersed in worldly concerns, all nights are the same. That night is marked by darkness. This night is marked by light. Spirituality is the lighthouse that spreads light for the man who is full of despair, immersed in insatiable desires. The name of God is the lighthouse. By chanting the name, the bearer of the name can be realised.

Man has to proceed from the body to the Divine. Man is a limb of society. Society is a limb of Nature. Nature is a limb of God. The *Aathma* is present in everyone. It knows no territorial barriers. It is omnipresent. To recognize the omnipresence of the Divine is the purpose of observing Shivaraathri. This purpose is not served by fasting and keeping awake all the night. These are mere auxiliaries to what is considered the ultimate goal. But God-realisation should not be put off to some distant future. It has

to be taken up here and now. That is the purpose
of Shivaraathri.

Concentrate Mind on God

But today, people have forgotten their Divine
destiny and are wasting their lives in worldly pursuits.
They have no faith in their future. Where there is
no faith, there is no Shiva. They lack the power of
Shraddha (earnestness). So Paarvathi is also not there.
Man's pathetic condition today is he has denied
himself the grace of both Paarvathi and Shiva. He can
obtain it only by cultivating human values. He has
to acquire the *Jnaana* (spiritual wisdom) that comes from
Shraddha (spiritual earnestness). The true values for
man are *Ichcha-shakthi, Kriya-shakthi,* and   *Jnaana-
shakthi.* These represent the triple aspects of the Divine:
Sathyam, Shivam, Sundaram (Truth, Auspiciousness and
Beauty). These are the eternal verities. Though
endowed with these divine powers, man goes after
petty trinkets. When the Divine is ready to confer
liberation, why get involved in the bonds of worldly
life?

Man should seek God alone. Once God's grace
is secured, all else will be got with ease. For this
purpose, man has to get rid of attachment, fear and
hatred. He must perform all actions as an offering
to God, who is omnipresent.

The vigil and fasting observed on Shivaraathri
night have become farcical. True vigil and fasting
consist in concentrating all one's thoughts on God
during the whole night. God's grace is a direct sequel
to one's actions. Each one has to examine for himself
in what spirit he is performing his worship. The

Divine can be realised only through *Shraddha* and *Vishvaasa*. The Divine is within everyone. Once man recognises this fact, he will give no room for bad qualities.

Embodiments of Divine Love! Dedicate yourselves to the performance of your duties. Do not waste your time or that of others in idle talk. Starting with the duties of the individual, man should aim at achieving oneness with the Divine as the ultimate goal. Shivaraathri is an auspicious occasion for concentrating the mind on God. Devote at least this one night entirely to the contemplation of God, to the exclusion of all other thoughts and worries.

Discourse in the Puurnachandhra Auditorium on 19-2-1993, Shivaraathri Day.

I am showing you by My example how you must fill every moment with useful beneficial activity. You talk among yourselves, "O, Svaami is having his rest hour; Svaami is sleeping." But I have never craved for a minute's rest or sleep or relief. Shall I tell you at what time I feel restful, relieved, content? When I know that you are all earning supreme bliss through detachment and spiritual discipline, not until then.

—BABA

CHAPTER 17

Serve the Divine: chant the Name

What can Kali or the forces of evil do
To one whose heart is filled with compassion,
Who wears the jewel of truthful speech,
Whose limbs are devoted to the well-being of others?

IF MAN is to be free from the sway of evil forces, he has to achieve the triple purity of thought, word and deed. It is only when the heart, the tongue and the body are pure that man can fully comprehend *Para thathva* (Supreme Principle.)

This world that is inhabited by man is called *Prapancha. Pra* implies that which is shining or blooming. It is a prefix. It is only when this *Pra* is prefixed to every sense organ that *Prapancha* (the world) emerges.

Prapancha and Paramaathma

There are the five basic elements (space, air, fire, water and earth), the five sense organs (relating to hearing, touch, sight, taste and smell), the five sheaths (*Annamaya, Praanamaya, Manomaya, Vijnaanamaya and Aanandhamaya*), and the five life-breaths *(Praana, Apaana, Vyaana, Udaana and Samaana)*. When the prefix *Pra* is added to each of these *Pancha* (five) categories, the *Prapancha* emerges. This means that the world is made up of the five elements, the five senses, the five sheaths and the five vital airs. Consequently, wherever you turn, you see in the world differences: differences among material objects, a variety among individuals, differences in experiences, etc. Wherever such differences exist, there are bound to be likes and dislikes, *Raaga* and *dhvesha* (attachments and aversions). If man has to transcend these differences, he has to recognise the all-pervading Divine principle. Only then both attachment and hatred can be totally eliminated.

The five elements are manifestations of the *Paramaathma* (Over-self). So are the five sheaths and the five vital airs. Hence, man cannot exist without these manifestations. That is why the scriptures declared: "His feet and hands are everywhere; His head, face, eyes and ears are everywhere." The omnipresence of the Divine can be experienced in the Cosmos.

When a man embarks on some undertaking, he imagines that no one is observing him. But no man can do anything unseen or unnoticed by God. Is it possible to deceive the Divine whose face and eyes are everywhere?' *"Sarvam Aavrithya thishthathi"*

(Encompassing everything, He remains). The Divine
shines in every object. It is a mark of supreme
ignorance to imagine that you can conceal anything
from God. Nor is that all. God is described as
"*Acharam Charameva Cha*" (He is non-moving and
moving). That is, though appearing to be moving,
He remains unmoving. God has no hands, but He
can grasp anything. He has no feet but He can move
everywhere. He has no eyes, but can see everything.
This is the significance of the statement "*Acharam
Charameva Cha.*"

Here is an example. Man in the dream states feels
that he is moving about. In the dream he wanders
over all places. He experiences many actions done
by the body. But despite the movements and activities
in the dream, his body is still and motionless on the
bed on which he is sleeping. The same body is moving
about in the dream. The Divine is in that body.
Equally the Divine is in the body that is motionless.
Thus, He is both the unmoving and the moving. It
is not easy to recognise this subtle *Jnaana* (spiritual wisdom).

Perception of One without a second is *Jnaana*

What does *Jnaana* mean? *Jna* means to know. *Na*
refers to that which cannot be known. *Jnaana* therefore
refers to that which cannot be easily comprehended.
"*Advaitha Dharshanam Jnaanam,*" declares the scripture.
Jnaana (Super-knowledge) is the perception of the One
without a second. Only the One exists. There is no
second. In such a situation, there is nothing to be
known. There is no knowledge, knowing or knower
(in that state). In comprehending the One, the nature
of the many has to be properly understood. Every

man has to recognise the Divinity that is present in all human beings.

God is one. That One is the Indweller in all beings. Did the Divine fragment Himself in a myriad ways? The answer is: without fragmenting Himself, the Divine is present in all beings. In his ignorance, man notices only the manifoldness around him.

This may be illustrated this way. The sun's image can be seen in an ocean, a river, a lake, a pond or a well. Everywhere the sun appears to be shining. Are there so many different suns? No. The objects reflecting the image of the sun are varied and different from one another. Likewise, names and forms say be different, but in all beings, the same God, without being divided, shines as the Indweller. Thus, although bodies may appear with different names and forms, the Divine in them is one.

Develop love, nearness and obedience to the Divine

To recognise this omnipresent Divine, man has to get rid of *Raaga, Bhaya,* and *Dhvesha* (attachment, fear and hatred). These three are worldly qualities. But, merely by shedding these qualities, man cannot have God-realisation or comprehend the Divine principle. This table before me has no qualities. Can it comprehend the Divine? The mere absence of bad qualities is not enough. There must be love. You must develop love towards God. But love alone will not serve to make one comprehend the *Aathmik* principle. One must move towards the Divine. But, here again, nearness to God is not enough. You have to carry out the injunctions of the Divine. It is only when love, nearness and obedience to the Divine commands are present that one can realise the *Aathmik* principle. Recognition of the Divinity inherent in the human state calls for spiritual *saadhanas* (disciplines) of various kinds.

Today man is enveloped in a certain disease. It is *Ashaanthi* (peacelessness). For curing any disease, there are normally three methods. One is to take the prescribed medicine. After taking the medicine, the prescribed diet regimen has to be followed. Taking the medicine without observing the diet regulations will not help to cure the disease. Adhering to the prescribed diet, without taking the medicine, will also not serve the purpose. Both medicines and diet control are essential to ensure a cure.

If the disease of peacelessness afflicting man is to be cured, he has to take the medicine of love and adhere to the diet of following the injunctions of the Divine. Only then will the mental unrest go.

Three different types of argument

It is true that many have love for God. But they do not live up to the dictates of the Divine. Those who follow the Divine injunctions in a formal manner, do not act with love for God. It is only when there is a union of love and obedience that man can recover peace of mind.

In this context, a *Vedhic* aphorism declares: "*Vaadhah pravadhathaam*" (Let the argument be expounded). There are three different ways of carrying on a *Vaada* (argument). Without attachment or hatred, with the desire to understand the *Aathmik* principle, with a sincere heart, engaging oneself in a spirit of enquiry, is termed a discussion, *Vaadhah* (purposeful argument). This means that one conducts the debate with a heartfelt yearning to know the truth, with a pure mind filled with noble thoughts.

Without such an attitude, if one is keen only to assert his own opinions and defeat the others in the argument by any means, condemning the beliefs of others and defending one's own views in an egoistic spirit—this type of argumentation is termed *Jalpa* (wrangling).

The third type of argumentation is condemning everything and indulging in such condemnation habitually, without any regard for one's own defects, finding faults in others perpetually, magnifying those faults and broadcasting them. Such an attitude is termed *Vithandavaadha* (perverse argumentation).

Of these three types, unfortunately these days we notice only the third type of perverse logic prevalent. *Vaadha* and *Jalpa* are not very much in evidence. One pretends to be all-knowing in any argument. Such people enter into an argument only for furthering their selfish ends. These persons can never realise the *Aathmik* principle even after any number of lives.

Strive to understand the inherent Divinity

The first requisite is the urge to comprehend the *Aathmik* principle. Only when this arises in man will his humanness become worth while. In spite of human birth and the inherent Divinity in them, men are failing to recognise their Divine nature. Man is learning all about other things, but is making no effort to understand himself.

What is the real meaning of *Jnaana?* It is to know the truth about one's self by a process of refinement.

What is spirituality? What is the refining of one's nature? It is discovering one's true self.

One is searching for something in a room. He sees everything in the room except himself. Likewise in this vast room of the cosmos, man is searching for everything and perceives all things. But he does not know himself and has no perception of what he is. He cries out: "Where is God? Where is God?" This query is like that of a man who asks others where he is. "Where am I? Who am I?" What is the meaning in putting such questions to others? He knows where he is. How can others tell him where he is?

"As is your feeling, so is the outcome"

Likewise, it is sheer ignorance to search for God. There is no need to search for God. He is everywhere, all-pervading, inside and outside. You have to know the Divine which is here, there and everywhere. The Bhaagavatha says: *"Dhuuraath dhuure anthike cha"* (He is farther than the farthest and closeby as well). There is none who is nearer to us than He. But there is also none who is farther from us than He. What is the reason for this nearness or remoteness? One's feelings alone are the primary reason. If you feel He is near, He is near; if you feel He is distant, He is remote. It is on account of this that the scriptures declare: "As is your feeling, so is the outcome."

God has been given three names: *Om Thath Sath*. Man has a fascination for names. When the name of his native place or his own name is mentioned, he feels happy. But with regard to the Divine, the name is not important. If the inner significance of all the different names of the Divine is understood, it will be found that they mean one thing alone. *Om* is *Parabrahma* (the Supreme Absolute). *Tath* is 'That.' *Sath* is the Real. *"Om Thath Sath"* means "The Supreme Absolute is that Reality." By describing *Om* as *Pranava*, made up of the three letters A, U, M and elaborately commenting in this manner, the pedantic expositors confuse the aspirants. By such expositions, devotion is weakened. Each one expounds these statements in his own way. When the question is asked whether these exponents practise any of the teaching they preach, the answer is in the negative. When such is the case, how can spirituality grow?

Hence, practice is more essential than preaching. When you practise the teachings, others will follow your example. When you preach to a lakh of people what you don't practise yourself, all of them lose their faith in the teachings and are indifferent to them.

Three stages to attain the Divine

Moreover, the *Aathmik* bliss to be derived from practising spiritual truth cannot be derived by any other means. No preceptor's teaching will be of any use. Nor will the reading of scriptures be of any avail. The gain from study or listening is precious little. It is only when you practise what you have seen and heard that you can experience *Aathmik* bliss. In the Geetha, Krishna declares: *"Jnaathum, Dhrashtum, Praveshtum"* (the three stages of knowing, seeing and experiencing in Self-Realisation). You have heard about something: that is *Jnaathum*. You wish to see what you have heard about: that is *Dhrashtum*. And then you wish to have the experience of what you have seen: that is *Praveshtum*. Only when these three take place can the human being attain the Divine. At present, you are merely studying the scriptures or listening to the expositions of scholars. You must embark on an undertaking to ascertain whether what you have heard can be found and put into practice. You have to begin the quest. But where is the quest to be made? Not outside you. Everything is within you. All that is outside is a reflection of the Inner Being.

Experience of the sages in realising the Divine

In ancient times, the great sages performed rigorous penances to experience the Divine. Some of them gave up the attempt after a time, considering the Divine as unattainable. Some others persisted in their attempts with the determination to achieve the goal. Thereby they realised the Divine. What did they proclaim to the world after their Realisation? "Vedhaaham etham Purusham Mahaantham Aadithya-varnam Thamasah parasthaath" (We were able to see the Lord, the Effulgent One, bright as the Sun). Where did they see God? "Thamasah parasthaath" (Beyond the Thamo-guna), came the answer.

Today man is enveloped in a thick cloud of Thamo-guna. The effulgent Lord can be seen beyond the Thamo-guna (the quality which is the cause of all man's ignorance and wrong doings). This Thamo-guna, which holds every man in its grip, should be got rid of. For this purpose, men should perform good deeds and render service.

In the Raamaayana, during an encounter between Hanumaan and Vibheeshana, Raavana's youngest brother, in Lanka, Vibheeshana asked Hanumaan why he (Vibheeshana) had not secured a vision of Raama

in spite of his chanting Raama's name. Hanumaan
replied that mere chanting of Raama's name was not
enough. Vibheeshana had failed to engage himself in
any act of service to Raamd. He had done nothing to
render help to Seetha, who was held captive in Lanka
by Raavana.

It is not enough to recite the Lord's name. One
has to render service to the Lord. Only then, there is
a unification of the Name and the Form and the Divine
is experienced.

People are chanting the name of the Lord today.
They are dwelling in the *aashram*. Why have they come
here? To secure Bhagavaan's grace and experience
Aathmaanandham (spiritual bliss). Those who have come
may be reciting the name of the Lord. But are you
engaging yourselves in any of the Lord's work? What
part are you playing in Svaami's work? Without
participating in Divine service, your stay here for any
number of years will be as futile as the presence of
a frog on a lotus. While bees coming from long distances taste the nectarine sweetness of the honey in
the lotus, the frog derives no benefit from its nearness
to the lotus. This truth is not recognised by devotees.

Duty of the *aashramites*

Hence, it is not enough to come to the *aashram*.
You have to take part in the *aashram* activities. You
must render service according to your capacity. You are
not asked to do more than that. Svaami does not ask
for your services. He is saying all this for your own
sake.

Hence, from today everyone staying in the *aashram*,
whoever he may be, should render service according

to one's capacity. There is no use merely in consuming food and taking one's seat in the *Mandhir* Verandah or the *Dharshan* (audience) line. Everyone must render service to the limit of one's ability. Those who cannot render such service should quit the *Mandhir*. Why have you come here? What are you doing? Consult your conscience for the answers. You have come from far away places, giving up all things. But despite this renunciation, what are you doing? You are wasting your time. This is a grievous mistake. Time is a manifestation of God. Time is consuming man. God is the consumer of Time itself. Therefore, you should strive to earn the grace of God. If you waste time, you will forfeit God's grace.

Embark on active work

Many persons are wasting their time in this manner. Whatever you tell them, they say: "Sai Raam! Sai Raam!" Even a tape-recorder can repeat this. What is the use of uttering the name? Embark on active work. Even for eating a *masala dosa*, you have to engage your hands and mouth in action. Likewise, you have to use your hands for service. Chant the name with your tongue. And experience bliss in your heart. Only when all these three are done will you qualify for God's grace.

Therefore, everyone who had joined the *aashram* should take part in service activities according to one's capacity. Some are doing this. There is one devotee who is 86 years old. He is engaged in some work or other right upto 10 p.m. in the night. For doing work earnestly, is age a bar? He has difficulty in climbing stairs or coming down. But he carries on his work by using a vehicle. There is another devotee who is also an aged person. According to his strength, he renders service in the Canteen by serving water. There is a third devotee. His energies have declined. Despite this, he is carrying on the editorial duties assigned to him.

Do service according to your capacity

Therefore, each one may do what lies within his power. But there are quite a few younger people who don't do any work. They take food several times. They sit in the verandah and do nothing. There is no room for such persons in the verandah. You have to work. Those who do not work, should leave. This is the import of the Geetha declaration: "Karmanyeva Adhikaarasthe maa phaleshu kadaachana" (You are entitled only to do your duty, not to the fruits thereof). Practise and propagate this Karma Maarga (the Path of Action).

When one is told to take up some work, he says: "I won't be able to do this." Now, what is it such a person can do? He must at least say what it is that he can do. He is not being asked to build walls or dig wells. No one is asked to do such arduous work in the aashram. All tasks are easy ones. We want persons who will take up such work. It is not for the development of the aashram. It is for fulfilment of your life. The work can always be got done by wage earners without your service. But if you do that work, get involved in Karma Yoga, aim at Dharma Yoga and merge in Brahma Yoga (union with the Divine), you will have Self-Realisation. This is the teaching of Svaami.

Grief follows happiness like a shadow

Dear devotees! All actions should be done with a view to achieving *Thrikarana shuddhi* (purity in thought, word and deed). Everything is in the heart of man. Divinity is installed in the heart. A foolish person is carried away by the wealth and pomp of the outside world. The conceit that accompanies the fascination for these possessions is not recognised. Grief follows happiness like a shadow. Under the shadow of *Adhikaàra* (Authority) flourishes the demon of *Ahamkara* (egotism). Do not be carried away by the lure of power. Self-conceit, which comes in its wake, will overwhelm you. Beware of its presence. Only then you will be well. Do not gloat over wealth and possessions. There is an ogress that will submerge them. That is *dhurabhimaanam* (self-conceit). You must take note of such dangers.

When there is a lightning, you see a sudden burst of effulgence. This is followed in the next moment by intense darkness. Darkness lurks all the time behind light. Hence, man is advised to treat pleasure and pain, profit and loss, victory and defeat with an equal eye. There is nothing in the world without these opposites. This is termed *Dhvaitha* (duality). Darkness and light, heat and cold, good and bad, sin and merit, truth and falsehood—these pairs are always there. Man has two eyes, two ears, and two nostrils in one nose.

Thus the world presents a picture of dualism. And because of this, we have the phenomenon of constant change in the *Jagath* (world). *Jagath* means that which "comes and goes" *(Ja + gath)*. Nothing is permanent. There is only one thing that is unchanging and eternal and that is Divinity. To experience that Divinity man must first of all get rid of his bad qualities. He must suppress his ego and render service to the Divine along with chanting the Lord's name. That is the way to redeem one's human life. Moreover, both the chanting of God's name and rendering of service should be done with a love-filled heart.

*Discourse in the Puurnachandhra
Auditorium on 20-2-1993.*

ౣ━━━━━━━━━━━━━━━━━━━━━━ ౪

I am ever engaged in some activity or other for your benefit. Things I could get done, I do not entrust to others; I do them Myself, so that they may learn self-reliance and get experience thereby. I have always your progress, your comfort, your happiness in mind. You can note it in the slightest act of Mine. I do all work pertaining to Me. I open all letters addressed to Me and they are legion.

—BABA

CHAPTER 8

New horizons for the Sai Institute

STUDENTS! Do not be proud that you have acquired scholastic knowledge. The true form of knowledge is humility. Eschewing pride and self-conceit, pursue the right goal.

Students today are acquiring considerable scientific knowledge. It serves only to promote civilised living in the phenomenal world. But what the students need today is the refinement of the heart. This is possible only through an internal process. Students who have imbibed modern culture should not only develop their intellects, but should also develop a broad outlook.

The students today have a two-fold duty: One is to face the challenges of modern civilization, the other is to protect and preserve the ancient spiritual and cultural heritage of the country. Students should shine as ideal citizens of the nation.

A complete education is that which makes a man compassionate. Besides giving appropriate exercises to the body, students should strive to cultivate the heart and keep it pure.

Two kinds of learning in educational system

There are two kinds of learning in the educational system today. One relates to information about various subjects. The other relates to the rectification of the individual's life. The first relates to the physical. The second relates to the spiritual. The former is concerned with earning a living. The latter is concerned with the basic goal of life.

In the first type of education, you have opportunities to investigate various matters and arrive at scientific truths. For instance, you find out that water is composed of two parts of hydrogen and one part of oxygen. You thereby know the composition of water. This enhances your scientific knowledge. But what is relevant from the social and spiritual point of view is how to ensure fair distribution of water among all people.

A national system of education calls for the cultivation of humility, devotion and obedience. When students go through such a national system, they will not only manifest the inherent divinity in them, but also develop discipline. If education consisted only of scientific knowledge, the world will be a hopeless place. Scientific knowledge alone does not constitute the content of education. Character is knowledge.

Character is power. Character is life itself. Character is the hallmark of true education.

Unfortunately, the student today fills his head with a lot of information, but his personality is impaired in the process. Filling his mind with physical facts and absorbed in physical investigations, he undermines his basic humanness.

Aim at cultivation of good qualities

Selflessness, humility, unostentatiousness are qualities that underlie the human personality. Along with academic excellence, a student should aim at the cultivation of good qualities. Education enables you to score marks, but you also need elevation of your personality. Qualities contribute to elevation. Education and elevation combine to develop the human personality.

Unfortunately, people today are only concerned about academic education and ignore the cultivation of good qualities. Today the progress of scientific and technological education has virtually destroyed the sacredness of the human personality. Even the great war leader and Prime Minister of Britain, Winston Churchill, once declared: "Man has conquered everything, but has not conquered himself." Prahlaadha reproved his father, Hiranyakashipu, by telling him that though he had conquered the three worlds, he had not learnt to conquer his senses.

Without being able to control the senses, what is the use of learning every kind of knowledge? All knowledge is useless, if one has not acquired Self-knowledge. Such a person may be regarded as intellectually clever, but cannot be called intelligent. The first step, therefore, is to know one's Self. Spirituality is the means to acquire knowledge of yourself. Hence, as much importance should be assigned to the promotion of good qualities in the educational process as is given to academic studies.

During the past two centuries, many marvellous and even dangerous achievements have resulted from the pursuit of science. Exploiting the resources of the earth, they are boasting about their accomplishments. They have produced atomic bombs which can cause terrible destruction. Is it a sign of wisdom to boast one's capacity to destroy the world? This is a demonic power. The Western nations are now worried about the consequences of their dreadful discoveries.

Vijnaana should be combined with *Prajnaana*

It is essential that the development of science should be accompanied by a corresponding development of the power of *Viveka* (discrimination). *Vijnaana* (Science) is, doubtless, necessary. But it should be combined with *Prajnaana* (divine wisdom). *Prajna* is the essential principle in man. This 'Integrated Awareness' in *Vedhaanthik* parlance, *Prajnaanam* has been equated with *Brahman* (the Supreme Absolute).

When science is combined with *Prajna*, discrimination follows as a corollary. By forgetting *Prajna* and pursuing *Vijnana* (science), man is making a mockery of his existence. It is not enough to make a mere man out of a person through education. Education should aim at making him a "full man".

It is well known that the Indian economy is passing through a critical phase. But this is not so grievous a problem as the decline in morality and character. If this moral decline is not reversed, education will be utterly ruined. Students therefore must endeavour to promote morality and ethics. Without these, the entire nation will be ruined.

Four-fold formula for developing human qualities

Earning of money should not be the primary aim of students. Education should be for developing human qualities, not for securing jobs. There are four requisites for promoting this attitude to education and life. They are: *"Thyaja dhurjana samsargam"* (Give up all association with the evil-minded), *"Bhaja Saadhu samaagamam"* (Pray for the company of the good), *"Kuru punyam Ahoraathram"* (Engage yourself in meritorious deeds day and night) and *"Smara nithya-anithyathaam"* (Remember what is permanent and what is transient).

You should run away from bad company. A bad company can spoil even a good man. A renunciant may be turned into a covetous man. This is the effect of bad company. The ancient sages considered association with the evil-minded as companionship with a poisonous snake. It was to escape from the danger of such association that they resorted to the solitude of forests. A snake may bite a person once in a way but a bad man infects others with poison all the time. A bad man is one who is filled with bad thoughts, speaks bad words and does bad deeds.

The Mahaabhaaratha offers four examples of bad men called *Dhushta Chathushtayam*. The first one is Shakuni (Dhuryodhana's maternal uncle). Shakuni was all the time filled with *Dhuraalochana* (bad thoughts). He is a total stranger to good ideas. He was always plotting something bad for someone or other.

Dhuryodhana was having Shakuni as his adviser. Dhuryodhana was engaged in *Dhuscharya* (bad deeds). They were comrades in evil.

Then came Dhusshaasana (brother of Dhuryodhana). In association with Shakuni and Dhuryodhana, Dhusshaasana became notorious for his *Dhushpravarthana* (bad behaviour). When these three evil-minded men came together, "even stars started falling during daytime," as the saying goes. The whole cosmos rebels against such evil-minded men.

Karna, out of a false sense of *Dhurabhimaanam* (bad attachment), joined this trio. Gratitude is doubtless a good quality. But because Dhuryodhana came to his rescue on a critical occasion, Karna developed a wrongful attachment to Dhuryodhana. Karna was a good-natured person. He was noble-minded. But because he was associated with evil-minded men he also became a bad person. Despite his valour, physical prowess and intellectual abilities, Karna met with disaster because he had made himself remote from God. What was the defect in Karna? *Dhurabhimaanam* (misguided attachment).

Four kinds of evil persons

Evil thoughts, evil deeds, evil conduct and attachment to the evil-minded—these are *Dhushta Chathushtayam* (the four evil persons).

Hence, students should, at the outset, give up the company of bad persons. Once you have achieved maturity in moral stature, you can associate with anyone. At this stage, when your hearts are tender and your minds are not developed, you should not move freely with all and sundry. When you are spiritually immature, you should not associate with one and all equally.

These four rules should be the guiding-posts in your life. If you adhere to these four rules, you will be able to acquire all knowledge, by the grace of the Divine. This is illustrated by the story of Padhmapaadha, who acquired spiritual knowledge from Aadhi Shankara purely by his devoted service to the preceptor, without any attention to scriptural studies. Service to the preceptor was the *Punyakarma* (meritorious deed) which he performed all the time. This sanctified his life. While bringing the clothes of his *guru* from the other bank of the Ganga, the river was in spate and rose to the level of his neck. He prayed to Lord Shankara to enable him to serve his preceptor. He could reach the other bank by walking over lotus shaped slabs which appeared on the swollen river. He got the name Padhmapaadha and received all spiritual knowledge from Aadhi Shankara by sheer grace.

Service to *Guru* sanctifies one's life

Let me relate the story of Ashvathaama, who secured the *Chuudaamani* (diadem) by the grace of his preceptor for his devoted service to the *guru*. The *Chuudaamani* which Ashvathaama wore on his head, saved him from being beheaded by Arjuna, who had taken a vow to cut off Ashvathaama's head for his crime of slaughtering the Upa-paandavas (infant children of the Paandava brothers). Though Arjuna was keen on carrying out his vow and took Ashvathaama before Dhraupadhi, she, out of the largeness of her heart and from the inspiration of Krishna, found a formula to punish Ashvathaama without cutting off his head.

She said that if a *Brahmana* was kept captive in a house and sent out as free man, it was equivalent to beheading him. She also told Arjuna that it was not *Dharma* to kill a *Brahmana* who carried on his head the precious jewel given to him by his *guru.*

Students have to bear in mind these four principles: (1) Give up association with the evil-minded. (2) Welcome the company of the good. (3) Do meritorious acts ceaselessly. (4) Remember always what is transient and what is eternal.

You must remind yourselves that you are human beings and not animals. You must give no room to bad thoughts. Develop the inner vision to realise the Divine within you. This is the significance of devotees closing their eyes when they are in the inner sanctum of a temple. They pray to the Divine to open their inner vision.

The unique Chancellor and Vice-chancellor

In today's programme, we regard two items as important: one, a send-off and the other, a welcome. That is not so. Both are welcome. There is no such thing as a "send-off" with Sai. Svaami will not stand in the way of those who wish to leave. But I will not ask anyone to go.

However, during the past two years, Prof. Sampath moved among the staff and the students as among the members of the family. The teachers, the students and others lived as members of the same family. In other educational institutions, the Vice-Chancellor puts in his appearance once a year. Chancellors are hardly to be seen at all. But in our Institute, even more than the Vice-Chancellor, the Chancellor is ever present.

The most amazing fact is that the Chancellor spends all twenty four hours with the students. How should they answer their examination papers? How should they face their examinations? Speaking to the students even about these simple matters, Svaami gives them joy. In the same manner, the Vice-Chancellor also, from the morning prayer, till late in the evening, discusses their problems with the students. Prof. Sampath is a devotee. He did not come here seeking an office. To lead a sacred life in close proximity to Svaami was the sole desire of the couple Mr. and Mrs. Sampath. Coming here, he carried on his duties, to the limit of his capacity, without any deficiencies on his part. This is his home, not mine. So everyone carried on his respective duties. It is not merely to praise him that I say all this. He performed his duties well. That is enough.

Need for research in harnessing solar energy

Do not consider that from this day he is relinquishing his post. Spending the rest of his life with Svaami, giving to the students the benefit of all his knowledge, he should contribute to the growth of our Institute in a unique way. He has specialized in electronics. In addition, he is interested in the harnessing of solar energy. Bhaaratheeyas revere the sun. The sun is an immense ball of hydrogen and helium. There is immense scope for harnessing a small fraction of the energy coming to the earth from the sun. My desire is that "Our Sampath" should remain here and make use of his knowledge to utilise solar power. The sun is the embodiment of effulgence. Wherefrom does this light come? How does it come? No scientist has yet found how this light reaches us. It comes from a Divine power. The Divine is fully effulgent. He has the splendour of a billion suns. Today you are not able to make use of the energy from a single sun. How can you measure the power of One who has the splendour of a billion suns? The solar system is like a candle to the effulgence of the Divine.

For harnessing the solar energy, with the realisation of its divine source, special efforts should be made in our Institute to develop research in electronics and solar energy. I desire that Prof. Sampath should ascertain what arrangement should be made for this purpose and carry on his work here in the years ahead.

Raamaayana should be enacted in the Sai Institute

The new Vice-Chancellor, Dr. Hanumanthappa, has been a devotee of Svaami for the past 25 years. When the Sai College was started in Brindhaavan, he used to come all the way from the city and hold classes in Commerce for our students. Nor is that all. He has been closely associated with our educational institutions from their inception. At that time our college in Brindhaavan was affiliated to the Bangalore University. From those days he has been rendering service in various ways. He is an ardent devotee. Both the outgoing and the incoming Vice-Chancellors should work in perfect harmony, make our Institute an ideal institution and do pioneering work in new fields for the progress of our students. They should be like Raama and Lakshmana. Our Institute should be like Seetha. When you have these three, Raama, Lakshmana and Seetha, our students will develop like Bharatha and Shatrughna. The Raamaayana should be reenacted in this form and presented to the world.

What is the inner significance of the Raamaayana? *"Sathyam Vadha: Dharmam Chara"* (Speak the Truth and follow Righteousness). Today, these two have to be upheld. Without these two, life is worthless.

Prof. Sampath honoured

Prof. Sampath could have continued for some more time. But official regulations have prescribed an age-limit, which has to be complied with. Therefore, he had to retire. But this is only in conformity with external regulations. He will not depart from Svaami's heart. For the signal service rendered by him during the past two years, he has to be appropriately honoured. We are binding him closer to ourselves. The bonds we are placing on him are that he should impart all the knowledge he has acquired to our students and offer to the nation the new discoveries by our institutions in Prashaanthi Nilayam.

I, therefore, fasten two gold Kadiyams (bangles) on the wrists of Prof. Sampath. Sampath! we are going to bind both your hands. Hence, you will be a bondman, engaging yourself to the full measure of your capacity in Svaami's work, and rejoicing in the service you render.

Discourse at a special function, unique of its kind, got up by Bhagavaan Baba, Chancellor of Shri Sathya Sai Institute of Higher Learning, on 4-3-1993, in the Institute Auditorium, to honour the retiring Vice-Chancellor, Prof. Sampath, and to welcome the new Vice-Chancellor, Dr. K. Hanumanthappa.

CHAPTER 9

Chaithanya and the 'Outcast'

ONCE, a mendicant with tattered clothes, unkempt hair and dirty body, came and stood at the threshold of Chaithanya's room and was meditating with closed eyes. On seeing him Chaithanya came out and asked him, "Who are you? You can come inside." On hearing these soft and sweet words, the mendicant opened his eyes and replied in all humility, "Svaami, I don't deserve to step into your room. I am a despicable person belonging to the caste of Chandalas (Untouchables). I am unfit to defile your sacred residence." Full of smiles, Chaithanya went closer to him and said endearingly: "My son, never say that you are mean, despicable or unworthy. Who is mean and who is sacred on this earth? All are sacred because the same God shines in every one's heart. So, please come inside without any hesitation."

Power of the Lord's name erases all fears

When the mendicant was still hesitating to go inside, Chaithanya questioned him about the purpose of his visit. The visitor replied, "Svaami, I am repeatedly chanting God's name but I feel it lacks *chaithanya* (spiritual power) just as a person in a state of coma has mere life without any consciousness. I seem to be mechanically chanting the Lord's name without experiencing the power of the Divine. I have come to you with the hope that if you initiate me in one of the Lord's names, it will be charged with spiritual potency and I will be benefitted by chanting such a name."

Chaithanya replied, "All the names of God are full of *chaithanya* (divine power). God's name is omnipotent and self-effulgent. Hence it is not proper for you to underrate the efficacy of any of the Lord's names. However, for your satisfaction, I will give you *Manthropadesha* (initiation into the sacred formula) as desired by you. Please step into the room." The visitor responded by slowly entering the room, full of humility, hesitation, nervousness and fear, and sat in one corner of the room. Noticing his plight, Chaithanya gently told him, "My son, why are you so full of fear? Freedom and fearlessness are the birth-right of every man. Freedom being your real nature, why do you give room for fear? You must recognise that the *Aathmik* power is behind all thoughts, and give up fear."

Saying this, Chaithanya came closer and closer to the mendicant. Seeing this, the mendicant cried out apprehensively: "Svaami, please don't touch me. If you touch me, both of us will be guilty of breach of the traditional norms of our society. I say so particularly because it is winter now, and if you touch me, you will have to take a cold water bath again and that will tell upon your health. I have accepted you as my *Guru* (preceptor) and since, according to the scriptures, the *Guru* is verily God, I shall be sinning against God by hurting you in any way. I have come to obey your commands and receive help from you, but not to hurt you in the process. Because of my sins in my past life, I am now born as an untouchable. I don't want to add to my load of sins by allowing you to touch me now."

There is no caste for any of the five elements

On hearing this, Chaithanya remonstrated: "What a simpleton you are! You are only betraying your ignorance by observing untouchability, ignoring the divinity inherent in every being. God has no distinctions of caste and creed. There is no caste for any of the five elements, namely, earth, water, fire, air and sky, all of which have emanated from God. Irrespective of the castes and creeds professed by men, all are equally sharing the bounties of Nature offered by the five elements. Therefore, there is no need to observe such differences of caste and creed. Come closer to me."

However, the mendicant could not shed his fear, because he had been nurturing this fear from his childhood. This shows that feelings such as fear, love, hatred etc., become ingrained in a person if he nurtures them for a long time from an early age in his life. Chaithanya told the mendicant, "God never endows man with fear. It is one's own weakness that fosters fear, because of some short-comings in one's self. One who has not committed any wrong or evil act will

have no fear and hence will not need any protection
or security. Fearlessness is the hall-mark of divinity.
One can become fearless through *thyaaga* (renunciation
or sacrifice). For example, if you have some valuables
with you, there is room for fear. But if you give up
those valuables, you will be free from fear wherever
you may be, even in a jungle infested with robbers.
My dear child, realise that your very nature is absolute
fearlessness in all circumstances. Remain true to your
nature."

Lord's name sanctifies and transforms

Saying this, Chaithanya hugged the mendicant. But
the latter began shaking with mixed feelings of bliss
and fear, bliss because of the embrace of such a holy
saint like Chaithanya, and fear because of the
misapprehension that Chaithanya would be polluted by
physical contact with him. He cried out, "O Svaami,
let not my sins pollute you." Laughing at this statement,
Chaithanya told him assuringly: "O innocent one, you
and I have now become one. We are no longer separate."
So saying, Chaithanya hugged him in a warm embrace
and whispered the Lord's name into his ear. The name
went straight into the old man's heart, and so
transformed him that he exclaimed in ecstasy, "Svaami
there is no one as lucky as myself. I have now become
sanctified, sacred and pure. I have got rid of my wrong
notion that I am only the body made up of the five
elements and have realised my true nature, because of
your grace and the grace of the Lord's name which
you gave me."

One's life becomes sanctified by treasuring the
Lord's name in one's heart with a feeling of intense

love. In the absence of such love, all so-called spiritual practices will prove futile. Various spiritual disciplines are necessary only for the purification of the heart. Once the heart becomes pure, there is no further need for study of the scriptures or spiritual practices. Explaining thus, Chaithanya exhorted his new disciple to give up fear henceforth. From then onwards, the mendicant became known as Haridhasa.

The moral of this story is that we should give up all differences based on one's birth and position in life and chant or sing the Lord's names with intense love and devotion. First, the Name should melt the devotee's heart; then only it can melt God's heart and draw His Grace upon the devotee. God does not care for how long and in what ways you have practised *Saadhana* (spiritual discipline). What He wants is sincere, whole-hearted and intense love for Him.

Discourse on 16-3-1993, when Bhagavaan chose for His theme a significant episode from the life of Chaithanya Mahaaprabhu to underline the truth that the Godly man should rise above differences of caste and creed.

೮ ———————————— ೞ

Love is the vital force. Love is the governing principle. It is only when the precious diamond of love is shining in one's heart that sacred and divine thoughts about God will arise in the mind.

—*BABA*

CHAPTER 10

The life of Samartha Raamadhas

IN a place called Baadar in the Aurangabad district of Mahaaraashtra, a son was born to a couple highly devoted to God. He was named Naaraayana. He grew up as a naughty boy, neglecting his studies and quarrelling with other children. At the age of eight years, he lost his father. His mother Ramaa Dhevi, found it difficult to control her mischievous and delinquent son. Her relatives and neighbours advised her to get him married so that he might realise his responsibilities and change for the better.

Although the boy was only 13 years old and too young for marriage, his mother yielded to the persuasions of others and arranged for his marriage. At the time of the wedding, a screen of thick cloth was held in-between the bride and bridegroom, according to the prevailing custom, and the *purohiths* (priests) removed the curtain to hand over the *Mangala Suuthram* (the sacred thread of wedlock) to the bridegroom for him to tie it round the bride's neck. Lo and behold! The bridegroom had disappeared behind the curtain, without anybody's notice. A thorough search was made to trace him out, but in vain. So, the marriage could not be performed.

Hanumaan's blessings showered on Raamadhas

The boy Naaraayana, who had escaped from the marriage hall, ultimately reached a place called Nasik near the source of the sacred river Godhaavari. He stayed there for sometime and then moved to a nearby mountain called 'Chithrakoota' which is considered holy, because Lord Raama lived there for nearly 12 years. There he selected an exquisitely beautiful spot by name Panchavati. The boy was enraptured by the grandeur of the scenery of the place, and its sanctity, associated with the stay of Lord Raama there during his exile, sent thrills of ecstasy in Naaraayana. He was always immersed in the contemplation of Lord Raama.

What was the cause for the naughty boy turning into a pious young man? Apart from the fact that his latent good *Samskaaras* (accumulated tendencies) were aroused by the sudden shock of the prospect of being saddled with the heavy responsibilities of married life, the boy, during his journey to Nasik, entered a famous Hanumaan temple enroute, and wholeheartedly prayed to the Deity to bless him with all the noble qualities for which Hanumaan was renowned. And he had an indication of his prayer being answered by way of gentle movement of the idol transmitting spiritual vibrations in the direction of the boy.

After 12 years of intense penance at Panchavati, Naaraayana gained the three-fold realisation of Lord Raama, as did Hanumaan, namely, when he had body consciousness, he was the servant and Raama the Master, when he was conscious of his being a *Jeeva* (individual soul) he was a part of Raama *(Visishtaadhvaitha)* and when he was aware of his being the *Aathma* he and Raama were one *(Adhvaitha* or non-dualism).

Raamadhas enters the arena of social service

After this realisation, he returned to Nasik from Panchavati. While there, he came to know that the country was in the grip of a severe famine. Then he began to reflect that to spend his time thinking of only his own liberation, when all his countrymen were suffering due to famine, amounted to extreme selfishness. So, he coined the *slogan, "Dhil me Raam, Haath me Kaam"* (Raama in the heart, and work in the hand), and entered the arena of social service with all his energy and zeal, giving to himself and his band of dedicated workers mottoes such as: *"Maanava seva* (service to man) is *Maadhava seva* (service to God)" and *"Graama seva* (service to the villages) is *Raama seva* (service to Raama)." He filled the tank of his heart with the holy water of *Raama naam* (Raama's name) which flowed through the top of his hands to quench the thirst of the multitudes of his countrymen.

Proceeding thus from village to village, doing social work, coupled with chanting of *Raama naam*, Naaraayana finally reached Raameshvaram at the southern tip of the Indian peninsula. From there he went to the pilgrim centres of Thirupathi (where he had the *darshan* of Lord Venkateshvara) and Hampi (where he worshipped Lord

Viruupaaksha). Ultimately he returned to Nasik. On
the way to Nasik, he saw Saint Thukaaraam, who
was singing the glories of Raama so melodiously that
a large number of people including Shivaaji, the
ruler of Maharashtra, were attracted to him. As
Shivaaji listened to Thukaaraam, and told him about
his decision to give up his kingdom and to devote
himself fully and whole-heartedly to the pursuit of
the spiritual path, Thukaaraam admonished Shivaaji
for his narrow-minded view of spirituality and
exhorted him to consider duty as God and work as
worship. Thereupon Shivaaji prayed to Thukaaraam
to give him initiation. Thukaaraam declined saying,
"Raamadhas is your Guru, not I, so you have to
receive initiation only from him." Rather disappointed,
Shivaaji returned to his capital.

Shivaaji's offer to Raamadhas

When Shivaaji came to know that Naaraayana alias
Raamadhas was in Nasik, he sent his Ministers and
other high dignitaries to invite Raamadhas to the royal
court with a band of music and other traditional honours
befitting a highly distinguished personage. When
Raamadhas arrived, the king received him with due
honours and reverence, arranged for his stay in the
palace itself, and after washing his feet, he sprinkled
the holy washings on his own head and submitted to
him in all humility: "O revered Master! From this
moment this kingdom belongs to you; and I too, am
yours."

Thereupon Raamadhas replied, "My son, I am an
ascetic who has renounced everything. I have neither
the right nor the desire for your limited kingdom.

God's kingdom is unlimited. The goal of my life is to help every one to reach that unlimited kingdom of God. So I don't want this kingdom of yours. I am now coronating you as the ruler of this kingdom which you have offered to me. From now onwards, you will be king with a difference. You should consider that the kingdom really belongs to God and that you are only His instrument or trustee administering the kingdom on His behalf."

From Raamadhas to Samartha Raamadhas

Since Raamadhas had the extraordinary capacity to do many great things, he came to be known as Samartha Raamadhas, the appellation Samartha meaning a man of versatile skills. There is an episode in his life which describes the context in which the title of "Samartha" was conferred on him. He used to dress himself and move about like *Kodhandapaani* (Raama armed with his bow and arrows).

Once when he was walking along the banks of the Godhavari in this dress, some *Brahmanas* who were taking bath there questioned him whether he belonged to the community of Koyas (hunters belonging to a hill tribe were called Koyas). Raamadhas told them that he was Raamadhas (a servant of Raama) and not a Koya. Thereupon, they questioned him why he was dressed and equipped with bow and arrows like Raama if he was only a servant of Raama. They heckled him saying, "What is the use of merely trying to imitate Kodhandapaani in appearance only? Are you capable of wielding the bow and arrows as Raama did?" Just then a bird was flying fast at a great height across the sky above their heads. The Brahmanas pointed the bird to Raamadhas and asked him whether he could shoot that bird. With Rama's name on his lips, Raamadhas immediately aimed an arrow at the flying bird and brought it down right in front of the *Brahmanas.* Seeing the dead bird, the *Brahmanas* accused Raamadhas saying, "There is no harmony of thought, word and deed in you and therefore you are a *dhuraathma* (a wicked person); you chant Raama's name and at the same time you have committed the sin of killing an innocent bird, to show off your skill." When Raamadhas replied that he shot the bird at their instance only, they remonstrated, saying, "If we ask you to eat grass, will you do so? Don't you have your own independent thinking or discrimination?" Then Raamadhas gently replied, "Sirs, past is past. Kindly tell me what I should do now?"

Raamadhas revives a dead bird

They asked him to repent for his sin. Raamadhas promptly closed his eyes and prayed to God wholeheartedly, repenting for his sin and asking for His forgiveness. Then he opened his eyes and pointed out to the *Brahmanas* that the dead bird had not regained life, in spite of his repentance. The *Brahmanas* said reprovingly, "What a madcap you are! Repentance cannot undo what you have done; but its purpose is to enable you to make up your mind not to repeat such misdeeds in future." "That is no repentance in my humble view," countered Raamadhas, "God and His name are so powerful that if we pray sincerely, His grace will bring the bird back to life." So saying, he picked up the dead bird, hugged it to his bosom, and with tears flowing down his cheeks, he wholeheartedly prayed, "O Raama, if I have been chanting your name with all my mind, heart and soul and if it is a fact that I have killed this bird out of ignorance and not with an intent to kill, may your grace either revive this dead bird, or take away my life also along with that of the bird." As he concluded his prayer, the bird fluttered in his hands. Then he opened his eyes, thanked the Almighty and released the bird into the sky. Astonished at this miracle, the *Brahmanas* exclaimed in one voice, "Revered sir, forgive us for not recognising your greatness. Since you have the capacity to kill a flying bird with a single arrow, and also the capacity to revive the dead bird, you will hereafter be known by the worthy name of 'Samartha Raamadhas.'

Raamadhas' visit to Pandaripuram

After this, Raamadhas visited Pandaripuram where he was an eye-witness to the ideal way in which a man by name Pundareeka served his parents as veritable gods, making Lord Paanduranga Himself wait in front of his house standing on a pair of bricks, till he completed his service to his parents.

Then he visited Shivaaji and gave him three things as mementos to guide him in his royal duties: one, a coconut to remind him that just as our intention in buying a coconut is to consume the white kernel inside, so also the purpose of owning and administering the kingdom is that the king himself should lead a *saathvik* life and also to ensure that the *saathvik* quality prevails in his kingdom; second, a handful of earth to remind the king and through him his subjects, about the sanctity of Bhaarath, their motherland; third, a pair of bricks to symbolise that just as bricks are used to construct houses for the safety of the inmates, the king should use his powers to protect the people and promote their welfare and progress.

Raamadhas' re-union with his mother

At this time the memory of Pundareeka's devoted service to his parents at Pandaripuram was revived in Raamadhas' mind and he hastened back home with the idea of serving his aged mother. When he reached home, his old mother could not recognise him, particularly because of his long beard and strange dress. He told her that he was her son, Naaraayana, who was popularly known as Samartha Raamadhas. Thereupon, his mother exclaimed ecstatically, "O my dear son, I have been hearing so much about Samartha Raamadhas and have been eager to see him for a long time. But I never knew that it is the popular name of my son, Naaraayana. I am proud of you and thank the Lord for making me the mother of such a great one. My life is fulfilled." So saying she breathed her last on her son's lap.

Raamadhas duly performed the obsequies of his mother. Shortly thereafter, he heard about Sivaji's death in A.D 1680 (just six years after he was coronated by Raamadhas in A.D 1674). He went to the King's capital, installed Sivaji's son as the king and blessed him so that he might rule the kingdom, following the foot-steps of his noble father.

Discourse on 19-3-1993, at Thrayee Brindhaavan, when Bhagavaan gave a detailed account of the life of Samartha Raamadhas, the great Mahaaraashtra saint.

CHAPTER 11

Through Self-enquiry to Self-realisation

The entire Cosmos is governed by God;
God is governed by Truth;
Truth is governed by the Supreme Wise;
Such a noble one is equally Divine.

THE entire cosmos is subject to the sway of the
Divine. The cosmic Divine Lord is governed by
Truth. That Truth is governed by a *Uthama* (supremely
wise person). Such a noble being is the very embodiment
of God—"*Uthamo para Dhevatha.*"

God is the embodiment of Time. Time is eternal.
It has no end. It is boundless. As against this eternal
Time, the life-span of man is very limited. Because of
his limited time-span, man is bound by the passage

of time in terms of hours, days, months and years.
All the latter are by their intrinsic nature transient. The
Lord declares: *"Akshaya Kaalah"* (I am the Eternal Time).
It is indeed a pity that this eternal time should be
considered as a fleeting moment. Man's actions are
governed by the change in time and circumstances.

In the procession of years, the present new year
is known as "Shreemukha." The past year was known
as "Angeerasa." To bid farewell to Angeerasa and to
welcome Shreemukha are considered a natural action
among common people. Not realizing the infinite and
sacred nature of Time, men set bounds to Time and
bid farewell to one year and extend welcome to a new
year. In this context, all actions of men appear to be
artificial.

On this day, when one person meets another, he
greets the other with the words: "Happy New Year!"
The other man replies: "The same to you!" These words
have no meaning at all. If, for one moment on one
day one wishes someone happiness, will he secure
happiness? People's entire lives are consumed by artificial behaviour.

Moving Time and the unchanging mind

Time is moving fast like a stormy gale. Man's life
is melting away every moment like a block of ice.
Months and years are rolling past in the Wheel of Time.
Everything around is undergoing change, but man's
mind and *Buddhi* (intellect) remain unchanged. Years
are passing before our very eyes. How many eras are
disappearing in our own epoch!

Eras come and go, epochs roll on, but man's mind
remains as before. What can the greeting "Happy New

Year" mean in the context of such a human predicament? It appears to be a scene in a drama on the worldly stage.

Elimination of desires leads to *Mukthi*

The practice of offering worship and revering elders (on New Year's Day) also appear to be artificial acts in a play on life's stage. When the source of all happiness is within you, if you go about seeking happiness from others, it is unnatural. If you desire to elevate yourself and attain a higher level, you have to adopt the appropriate means. This does not mean trying to fly like birds. What you aspire for is *Mukthi* (Liberation). The *Vedhas* declare: Liberation will not fall from the sky. Nor is it to be found in the Nether World or on the earth. It can be got only by the elimination of desires which constitute knots in the heart.

To take an illustration from daily life: Bits of paper or pieces of cotton float in the air because they are lighter than air. Man is unable to go up spiritually because he allows himself to be weighed down by the heavy loads of his *Mamakaara* and *Ahamkaara* (possessiveness and pride). Man is becoming heavier every day. His desires are getting insatiable. His selfishness and self-interest are reaching the skies. How can a heavy-loaded mind and over-burdened senses help man to attain liberation? This is impossible.

A man seeking liberation cannot attain it by merely revering elders or practising meditation. These are formal acts. By these artificial means one cannot realise the sacred, subtle and boundless experience of the Divine.

Moksha (Liberation) is not a specific place. Nor is it something that can be got from any preceptor or other person. To realise one's own true Self is Liberation. Obsessed with the external world, preoccupied with the acquisition of external objects, man's life is becoming more and more burdensome every day. Only by getting rid of these burdens can one hope to ascend spiritual heights.

Spirituality is associated today with exercises like attending religious discourses, reciting slokas, counting beads and conducting *bhajans.* It is imagined that by these means Liberation can be secured. This is not real spirituality. At the outset, the animality in man has to be got rid of. Getting rid of the animal qualities, entering into the human estate, man should embark on the realisation of the Divine.

Man should be engaged in perpetual enquiry

In every man, animality, humanness and Divinity are present. Today what is happening is the growth of the animal tendencies in man. As a consequence, qualities like kindness, compassion and sympathy are not to be seen anywhere. Selfishness and self-interest are animal qualities. An animal is only concerned with external objects. It has no internal vision or any power of discrimination. Man, however, is endowed with internal vision as well as the power of discrimination.

Man, unlike an animal, is endowed with a mind, which confers on him *Vichaarana Shakthi* (the power to enquire into the how and why of things). Man, therefore, should undertake an enquiry into what is permanent and what is temporary, what is truth and what is false, what is bad and what is good. Only when man transcends the animal tendencies can he become truly human. Then, his divinity will manifest in due course. This Divinity is inherent in man. It is not got from outside from anyone. It has to manifest itself from within.

Man's inherent quality is divinity. It has to be realised by him by his own efforts. The *Aathmik* principle is not derived from an external *force*. It is based on an internal *source*.

Man should be engaged in perpetual enquiry. He has to realise his humanness. Because of the influence of the *Kali* age, humanness has declined. Wickedness, immorality, cruelty and other vices are growing beyond all limits. Men are behaving worse than animals. They are harassing the innocent and the ignorant. They are behaving as demons.

Realise that the same spirit dwells in all beings

To get rid of the demonic qualities, man has to embark on self-enquiry: "Who am I?" Scriptural scholarship is of no avail in this enquiry. *Aathmik* bliss (*Aathma-Aanandha*) can be realised only by recognising that the same spirit dwells in all beings. This realisation can be got only by spiritual enquiry. Conning the *shlokas* of the Bhagavath Geetha will not rid a man of his sorrow. The transformation must take place within.

Today is celebrated as Yugaadhi because it is the first day in the first month of the new year, marking the beginning of *Vasantha Rithu* (Spring season).

Of the four *Yugas—Kritha, Thretha, Dhvaapara* and *Kali—*the present *yuga* is called *Kali yuga*. In truth, it is *Kalaha Yuga*, the Age of Discord. There is discord everywhere—between husband and wife, between preceptor and pupil, and in every other relationship. What is the reason for this discord? The absence of mutual trust. No one trusts another. As a result, hatred and bitterness are growing in the social, ethical, political, economic and every other field. There is discord even in the scientific field. The lack of trust has blinded people towards each other.

Believe in the sacred pronouncements of *Vedhas*

People have belief in things which should not be believed, but do not believe that which they ought to believe. People are ready to believe in the statements of the author of an almanac or the predictions of a parrot kept by a pavement astrologer or a roadside palmist, but will not believe in the sacred pronouncements of the *Vedhas.*

The *Vedhas* have declared: *"Thath Thvam Asi," "Aham Brahma-asmi," "So-Ham"* ("Thou art that," "I am Brahmam," "I am He"). The *Vedhic* dictum, *"So-Ham,"* is confirmed by the inhaling and exhaling that go on in everyone. But no one believes in it. People believe in the films, in novels and newspapers and many other sources. But one does not believe in the truth of his own *Aathma* (Self). As a result, man is growing weaker and losing his humanness because of the lack of faith in his own Self. A man without *Aathma-Vishvaasa* (self-confidence) is no man at all. Without self-confidence, how can he get self-satisfaction? Lacking self-satisfaction, how can he hope for Self-Realisation? This is impossible.

Hence, the mansion of Self-Realisation has to be erected on the foundation of Self-confidence, with the walls of self-satisfaction and the ceiling of self-sacrifice. Confidence is at the root of it all. Live with faith and confidence.

Beauty of Spring is called 'Vishnupriya'

The New Year Day begins with Nature shining in all her glory, decked with flowers, with the tender leaves rustling in the wind and the cuckoo calling to its mate in mellifluous notes. *Vasanhta Rithu* (Spring season) has come in all its beauty and freshness. It is the season when nature presents her most beautiful and glorious appearance. The beauty of the Spring season has been dubbed *Vishnupriya* (Beloved of the Lord). Indeed, it is not merely dear to the Lord, it is the very form of the Lord. There are well-known sayings: *"Alankaara Priyo Vishnuh"* (The Lord loves adornment), *"Namasakaaro Arunapriyah"* (The sun loves salutation). The Lord loves the advent of Spring when every tree is in bloom.

Today we are welcoming this Spring. But it is not enough to greet it on one day. Some people figure the position of the planets at the commencement of the new year and try to predict the shape of things to come. The new year should not be judged by its name Shrimukha. It is well known that there are many who belie their names. "Shri" means happiness, honour, auspiciousness. The year makes its appearance with a happy, respectful and auspicious face. But, the prospects for the year are the very opposite of what the name suggests.

Astrologers make their predictions on the basis of the relative position of the planets. The sun is expected to confer *Sauryam* (valour). The moon is said to confer prosperity. *Rahu* is expected to confer inner strength. *Rohini* will confer happiness. *Sani* (Saturn) will confer physical fitness. But during this year, the results will be contrary to these beneficial effects.

The dangers that the country is to face

One of the consequences is the thinning of the ozone layer above the earth. As a result, there is the threat of fire disasters. There are also threats from bomb blasts of the kind you have noticed in newspaper reports. The country is faced with such dangers from man-made calamities.

These dangers can be averted if men realise the sacredness of human existence. People have to ask themselves how they are using the time that is given to them. In a year there are 3,15,36,000 seconds. How is man using these precious moments? How many seconds is he devoting to respecting elders and honouring his parents? How many seconds does he spend for earning his food? And how many is he wasting on useless activities? How many is he devoting to seeing films and T.V? How many is he spending on reading meaningless novels? And how many on studying worthwhile books? How many does he devote to God? How many to rectify his inner feelings?

If this sort of enquiry is made it will be found that the average man spends most of his time on mundane activities. Not even ten minutes or ten seconds are devoted wholeheartedly to spiritual enquiry or self-examination.

All are ostensibly engaged in the pursuit of Truth, all are devoting their time to God. They go on pilgrimages. But even in these trips, they do not concentrate their thoughts on God for a few moments. They don't make any internal enquiry.

To seek the Truth and experience God, there is no need to go out anywhere. By going to a forest or visiting temples, the inner being is not purified. Renouncing all worldly things, one must explore his inner life. This prescription of sacrifice is what the *Vedhas* recommended for attaining immortality.

Practice is more essential than precept

Those who claim to be *Saadhaks* (spiritual aspirants) are really striving for selfish ends. The Divine is omnipresent. To experience the Divine, you have to undertake an enquiry with a steady mind. People today pursue studies all their life, but hardly practise what they have learnt. Practice is more essential than the mere acquisition of knowledge. It is not accumulation of information that is important, but the transformation of himself. Of what use is all the information you have gathered? How much of it have you put to practical use? How much bliss you have derived from it? The answer will be: a hero in gathering information; a zero in putting it into practice. In this way, life is being wasted rather than being purposeful.

The first step is for each one to comprehend his true Self. In many cases, as they grow in years and study more and more books, they develop doubts. Apart from filling their minds with bookish lumber, of what use is all their studies? There is no difference between books without consciousness and minds filled with bookish knowledge. Both are equally sterile. It is a case of "living death" for both. Book knowledge without practice may be useful for teaching others, but is of no value to the man himself. A man who does not practise what he preaches is wasting other people's time. To begin with, make right use of your time. In this context, I repeatedly advise students and others to reduce their talk. Engage yourselves in spiritual enquiry and practise at least a fraction of what you learn.

Today we are supposed to bid adieu to the old year Angeerasa and to welcome the new year. But, in fact, we should not bid farewell to Angeerasa because the name suggests the presence of the Divine in every *anga* (limb) of our body. Welcome all the years. Don't give a send-off to any year. Develop equal-mindedness towards everything. Do not brood over the past.

The joy experienced will be in inverse proportion to your desires. The greater the desires, the less the happiness you will experience. Therefore, try constantly to reduce your desires. In the journey of life, as in a railway journey, the less luggage (desires) you carry, the greater comfort you will have.

Meaning of true *Moksha*

Embodiments of Love! Recognise what holiness is associated with human life. But because of the vagaries of the senses, man develops attachments to various objects and persons entirely for selfish reasons. All the love he professes is not out of affection for others but out of self-love. If this selfishness goes, there will be real oneness. Both love and hatred will be absent. There will be *Samathvam* (equal-mindedness). There will be no sense of separateness. That is true *Moksha* (Liberation).

Moksha does not mean attaining some divine state. Divinity is within you. All you have to do is to manifest it. That which does not exist, will not come forth. That which exists will not go away. Everything is present here and now. Hence, there is no need for any search or for any *saadhana.* Whatever you do, do it as an offering to God. Do not make a distinction between "my work" and "God's work." When you make a division, you give rise to enmity, because of differences. Where there is enmity, there is no room for Divinity, purity or unity.

When you install God in your heart, there is no room in it for anything else. But today's aspirants treat the heart as a musical chair. They go on from one "Svaami" to another and shift from one kind of *saadhana* to another. Of what avail is this kind of merry-go-round? It is a waste of time and of life itself. One heart, one thought, one God, one Goal. Whether you utter the name of Allah or Jesus, Buddha or Zoroaster, or Guruji (Naanak)—it is all the same. Today is sacred to the memory of Guru Naanak, who commenced the propagation of his teachings on a Yugaadhi day.

Purity, unity and divinity

We celebrate Yugaadhi today. But each one can choose his own day for celebration of the new year. God is one. All names are associated with the Divine. You should have no aversion to anything. You should develop this feeling of equality. Only then will you be aware of the unity that underlies the diversity.

Today, you must concentrate first on purity. For this, you have to reduce your desires gradually. It is not practicable to give up all desires totally. But limit your desires to the essential minimum. Do not cherish excessive or endless desires in respect of wealth or other possessions. Promote *Thrupthi* (sense of contentment). The discontented man loses everything. Only the contented man can experience real joy. The man with endless desires is the poorest man. The man with no desires is the richest man. The rich man can have no sleep. You must no doubt earn enough to meet your reasonable needs. But excessive wealth is undesirable.

Cultivate human values

People have been listening to spiritual discourses. How far are they practising the teachings? Without the cultivation of human values, all studies and spiritual exercises are of no use. If each examines himself, he will find how far he has failed in this respect. Raamakrishna Paramahamsa once slapped Raani Rasmani on the cheek at a spiritual gathering when he noticed that while appearing to follow his discourse, her mind was thinking about some legal matters. Many resented Svaami Raamakrishna's action, but after his explanation, the Raani admitted her lapse. Today no one can inflict punishment on erring devotees. Each has to examine his own lapses and correct himself.

It is not very important that you should rejoice over the advent of the New Year. You should develop new ideas and ideals. Feel your oneness with all, because the same Divine dwells in everyone. Do not hate anyone or any religion.

Embark on self-enquiry to acquire self-knowledge. For the refinement of the heart, the first requisite is seeking *Sathsangam* (company of the good). It is because you have assembled here that you have been able to derive the benefit of Svaami's message. Along with good company, you must listen only to what is sacred.

Discourse on 24-3-1993, Yugaadhi day,
at Brindhaavan.

ॐ ━━━━━━━━━━━━━━━━━━━ ☙

Raamaayana and Mahaabhaaratha are very sacred books, which will directly tell us about many things, especially the ways in which we have to conduct ourselves. Raamaayana and Mahaabhaaratha will help us in our daily life, like our two eyes. We are not able to know the true value of these jewels and we think that Mahaabhaaratha is mrely a battle between the sons of two brothers, and that Raamaayana is a story wherein a demon stole away the wife of Raama and Raama again won her back. It is not like that and these two epics are like the heart and the head of India, are as vital to India as the heart and the head are to a human body.

—BABA

CHAPTER 12

The martyrdom of Mansur

ABOUT 400 years ago, there was a man by name Mansur in the city of Benaras. By virtue of his good *samskaaras* (inherited tendencies) and his preceptor's teachings, he had developed firm faith in the *Vedhic* dictum: *"Aham Brahmaasmi"* (I am God). When people heard him always repeating this aphorism, they questioned him whether he was really God. He used to emphatically tell them thrice, "Yes, I am God." In course of time, he became the target of envy and hatred among the prominent men in Benaras, including *Vedhic* scholars and heads of religious institutions. They went in a body to the King of Benaras and complained against Mansur, saying that he had no knowledge of Sanskrith or scriptures but was going about shouting, "I am God," thereby insulting eminent scholars and *pandiths*. The King summoned Mansur to his court

and asked him, "Who are you?" Promptly came the
reply, "I am God." The King got him examined by
medical experts and found that he was not   insane.
Then the King advised him to give up saying "I am
God," in view of the complaints from scholars and
Mataadhipathis that he was guilty of blasphemy. Mansur
firmly refused to obey the King's command and declared
that he would sooner give up his life than forswear
his unshakable faith and firm conviction in his oneness
with the Divine. He questioned the King boldly, "Why
do you want me to give up truth? The truth is: I am·
God; you are God; everyone is God."

One with purity of heart will find God in all

As he did not change his attitude despite all kinds
of persuasions and threats, the King ordered that his
hands should be cut off for the offence of disobeying
the King. As the King's minions held Mansur tightly
and raised their gleaming swords to cut off his hands,
Mansur went on boldly shouting aloud: *"Aham Brahmaasmi"* unceasingly and smilingly. After severing both his
hands, the executioners went to the King and reported
that Mansur was fearlessly and smilingly repeating his
declaration even after his hands had been cut off and
he was bleeding profusely.

The King went to the scene of Mansur's ordeal and
found that the place was reverberating with the sacred
sound of *"Aham Brahmaasmi"* coming unceasingly from
the tongue of the smiling Mansur as well as from
the blood flowing profusely on the ground from his
hands. In a short while, Mansur fell down dead with
a smiling and calm face and *"Aham Brahmaasmi"* on
his lips.

The King was deeply moved and he prostrated at the feet of Mansur. He sent for the scholars, priests, *pandiths* and heads of religious institutions who had complained against the saintly Mansur. On their arrival, he reprimanded them saying, "What is the use of your book learning? You could not recognise or understand the greatness of Mansur. He was a man who established unity in thought, word and deed. You don't practise what you read and teach. You are all a pack of conceited book-worms, envious of truly great persons. Misled by your complaints, I have committed the sin of virtually murdering such a saintly person. However, he has become a martyr in upholding the highest truth of *"Aham Brahmaasmi."* In order to teach you a lesson and to provide a source of inspiration to you and your progeny, I am building a memorial for Mansur in your *Agrahaaram* itself."

The criterion for true devotion is not proficiency in scriptures or routine performance of so-called spiritual practices, but the realization of the divinity in oneself as well as in all others which can be attained only through steadfast adherence to truth, purity of heart and universal love. Where there is *Chittha Shuddhi* (purity of mind and heart), there will be *Jnaana Siddhi* (attainment of wisdom). One with *Chittha Shuddhi* need not go to the forest or pilgrim centres in search of God. He will find God in himself and in others too.

Discourse in Thrayee Brindhaavan on 26-3-93 relating the story of Saint Mansur, who died as a martyr four centuries ago with the manthra, "Aham Brahmaasmi" on his lips.

CHAPTER 13

Sparks from the Divine Anvil

*Bhagavaan Baba gave discourses at "Sai Shruthi,"
Kodaikanal, from 5th April to 26th April 1993,
before a large audience exceeding three thousands
including a considerable proportion of overseas
devotees hailing from U.K., France, Germany,
Italy, Holland, U.S.A., Latin America, Canada,
Australia and New Zealand. Produced below are
excerpts from discourses delivered from 5-4-1993
to 12-4-1993.*

THOSE who assemble here come for *sathsang* or
good company so that they can advance in the
spiritual path. They should shed some undesirable
habits like smoking which retard their progress in the
spiritual path. The fire in the cigarette is so mild that
if you pile up two or three pieces of fire-wood on it

that fire will be put out. But, when a huge jungle-fire is raging, it can burn even green banana plants that are thrown into it. The power of the physical body is like the fire in the cigarette tip while spiritual power is like the forest fire. Once you are advanced in spirituality even the association with evil persons may not affect you. But, when you have not developed your spiritual power you should avoid bad company just as you spit out unpalatable food even at the first taste.

From concentration to meditation

Devotees are generally confused about meditation. Just as you can't receive the radio programme broadcast from any station clearly unless you tune to the appropriate wavelength perfectly, even in meditation you will not get the desired communion with God until you attune yourself to the Divine perfectly. Some aspirants mistake concentration for meditation. Concentration is needed for every activity in your daily life such as reading, writing, walking, talking, eating, etc. Concentration is below the senses, contemplation is in the middle and meditation is above the senses.

Meditation, in fact, is transcending the senses and the mind. During meditation, the mind is actively thinking of several things of the past, the present and the future. The thoughts are running fast. Scarcely does any one concentrate on the Divine even though one sits in the *Padhmaasana* (lotus pose) and closes his eyes. There is no need for sitting for meditation and wasting time in this manner. One can transform every act in daily life as worship of the Divine. Daily chores like making chappathis can be transformed into acts of worship of the Divine. Since the body is an instrument, you can make God happy through this instrument and enjoy happiness yourself in the process. In this way you practise meditation in your daily duties.

Three phases of enjoying happiness

There are three phases in the act of securing a desired object and enjoying happiness out of it. They are *Priyam, Modham* and *Pramodham. Priyam* is the desire to experience happiness from a particular object. *Modham* is the initial satisfaction derived from getting the desired object. *Pramodham* is the experience of *Aanandha* or happiness out of the object. It is not enough if you get the object which you desired to have, but you should experience the joy of using it. For example, you like to taste a mango fruit. The first phase is to buy it, the second is to hold it in hand (possessing it) and the third phase is to eat it. It is only while eating the mango that you derive the fulfilment of your desire. It is also described in the Bhagavath Geetha as *Jnaathum* (knowing), *Dhrashthum* (seeing) and *Praveshthum* (experiencing).

For instance, you hear about Sai Baba and come to know that He is at Puttaparthi, situated in Andhra Pradesh in India. You make preparations to undertake the journey to the place and have His *Dharshan*. The fist phase is getting the knowledge about the place where He is and how to get there; the second phase is making the journey and coming face to face with Him (Seeing) and the third phase is *Praveshthum*, that is getting practical knowledge of and experiencing the Divinity. All the scriptures of different religions (the

Bible, the Quoran, the Geetha, etc.) explain how to reach the same goal but through different paths.

Here so many of you have assembled in one place though you are coming from different countries like U.K., Italy, France, Germany, U.S.A, Canada, Australia, New Zealand, Madras, Delhi etc. Though all of you followed different routes to come to this place, all of you have the common goal of meeting here. You should realise that there is only one God who is Omnipresent, only one language, that of the heart and only one caste, that of humanity. You are all bound by one thing and that is Love. Love is God, live in love. The relationship with God breeds love alone and nothing but love. All other relationships with your mother, father, spouse or children are temporary. So you should have confidence only in the one relationship that is ever-lasting and that is with God.

Excerpts from Discourse on 5-4-93.

Vision should be good

The paradox of human behaviour is that, having the power of discrimination to identify good and bad, man is not able to get away from bad pursuits. This is due to the weakness of the human mind, which is in turn the result of desire and anger. Take the example of Raavana, who was a great scholar and master of many arts. Raavana looked at Seetha with a bad vision. The eye is a sacred organ. Good vision generates good thoughts. In Raavana, the bad look created bad thoughts, which led to his downfall.

Desire is all right as long as it is within reasonable limits. For example, if you feel thirsty, it is a reasonable desire to seek water to quench the thirst. Not satisfied with water, if one seeks cool drinks it is tantamount to excessive desire.

To illustrate the disastrous consequences of excessive desire, I will narrate a story. Once a wayfarer, who was making a long journey by foot in the hot sun, was feeling tired and sought the shade of a tree to rest for a while. It so happened that the tree was a wish fulfilling tree. Sitting under its shade, he wished for a cup of cold water for quenching his thirst. To his astonishment a cup of water was placed before him. After quenching his thirst, he felt that it would be good if he could get a bed to recline on and enjoy a siesta. Immediately a bed was provided from nowhere. Then he thought how nice it would be if his wife also was there. In a flash, he found his wife there. At this stage, he had a doubt in his mind as to how his wife, who was far away at home could come there and thought that it might be a demon in her form which might even devour him. As he thought in this manner, the woman turned into a demon and devoured him! This is the result of excessive desire, which is the enemy within you.

Excerpts from Discourse on 6-4-1993.

Will-power and Meditation

Developing good thoughts fosters the *Ichcha Shakthi* (will-power). *Ichcha Shakthi* fosters *Praana Shakthi* (Life Principle), *Medha Shakthi* (Intellectual power), *Grahana*

Shakthi (Power of understanding), *Nirnaya Shakthi* (Power of determination) and *Vaak Shakthi* (Power of Speech).

One who uses one's will power in the right manner shines as a virtuous person, but one who uses it in the wrong direction becomes wicked. The will power increases as and when one reduces desires. When excessive desires are entertained, the will power declines. By reducing just one of your several habits like smoking or coffee addiction, you can experience an increase in your will power and intellectual ability.

When the will power is weak, even when one sits in meditation he cannot steady his mind and it will only be a waste of time. One should reduce desires to progress in spiritual *saadhana*.

Excerpts from Discourse on 7-4-1993.

Ignorance is the cause of ego

Man is bound by seven types of ropes. They are (1) *Dheham* (body); (2) *Kaamam* (desire); (3) *Krodham* (anger); (4) *Ahamkaaram* (ego); (5) *Karma* (fate); (6) *Ajnaana* (ignorance) and (7) *Aviveka* or *Avidhya* (lack of discrimination). Ignorance is the cause of ego, which breeds *Raaga* and *dhvesha* (attachment and hatred). For getting liberation one has to get rid of the ego, ignorance and attachment. The ego gives rise to *Raaga* (desire) which plunges man in *Karma* which, in turn, causes *Janma* (birth).

Ego is like an inflated football. When one is inflated with the air of ego, both the good and bad qualities kick the body. The moment ego is gone, the kicking stops and one attends to his legitimate duties with the feeling that he does not do anything but is only an instrument.

In spirituality, experience is the method of gaining wisdom while in science it is experiment. When you put some sugar in a glass of water you can't see it or touch it as it gets dissolved. But you can find out its presence by tasting the water. Similarly you can realise Divinity, which is present in every being and within you, only by experiencing Bliss by *Saadhana.*

When fire on a piece of charcoal is left unattended for some time, you find that ash is covering the fire. This ash came out of the fire only because of negligence. If you blow off the ash you can see the fire. You are not bringing it afresh from outside. Similarly, *Jnaanaagni* (the fire of wisdom) in you is covered by the ash of *Maaya* (illusion) which obscures it from your vision. Just blow off the ash of *Maaya,* covering the fire of wisdom, by *vairaagya* (renunciation or sacrifice), you can realise the wisdom within you, which is constant integrated awareness.

Everyone is busy in protecting, decorating and painting the chariot of the body but does not have any concern for the charioteer. How do you expect it to move without the direction of the charioteer? The senses are the horses of the chariot of the body, the mind is the rein to control them.

The way to realise the Divinity that is in everyone is to cultivate love, which is the only divine trait. There are three sides to love forming a triangle. They are: (1) Love gives and never receives; (2) Love is fearless; (3) Love is changeless. The love that develops between a mother and child or a husband and wife is subject to change as it pertains to the body. It is only *Bhrama* (illusion). You should become *Brahman* shedding *Bhrama*.

The divinity in you is changeless, blemishless, without beginning or end. Just as a dhoby removes the dirt in a cloth and restores its original whiteness by washing with soap beating it on stone, man should try to regain his vision of the pure effulgent *Aathma* by washing his heart in the water of love with the soap of *Shraddha* (earnestness) on the stone of *Thyaaga* (sacrifice). This is the way to realise one's Inner Reality, which is *Sathyam, Jnaanam, Anantham* and *Brahma*.

Excerpts from Discourse on 8-4-1993.

Shuka teaches Vyaasa

Air is all-pervasive. It is within you and outside as well. Similarly God is pervading everywhere in the Universe. If you look at everything with the divine feeling you will not fail to see Divinity, pure and unsullied. If you see the idol of Krishna in this hall with a divine feeling, you feel you are seeing the form of Krishna.

But if you are keen on finding out the material from which it is made, you see only the bronze or other metal of which it is made and not Krishna. You can realise that what you visualise depends on the nature of your vision—*Dhrishti* is *Shrishti*. If you look at the world with coloured glass you see everything differently and not in its real colour. The mind is the cause for feelings. If you see with the feeling that this *Vishvam* (Universe) is *Vishnu Svaruupam* (embodiment of God), it will be so!

Every object has a *Svaruupam* (its own form) and *Svabhaavam* (its own nature). Man is completely unaware of his real nature, which is love and compassion. He is so much immersed in selfishness that he only does every action to further his own self-interest and accumulate possessions for himself. Even the love that man exhibits today towards other persons or objects is only with a selfish motive to gain something out of them and not for their sake.

Once Shuka, son of Vyaasa, wanted to leave his home and go to the forest to undertake *thapas*. Vyaasa, overcome by parental attachment, entreated him not to go to the forest but to remain there and serve his parents as it was his duty to serve them.

But Shuka told Vyaasa: "Oh! Vyaasa! you are not my father. I am not your son. We came from Bliss. Everyone wants to be blissful. I am going to seek the Bliss which is our common source. These names and forms and relationships are only ephemeral." By this he was referring to his Inner Reality which is the same in all beings.

Excerpts from Discourse on 9-4-1993.

Divine action

Everyone should remember that the purpose of human life is to do one's duty without regard for results, which will automatically accrue. When there is rain, water will flow in the river and one need not pray for both. It is enough if you pray for rain. Man can't live without activity even for a moment, as blood circulation and breathing are going on non-stop as long as one lives, whether one is sleeping, walking or sitting. It will be folly to attribute these natural activities to man's efforts. It is Divine action. Krishna spells this out in the Geetha: *"Aham Vaishvaanaro Bhuuthvaa Praaninaam Dehamaashrithah. Praanaapaana Samaayukthah Pachaamyannam Chathur Vidham."* God is in every being as Vaishvaanara, aiding digesting of all types of food.

God is described as Eesha, Gireesha, Naresha, Paresha and Bilvesha. The term Eesha means *sakala aishvarya sampanna* (master of all types of wealth). *Aishvarya* includes not only property, movable and immovable, but also strength, knowledge, skill, intelligence and prosperity. Eeshvara is the master of all wealth.

Gireesha: Gireesha means master of Giri or Hill. What does this signify? People often go to Thirupathi Hills and offer their hair in fulfilment of vows. The inner significance of this sacrifice of hair must be understood. God is not expecting your hair, which is of no value at all. Does He relish this lowliest of offerings? Certainly not! The head is the peak of the human body. Ignorance or *Thaamasik* quality is supposed to be dark or black. The black hair is enveloping the peak of the human body which is the head. By removing the hair on the head you expose the white surface of the peak. This is symbolic of surrendering the dullness or *Thaamasik* quality. This is an age-old practice, which is followed without comprehending its inner significance. Since God is the master of the light of wisdom, as opposed to dullness on the head at the top of the human body, He is termed as "Gireesha."

Naresha: In the term Naresha (master of *Narah*) 'Na' means no, 'Rah' means ignorant of one's sacredness. *Narah* means 'man' who is not ignorant. He is not a sinner. He is the embodiment of pure *Aathma*. The Master of man is Naresha.

Paresha: 'Para' means "above all." God transcends all. He is *Akhanda* (limitless) and *Anirvachaneeya* (beyond description by words). As God transcends the three stages of time—past, present and future—and transcends space, pervading everywhere, He is termed Paresha.

Bilvesha: He is termed Bilvesha—the lover of the Bilva leaf which is having triple leaves in a single stalk, Thrinethra—one with three eyes and Thriguna— transcending the three *gunas* (qualities of *Sathva, Rajas* and *Thamas*). His weapon is Thrishul, the three-pointed Javelin. One should offer the three qualities to God, symbolised by the offer of the triple-leaf Bilva for worship. One should do worship with full understanding of the inner significance of the rituals.

Excerpts from Discourse on 10-4-1993.

God realization

You are all embodiments of Divinity, which is within you. God is in the form of Vaishvaanara to digest your food. You listen to such teachings many times but don't practise. Instead of having tons of knowledge an ounce of practice is enough. *Saadhana* is essential to realise divinity. *Saa* means *Dhaivathvam* (divinity). *Dhana* means wealth. The acquisition of the wealth of divinity is *saadhana. Saalokyam* is entering the world of God; *Saameepyam* is going nearer to God; *Saaruupyam* is acquiring the feeling that you are part of God and *Saayujyam* is final merging with God.

You know there is butter in milk. But you have to subject it to the process of turning into curd and then churning it to get butter. Similarly, in the pot of the body there is the milk of Divinity. You have to churn it using *Buddhi* as churning rod and *Bhakthi* as the rope. Out of the churning, comes butter which is Self-realisation. You got it from what is already there inside you.

You should never divorce spirituality from worldly life. The cloth in my hand (a kerchief) is spirituality. It is made up of threads which represent worldly life. The cloth is there only because of the threads. If you segregate the threads there will be no cloth.

"*Thvameva Maatha, Pithaa thvameva.*" We say, God is father, mother, friend, relative, knowledge, wealth and all. God is the energy which drives us to action. We should not waste our energy on useless things.

Excerpts from Discourse on 11-4-1993.

The senses and values

The five values of *Sathya* (Truth), *Dharma* (Righteousness), *Shaanthi* (Peace), *Prema* (Love) and *Ahimsa* (Non-violence) are related to different inner instruments of the body.

The value of Truth is expressed through speech or words. The value of *Dharma* is expressed through the body. This is related to the *Annamaya kosha* (physical sheath). *Shaanthi* can be experienced only in the mental plane—*Manomaya kosha* (Mental sheath). For *Sathya*, *Dharma* and *Shaanthi* one has to purify the instruments of speech, body and mind. This is called purity of

"*Mano, Vaak, Kaayam.*" *Prema* (Love) comes out of *Aanandhamaya kosha* (mental and bliss sheath). *Ahimsa* (Non-violence) comes from Bliss sheath. *Prema* flows as an undercurrent in all the inner instruments and purifies them. So all the five values are having relationship with the five sheaths.

Now these values are mostly absent in human beings. Thinking in one way, talking in another way, and indulging in action not related to the talk or thought is the mark of a wicked person. He may be in human form but he is to be deemed to be a demon only. Because such people are in abundance, the world is in turmoil. *Sathya* is full of sanctity if one deeply enquiries into this value. *Sath* means *Praana* (life force). *Ya* means *Aahaaram* (food). "M" stands for Sun. It is a combination of life, food and sun. For life, food is essential and food comes from the sun. The greenery in the world subsists because of Sun's rays. It is the duty of man to make use of the food created by the Sun to sustain life. If you analyze this word *Sathya* in the reverse order *ya* stands for *Yama, tha* stands for *thapas* and *sa* stands for 'Sarveshvara'. It conveys the truth that by practising *Yama* and *thapas* one can realise the Almighty. *Yama* is not the God of death but is the five-fold discipline one should maintain. They are *Ahimsa, Sathya, Brahmacharya, Astheya* and *Aparigraha* (Non-Violence, Truth, Celibacy, Non-stealing, and Non-covetousness).

God is said to be of blue colour. It does not mean that His skin is bluish! He is *Jnaana Bhaaskara* (the embodiment of wisdom or shining with the light of wisdom). He is also *Anantha*—endless like the sky or fathomless like the Ocean. Since both are of blue colour

God is also described as bluish. He is not born with blue-coloured skin. He is infinite and fathomless.

The heart of the human being is like the sky in which the 'Self' is the sun shining constantly. Just as passing clouds obstruct the vision of the sun temporarily, attachment to world and worries and troubles will obstruct the vision of the Inner Self but once the clouds clear, you can have vision of the Inner Self which is resplendent within. By means of *Dhyaana Shakthi* and *Praana Shakthi*, you can experience Divinity in the Bliss sheath, which fosters the five human values.

Shaanthi Comes from Manomaya kosha.
Sathya comes from Vijnaanamaya kosha.
Dharma comes from Annamaya kosha.
Prema comes from Praanamaya and Manomaya kosha.
Ahimsa comes from Aanandhamaya kosha.

In these five sheaths are encased three types of bodies: *Sthuula* (Physical), *Suukshma* (Subtle) and *Kaarana* (Causal) *shareeras* (bodies). *Annamaya Kosha* represents physical body. It is like the tyre of a lorry. If you increase intake of food it grows and the weight of the body increases.

Divinity is there in all the sheaths of the body. It is Constant Integrated Awareness in different forms in speech, action and feelings.

Excerpts from Discourse on 12-4-1993.

CHAPTER 14

Trust in God : the Sole Protector

A person who has a compassionate heart,
Whose words spell truth and
Whose body is utilised to serve others
Will never be affected by any evil forces.
Such a person's life will be truly sanctified.

SANDALWOOD gives more and more fragrance
when it is subjected to more and more grinding,
so does sugarcane yield juice as it is chewed more and
more. Gold gets refined when it is burnt and melted
in fire. So also a true devotee will never falter in his
love for God even when he faces troubles and obstacles
in his life. God tests His devotees only to lift them
up to a higher level in the spiritual ladder. A true

devotee leads a sacred life which is sanctified when he faces the obstacles and problems with full faith in the Divine. The body is only for leading a sacred life.

"I am the infinite Time" says Krishna. Time has no measure, and it is unlimited, infinite. It is experienced by man in his life by dividing it into years, months, weeks, days, etc. It is only to facilitate man to pursue his daily activity that time is brought under some convenient standard division.

God is as a spark in everyone

"Mamaivaamsho jeevaloke jeevabhoothah sanaathanah." God is as a spark in every one. To recognize this Divinity man has to do some *saadhana*. A mirror though clean may not reflect your image if it is not having the mercury coating behind it. So also the heart may be pure but there should be the coating of love behind it to facilitate reflection of God.

There are multitudes of waves in the Ocean which are not all alike and vary in shapes and forms, but there is no difference in the sea-water that is contained in every one of these waves. Similarly names and forms of people are different but the spark of Divinity that is *Sathchithaanandha* is the same in every one. Every one, in fact, is an embodiment of *Sathchithaanandha*. When we realise this, sacred feelings will prevail and no petty ideas will arise in the mind.

God manifests in man in three forms described as, *Bhur-Bhuvah-Suvah. Bhu* is the *padhaartha* (material form). *Bhuvah* is *Spandhana Shakthi* or *Praana Shakthi* (Life Principle). *Suvah* is the form of *Prajna. Prajnaa Shakthi* is the radiation which, through *Praana Shakthi* (vibrating power) gives the material form represented by the body. God manifests in all these three forms. The body is a combination of water, iron, lead, phosphorus and other things which are but inert matter. The body is inert but is made to function actively through vibration or the Life Force. *Prajnaa Shakthi* (radiation) causes vibration to act. This *Prajnaa Shakthi* is conscience. It occupies a special place in the body. God, in the form of conscience, activates the body. If only man understands this truth of spirituality he will never indulge in bad deeds. The functioning of the body is itself a mystery.

Realise the effulgent divinity within

We use old newspapers generally to wrap different types of articles purchased in a shop. If jasmine is wrapped in the paper, the paper smells sweet like jasmine. Another person may wrap some edible like pakoda and the paper gives that smell. If dry fish is wrapped, the paper emits the smell of dry fish. Though the paper has no smell of its own it takes on the smell of the thing with which it is associated. In the same way our mind, too, gets polluted because of the illusion of body consciousness and attachment. When you think of a material object, it gets object oriented but if you turn the mind towards the Life principle it makes the life sacred. If you turn it towards the world, it is binding you to the world. If you turn it towards Awareness, which is *Brahman*, you become *Brahman*.

Embodiments of Love! If you enquire carefully you will find that the entire universe is pervaded by God—*Vishvam Vishnu Svaruuopam*. The human body is bound by time, *karma* (work) and duty. Everyone has the responsibility to do his duty. The effulgent Divinity within is not realised by man and he leads a useless life indulging in mundane pleasures. The entire universe is made up of matter which is transient and subject to decay. Therefore, one should develop devotion to the Lord who is the permanent Reality.

Absence of self-confidence is the cause of all miseries and troubles man encounters in the world. One should have confidence in his own inner Self that is the *Aathma*. If one has this self-confidence, he will have self-satisfaction, which will lead to self-sacrifice. Self-sacrifice leads to liberation or Self-Realisation. Everything is based on "Self" and everyone is *Aathmaswaruupa* (embodiment of the Self). The body is just an instrument. There is water in the tumbler before me. Without the tumbler water can't be kept; the tumbler is the basis for the water which is needed to quench the thirst. So also the body is the vessel to hold the water of Divinity. To drink the water is *Saadhana*. Your thirst for realising Divinity is quenched by *Saadhana*.

Significance of the New Year "Shreemukha"

You call this day as New Year Day. There is nothing new. It is as old as any other·day. We take it as a new year every time one year ends and another begins. The time is divided on the basis of the motions of Moon and the Sun. The former is called *Chaandhramaana*, which is followed by some people, and the latter is called *Souramaana*, which is followed by another section of people. Today, we bid farewell to the year Angeerasa and welcome the year Shreemukha. *Shri* means very sacred. It is the highest among the eight types of *Aishvarya* (wealth) of which God is described as the master. *Shabda brahmamayee, Charaachara mayee,*

Jyothirmayee, Vaangmayee, Nithyaanandhamayee, Paraathparamayee, Maayamayi and *Shreemayi* are the eight-fold wealth of which *Shri* is the most important. In order to foster immortality in mortals it is customary to use 'Shri' as prefix to the names of males and 'Shrimathi' to those of females. Even when God comes down to earth as Divine Incarnation such as Raama and Krishna, the prefix 'Shri' is added to their names and we call them as 'Shri Raama' and 'Shri Krishna'. The purpose is to signify the immortality of God even when he assumes the mortal human form.

God is the lighthouse for the ocean of life

The name of this year is 'Shreemukha'. The name implies that it should give brilliance to all faces. But you will not find this year as favourable as its name indicates. One should not get discouraged by these prospects. You cannot always have pleasure. Pleasure is an interval between two periods of pain. They are like sunshine and shadow. You should make efforts to look on both with equanimity. Man wants to get all that he desires and gets disillusioned and disappointed. The lighthouse of hope for this ocean of life is God, who is the only permanent entity. This lighthouse never fails. So you should engage yourself in Godly activities with unstinted devotion.

God is omnipresent. He has hands, legs, mouth, faces everywhere and pervades the entire Universe. Where is the need to search for Him? Such a search may be termed as folly. All forms of God are in you. Any time is auspicious to realise this. You need not wait for the New Year. There is no need for a new religion or a new culture or a new philosophy. What is needed is only a pure heart. You should not give room for impurity or pollution in the heart. You can make your life sacred by following the golden rule: "Help ever; hurt never."

Supreme Lord is the only one who can protect you

Speak softly, sweetly and truthfully. There are two eyes to see different things, two ears to hear good and bad, there are two hands to do good and bad, but there is only one tongue to speak only the Truth.

Real bliss consists in sanctifying the senses. The ornament for the hand is charity, that for the tongue is truth and that for the ears is listening to divine scriptural talks. What other ornament is needed than these! *"Aanandhame Andhamu"* (Bliss is beauty). It is the nectar of life. You should enjoy the sweetness of bliss.

Embodiments of Divine Aathma! Spend your life in cherishing sacred thoughts, listening to good things, speaking good words, and doing good deeds. If all of you adopt this path, happiness and prosperity will reign in the world. No government or politician or any one in the world can protect you from troubles and disasters. There is only one who can protect you and that is Supreme Lord. To seek His protection, all of you must wholeheartedly pray *"Lokaas-samasthaas-sukhino-Bhavanthu"* (Let all people in the world enjoy bliss).

Discourse at Sai Shruthi, Kodaikanal, on 14-4-1993.

CHAPTER 15

The juice, the sugar and the sweets

*E*MBODIMENTS *of the Divine Aathma!* From ancient times, the culture of Bhaarath has been upholding high ideals. Foremost among its teachings was the concept of reverence for the mother and the father as embodiments of the Divine. *"Maathru Dhevo Bhava! Pithru Dhevo Bhava!"* (Esteem the mother as Divine, adore the father as Divine).

Human life is indeed extremely sweet. Without this sweetness, life will be worthless. Man struggles in a myriad ways to secure sensual enjoyment, but there is sweetness which transcends these physical pleasures. This is the precious fruit of Bhaaratheeya culture.

Realise the sacredness inherent in motherhood

The mother sacrifices her all for rearing the child, protecting him and bringing him up well. Hence, the sweetness manifest in material love cannot be found in any other object or experience, "What greater sweetness is there in our land than a mother's love? One's honour is greater than one's life," goes the saying. Everyone should realise the sacredness inherent in motherhood.

When Raama went to the forest with Seetha, one day he told her: "Bhuujaatha! In this world there are no greater adorable deities than one's mother and father. When one has near to him a loving mother, who cares for him continually and fosters his well-being, without adoring her as Divine, how can a man contemplate on a Being that is subtle and beyond his daily experience? The Divine transcends all human understanding. How can this be recognised? People who cannot comprehend the hearts of parents who are close to them, whose love they experience in daily life, how can they comprehend the Absolute, which the Upanishaths declare is beyond the reach of speech and the mind? Hence, the injunction that the mother and the father should be adored as Divine. It was my foremost duty to carry out the will of my father."

However, if we wish to understand the Divinity that transcends the human understanding, we should seek to reach a level above the human. Till that is reached, we have to experience everything at the human level alone. Living as a human being, how can one recognize That which transcends the human capacity?

Therefore, in the first instance, man must try to live as a human being. He has to recognise the divinity that dwells in the human form. Man has to cultivate faith in the truth and live accordingly. Leading a life of dedicated service, man must enjoy the fruit of *Prema* (Divine Love). The best way to love God is to love all and serve all.

Svaami was telling the students the previous day that though the Divinity that resides in all human beings is one and the same, the capacities and personalities of various individuals are different. Depending on the ripeness of their experience on the cultural practices they have pursued, on the nature of their spiritual disciplines, and on their parental background, these individuals have a wide or narrow outlook. The attitudes of individuals are determined by their day-to-day experiences. Hence, people should engage themselves in good deeds. Only through hard striving can the Divinity in man be realised, like the fire that emerges from the rubbing of two sticks and butter from the churning of butter-milk.

Aadhi Shankara's *Adhvaitha*

Aadhi Shankara, at the age of five, after the performance of his *Upanayana* (spiritual initiation) ceremony, approached his preceptor and within three years was able to master the four *Vedhas* and the six *Shaasthras*. Through earnestness, anything can be accomplished. From his studies, Shankara realised that *Ekathvam* (oneness) is the essence of all knowledge. This is the doctrine of *Adhvaitha*. "Ekameva Adhvitheeyam Brahma" (The Absolute is one alone, not two). There is no second, but there is the appearance of an enormous multiplicity. How, then, can oneness be claimed? Here is an example. You have the number one and the

number nine. Of the two numbers which is the bigger?
The natural answer will be: nine. But this is not so.
One is really the bigger number 1 + 1 + 1 + 1.....up
to nine, make up nine. Hence, the *Vedhas* declare:
"Ekoham bahushyaam" (I am One; I willed to be many).
Only the one exists. But it has assumed numerous forms.
Shankara declared that *Anekathvam* (the many) is
subsumed by the one—this is the unity in diversity.
There may be many stalks of sugarcane, but the juice
from all of them has the same sweetness. Beings are
many, but the breath is the same. Nations are many,
but the earth is one.

In this manner, Shankara proclaimed to the world
the unity that underlies the apparent diversity. He used
the analogy of the same sweet juice that is present in
all sugarcane stalks.

Vishishta-Adhvaitha and Dhvaitha

Raamanuja asked the question: "How long can the
sweetness of the juice last?" Not for long. If the
sugarcane juice is converted into some other lasting
form, it could be used for sweetening many things. The
conversion should be in the form of sugar, which could
then be used for making any sweet preparation. Without
the sugarcane juice there can be no sugar. The sugarcane
juice represents the *Adhvaithic* principle and sugar
represents the *Vishishta-adhvaitha* principle.

Then came the declaration of Madhva: *"Pishtaadhi
gunasamparkaath."* The variety of sweet preparations is
the result of the bringing together of *Pishta* (flour) and
sugar. Without some kind of flour, the sugar by itself
cannot appear in different forms. Flour of the sort or
another, combined with sugar, can serve to produce

any number of sweets. However, it is not the flour that is the source of sweetness. It is the sugar in the sweet that is made out of the flour which accounts for the sweetness. This is the analogy employed to explain *Dhvaitham* (the dualistic doctrine).

Commmon sweetness in all the philosophies

Shankara, as the exponent of *Adhvaitha* (Non-dualism). Raamanuja as the exponent of *Vishishta-adhvaitha* (Qualified Non-dualism) and Madhva, as the expounder of *Dhvaitha* (Dualism), stood out as great teachers who taught the path of spirituality to the world. However, there is common sweetness in all the three schools of philosophy.

Shankara insisted on the recognition of the unity that underlies all diversity. *"Eesha, Gireesha, Naresha, Paresha, Bilvesha namo Saamba sadhaashiva Shambho shankara sharanam mey thava charanayugam,"* declared Aadhi Shankara, in praise of Shiva. In listing the different attributes of Shiva, the Aachaarya declared that Shiva is everything, by whatever name He is called. Thereby, the omnipresence of the Lord is proclaimed.

The *Adhvaithic* doctrine of Shankara propagated the view that bodies are manifold, and in these separate bodies the one Divine is present. With regard to *Adhvaitha*, however, it is possible only to experience it as *bhaava* (a conscious feeling), but not to apply non-dualism on carrying out one's activities in daily life. There is the divine in a tiger, a snake and a human being. You can recognise this as a concept, but on that account, you cannot go and embrace a tiger. The tiger must be treated as a tiger and a snake must be treated as a snake. The human being must be given the status that is appropriate to the human. You must have the faith that the same Divine dwells in all beings. This is indicated by the presence in all beings of three divine characteristics: *Asthi, Bhaathi* and *Priyam,* (existence, recognisability and utility). This is also expressed in other terms as: *Sath-Chith-Aanandha* (Being-Awareness-Bliss). *Sath* refers to That which is unchanging. This is a Divine attribute. *Chith* refers to total Awareness to know the complete nature of anything. When *Sath* and *Chith* are together, there is *Aanandha* (Bliss). This Bliss is unchanging. It is described as *Brahmaanandham* (Supreme Bliss). It is like mixing sugar with water, resulting in a syrup.

Sath-Chith-Aanandha (Being-Awareness-Bliss) is Divinity that is unchanging. Forms and names are continually changing. They are transient and momentary. The forms of tiger or a snake are impermanent. They have, therefore, to be dealt with as transient.

If you sustain a fall, your foot may suffer a fracture and you may have a bandage. But irrespective of the love your mother bears for you, she cannot bandage her leg to relieve you of your pain. She may feel sympathy for you, but she cannot take over your fracture by bandaging her leg. In the phenomenal world, such differences are inherent.

Discourse at Kodaikanal on 26-4-1993.

CHAPTER 16

What great mothers mean to the nation

The father, to teach the child the truth,
May chide, reprove or beat.
The mother may pinch the cheek
To make the child drink the milk.
Forget not at any time
These marks of paternal Love.
Doing good deeds, one will never reap bad results;
Wickedness will never yield good fruits;
Will the neem seed produce mango fruits
Or the mango seed yield neem fruits?

*E*MBODIMENTS of Love! The earth is one. But, if you sow neem seeds, you will get only bitter fruits. If you plant sweet mango seeds, you will get sweet mangoes. The earth makes no difference between them.

Only the differences in the seeds account for the differences among the fruits. Likewise, the womb of a mother is like the womb of Mother Earth. The thought which prevails at the time of conception results in the kind of child that is born. If the parents desire to have virtuous, exemplary and noble children, they have to observe righteous practices and lead virtuous lives.

Mothers should possess good qualities

It was because Aryamba was a devoted and pious woman and observed sacred practices that the great world-teacher, Aadhi Shankaraachaarya was born to her. For Vivekaanandha to achieve world-wide renown, his mother's sacred life was responsible. Raamakrishna Paramahamsa was able to preach the sacred doctrine of love to the world and achieve greatness because of his mother's good qualities.

Gaandhi earned the appellation of "Mahaathma" because of the sacred *"Kokila Vratha"* observed by his mother. Gaandhi's mother used to observe everyday a vow ritual known as *"Kokila Vratha"*. As soon as she completed the ritual, she would wait for the call of the *Kokila* (the Indian cuckoo) to have her breakfast. However, on one day, she waited for a long time, without taking food, for the call of the cuckoo. Noticing this, the young Gaandhi went out of the house, imitated the cooing of the cuckoo and then told his mother, "Now that the cuckoo has made its call, please, mother, take your food." Unable to contain her grief, the mother slapped on the cheeks of Gaandhi and wailed: "What sin have I committed that such a liar should be born to me! What a great sinner am I to have begotten such a wicked liar as son, Oh Lord!" She was shedding tears as she spoke. Deeply moved by his mothers's words, Gaandhi made a promise to her "In my life, henceforth, I will not utter falsehood."

In those days, the mothers used to watch the behaviour of their children and strove to keep them on the right path. Gaandhi became a 'Mahaathma' because of the severe punishment meted out to him by his mother.

Gaandhi's mother Putlibai, had a maid called Rambha. One day, Gaandhi came running to her saying: "I am afraid, I am afraid!" Rambha was a worthy maid of Putlibai. She told the young fear-stricken lad: "Don't have any fear. Whenever you feel afraid, repeat the name, 'Raam, Raam,' and your fear will leave you." That teaching was remembered by Gaandhi all his life and he died with the name of Raama on his lips.

As is the seed, so is the plant

Mothers of those days led a pure and pious life, cherishing sacred thoughts, fostering virtues and setting an example to the world. Parents today get up from their beds quarrelling with each other. When the parents wake up hurling abuses at each other, the children wake up levelling blows at each other. As is the seed, so is the plant. Parents today should ponder over the sacred ideas cherished by parents in the olden days. For all the bad ways followed by youth today, for all their wayward behaviour and bad conduct, the parents are to blame. If the mothers are good, there will be no room for bad behaviour by the children. Although parents may appear innocuous like fig fruits, they are responsible for the misbehaviour of their children, like the worms inside the fruits.

Will of the Divine in shaping the children

However, in some cases, through the grace and intervention of the Divine, some children are rescued from going astray and are guided on the right path despite the desires of their parents. For instance, King Shuddhodhana adopted many methods to prevent his son Siddhaartha (who became The Buddha) taking to the path of *Vairaagya* (renunciation). But he could not prevent it. This is due to the Will of the Divine. It is only when human effort and Divine Will are in unison that the great consummation takes place.

Ranthideva declared, *"Jeevanam Sarva-bhuutheshu."* He proclaimed the truth that he who regards food as the primary thing in life is ignorant, while the wise one is he who regards the Spirit as primary. How many of those who have plenty of food taken to wrong ways? Even with abundance of food, lacking the spiritual urge, these men have become destitute. Food may sustain the body, but it will not nourish the soul.

Chaithanya, the son of Satheedhevi, once went to Puri and had *dharshan* of Lord Jagannaath. He worshipped Jagannaath with these words: "Oh Lord! You are not merely the Lord of the earth. You are the Lord of the Universe! You are the Lord of Life! You are the Lord of Love! Svaami! I do not need wealth or vehicles. Even less do I seek devotion, wisdom or renunciation. I do not aspire for worldly pleasures or possessions. It is enough if I am endowed with the love to love you. If I have that love, all other things will come of their own accord. The only thing I seek is love towards you. Grant me this boon."

Young people do not realise that there is this Divine spirit in human beings. They consider human existence as nothing more than living like birds and beasts. This they consider as the primary purpose of life. This is wrong. They should realise that beyond the *Annamaya, Praanamaya, Manomaya* and *Vijnaanamaya koshas* (the physical, the vital, the mental and the supramental sheaths associated with the body), there is the *Aanandhamaya Kosha* (the Sheath of Supreme Bliss). When do you attain this Bliss?

The real meaning of *Mahaaraaja*

He is not a great ruler who possesses all kinds of wealth. The real *Mahaaraaja* (great ruler) is one who has surrendered everything to the Divine. He is a *thyaagi* (renunciant), he is a *yogi* (one who is in communion with the Divine). It is for this reason that in Uttar Pradesh, whatever sacred shrine you visit, you will find pilgrims greeting the *saadhus* and ascetics as *Maharaaj*. They are hailed as *Maharaaj* because they have renounced everything, taken refuge in the Lord, sought to merge in the Lord and practised spiritual disciplines for this purpose.

Chaithanya declared: "My property is not 'Shri' but 'Hari'. I value not Lakshmi (the Goddess of Wealth), but the Lord of Lakshmi (Vishnu)." If you aspire for the Lord, you will not suffer from any want. There is no greater wealth than love of the Lord.

> *What gift is greater than the gift of food?*
> *Is there a greater deity than one's parents?*
> *What virtue is greater than compassion?*
> *What is more valuable than good company?*
> *Is there a worse enemy than anger?*
> *Is any disease worse than debt?*
> *Can any death be worse than infamy?*

What can be grater than a good name?
What wealth is greater than God's love?

It is to acquire this supreme wealth that man has taken birth on earth.

There have been many mothers in the world who have sought, by their strenuous endeavours, noble thoughts and sacred practices, to bring up their children in the path of righteousness. In the city of Calcutta, there lived a mother and his son. For the education of the son, the mother made many a sacrifice. She, however, impressed on the son one lesson: "Dear son, do not be concerned about worldly education. The foolish ones acquire all kinds of scholarship, but have no understanding of what they are. By study alone, a man does not get rid of his lowly ways. Through scholarship, one learns only to engage himself in controversy but does not acquire complete wisdom. Why pursue studies which end up only in death? One should study that which frees him from death. Only spiritual knowledge can lead to immortality. It is enduring. Worldly knowledge is temporary. For earning one's livelihood, worldly education is necessary. But this education should be acquired only to lead an independent life, with limited desires. Therefore, dear son, while pursuing studies, embark also on the spiritual quest."

Human life should be used for service

Prahlaadha told his father that he had learnt the essence of all education, namely, to adore the name of Naaraayana. For the realisation of the four *Purushaarthas*, there is no need for any education. Maithreyee told King Janaka that there was no purpose

in having a human birth, only to lead a sensuous life
like that of birds and beasts. Human life should be
utilised for service and sacrifice. The mother taught her
son in this manner the true aim of education.

The boy completed his education and took up a
small job. One day, in that village, there was a folk
festival (Jaathra). The womenfolk of the village donned
their best clothes and jewellery to attend the festival.
The mother also went with tattered clothes. The son
could not bear to see that sight. He said, "Mother,
you have no good clothes or any jewellery. I am
distressed to see you like this. Please let me know
what ornaments you wish to have, mother!" The
mother replied: "This is not the right time. I shall
let you know at the proper time."

The three ornaments sought by the mother

Thanks to the good behaviour and diligence of the
lad, he rose to higher positions in service. Once again,
he returned to his mother and asked what ornament
she desired. "I shall get them as far as I can," he said.
The mother told him that she wished three ornaments,
but she would disclose what they were later on.

The son in the course of years reached a very
high position. Once again he entreated: "Mother, I
have now some money. Please let me know what
jewels you would like. I shall get them for you." The
mother said "Dear son! I am now not in a state when
I can wear jewels. However, there are some ornaments
in which I am interested and I shall tell you what they
are."

Drawing the son nearer to her, she said, "In our
small village, I am grieved to find that the children

have to go to distant places for education. My first ornament I desire is that you should set up a primary school in the village. Secondly, our people have no facilities for medical relief even for small ailments. I spend sleepless nights thinking about their plight. If you set up a small hospital for the village folk, that will be your second ornament for me. The third ornament is something which you have to do by yourself. In the days to come, your reputation may grow. If anybody asks "who is your mother?," you may mention my name. Your conduct must be such that you will uphold your mother's name. You must share with others the benefits of the education you have received. Do not go after wealth. The worshipper of Mammon will not yearn for God. The seeker of God will not seek for wealth. Observance of this is the third ornament I desire from you."

The young man who heard these words from his mother and later became famous and earned the people's esteem was none other than Eeshvar Chandhra Vidhyaasaagar. He earned a great name in Calcutta.

The hall-mark of education is humility

Once he was proceeding to a neighbouring village to deliver an address. People used to gather tin large numbers to listen to his lectures. A young officer, who wanted to listen to Eeshvar Chandhra Vidhyasaagar's lecture, got down from a train with a suitcase to go to the lecture-hall. Eeshvar Chandhra Vidhyaasaagar also get down from the same train. The young officer was calling for a porter to carry his suitcase. Eeshvar Chandhra went to him and said, "Why do you need a cooly to carry this small suitcase? Can't you carry it yourself and save the money?" He replied. "It is not in keeping with my dignity to carry my suitcase. I am an educated person." Eeshvar Chandhra told him: "The hall-mark of education is humility, not pride. If you cannot carry your own bag, how are you carrying your body? If, however, you cannot carry your bag, I shall do so." And Eeshvar Chandhra carried the officer's bag. He acted on the motto: "Plain living and high thinking." Eeshvar Chandhra left the bag where the officer got off. The young man wanted to offer money to his "Porter". Eeshvar Chandhra told him. "To serve you is my reward."

The young officer left and was later proceeding to the venue of the meeting. There people were offering garlands to Eeshvar Chandhra Vidhyaasaagar to welcome him to the meeting. The young officer realised that the man who had offered to carry his bag at the station was none other than the respected lecturer of that evening, Eeshvar Chandhra Vidhyaasaagar. He felt ashamed that he had made such a great man carry his bag. He reflected: "What is his education and what is mine? I have behaved like a little monkey. I am like a glow-worm before the Sun."

The joy of the mother

Eeshvar Chandra's mother shed tears of joy when she realised the great fame her son had achieved. "Having begotten such a son, my life has been redeemed. It does not matter what happens to me hereafter," she said to herself. That is why, the saying goes: "The father does not rejoice merely at the moment of a son's birth." These days, the petty-minded people celebrate the birth of a son with the distribution of sweets, etc. This is not a sign of wisdom. It is said: "The father rejoices when people praise his son for his great qualities." The father may feel that a son has been really born to him when he hears the praises of his son for his character and good qualities.

The *Kali* age has become the *Kalaha* age

In this manner, from ancient times the relations between mother and children have been hallowed as a result of the purity, the virtue and the integrity of the children. The relationship was full of love, mutual esteem, intense devotion and nectarine sweetness. The children had deep love for the mother. Today the children have no respect for the mother. Mothers have also little concern for the children. With the result, the *Kali* age has become *Kalaha* age—the age of discord.

Who are responsible for this situation? The mothers are the root cause. It is because of the pampering of the children in all sorts of ways by the mothers that the children tend to go astray.

After the Burma war (in the Forties), a mother and her son came to Madras as refugees. This son used to go out begging for food and bring it home for both of them to eat. Seeing the pathetic condition of the young one, the mother said that from the next day she herself would go out for getting food, leaving the boy in the shed. Moreover no mother would like to see her son going out as a beggar. For this reason also she decided to go out herself. For some days she went out begging, but could manage to get only a small amount of food. She gave the food to the child and starved herself, but told him that she had already eaten. After some time the woman was too weak to go out begging. The son started going out to beg for food and kept feeding his mother. Her condition deteriorated from day to-day. She could not bear the pangs of hunger. The son went out and begged for food at an officer's residence. The officer, who was glancing through the day's newspaper, heard the boy's cry for food to appease his hunger. The Officer brought some food and gave it to the boy and asked him to eat it in his presence.

The boy said he would not eat there, but take the food home. The Officer questioned him why he would not eat there when he was hungry. "You are not really hungry. You are lying," shouted the officer. The boy was too weak to stand and dropped down at the feet of the officer with the food in his hands. The officer noticed that the boy was muttering some words to himself. He went close to the boy's mouth and heard him say: "First for mother, first for mother." Saying those words, the boy passed away.

Children should abide by mother's injunctions

What an example is this of the love of a mother and the devotion of a son. Even though he was hungry, he wanted to give the food first to his mother. Does this kind of feeling exist even a little among students today? Of what use is education or office, wealth or authority? Children who have no love for their mothers have no reason to live at all.

We must have children who revere the mother as God. Abiding by the mother's injunctions, you may do anything.

Bhaarath has become a prey to numerous troubles because of the lack of exemplary mothers. What is it the mothers ask for today? Not compassion, good character, integrity and such virtues. They want their children to get educated, secure a big job, marry a wealthy girl and lead a comfortable life. Is it this kind of animal existence that one should seek? "Earn a good name. Become an ideal son. Use your wealth in righteous ways. Develop compassion. Lead a just and moral life." This is what mothers should impress on their children. Such high-minded mothers have become rare these days. Integrity and morality are going down day be day in the country.

Nation needs mothers who lead an exemplary life

The nation needs noble mothers who lead an exemplary life. They should manifest in their life the great culture of Bhaarath. Then, the culture will be transmitted to their progeny. Many great men in the past brought up such worthy children and enhanced the name and glory of Bhaarath. Today the children are being spoilt only by the parents. If the children are brought up on right lines from childhood, they will grow up properly. The fathers today are behaving like Dhritharaashtra (the father of the wicked Kauravas). The mothers today are behaving like Kalakanthi (the woman who had Chandhramathi's son bitten by a serpent). The fathers, instead of chastising children who take to wrong ways, pamper them and encourage them. Children who misbehave should be severely dealt with. Youth today are forgetting God, revelling in sensual pleasures and ruining their lives. They have no reverence for the mother or the Motherland.

After the war in Lanka, when Raama was
entreated by Vibheeshana and others to crown himself
as ruler of Lanka, Raama told them that the mother
and the Motherland were greater than Heaven itself
and nothing on earth would tempt him to give up
his love for Ayodhya. How many today are observing
the great teachings of Raama regarding love of the
Motherland? There are today many sons who will
deprive their mothers of their earnings and spend
the money for their own pleasure Are such sons
human beings? They are not human at all. Their
education is a waste. Of what use are they to the
nation?

Develop healthy patriotism

Students today should develop a healthy patriotism.
They must honour their mothers. Only then will they
be ideal men. Today corruption and dishonesty are more
rampant in cities with universities, high courts and all
other paraphernalia than in forest areas where illiterate
tribal people live. There is greater co-operative spirit
among the hill tribes than among the denizens of
metropolises.

The spirit of sacrifice should grow among students.
They should develop a broad outlook.

Once Raama told Seetha, while they were staying
on the Chithrakootha mountain, that as few could
comprehend the subtle principle of Divinity, people
should adore their parents as the visible embodiments
of God.

Only when there are good mothers and good sons
will the nation be free from troubles. Otherwise, the
nation will break into pieces. This is the lesson of

the Mahaabhaaratha where the wicked Kauravas brought ruin upon their entire clan by their evil ways.

What the nation needs today is not material prosperity or high education. It needs men and women of character.

The people should develop faith in God, have concern for the good name of society, cherish fear of sin and dedicate themselves to Godly activities. Then the nation will enjoy peace and security.

Every mother should be regarded as an embodiment of the divine. Then every son will enjoy peace and prosperity.

Discourse in the Sai Ramesh Mandap, Brindhaavan, on 6-5-1993, Easwaramma Day.

ಹಾ ———————————————— ಲ

The act of service is not to be judged according to the cost or publicity it entails; it may be only the offering of a cup of water in the depth of a jungle. But, the need of the recipient, the mood of the person who offers—these decide whether the act is gold or lead.

—BABA

CHAPTER 17

Man, the mind and the *Aathma*

*S*TUDENTS *and Teachers!* Man struggles hard
ceaselessly night and day for the sake of bodily
pleasures. One who recognises that the *Aathma* (Spirit)
is distinct from the body will not be a prey to any
troubles. If, indeed, every person in the world recognizes
the nature and purpose of human existence, these
difficulties will not arise. The Upanishaths declare that
if one, who is born as a human, grows up as a human
in society, does not know the meaning of the term
maanava (man), he is worse than birds and beasts.

Humanness is a marvellous thing. It is boundless.
It is significant. The term "man" does not refer only
to the physical body. A human being is a composite
of body, mind and *Aathma.* To perform with the body,
to understand them through the mind, and to have
the *Aathma* as a witness to both these—these three

constitute *Maanavathvam* (human existence). Action, Awareness and Realisation—these three manifest the inner meaning of human life.

It is a sheer ignorance to equate human existence with the body alone. Students have to understand at the outset how a man should grasp the nature and aim of human existence and have to lead a meaningful life.

First of all, there is the mind. Only the one with a mind can be called man. "As a man thinketh, so he becomes."

The five sheaths that envelop man

Man is enveloped by five sheaths: *Annamaya* (Food), *Praanamaya* (the Life Force), *Manomaya* (the Mental), *Vijnaanamaya* (the Integral Consciousness) and the *Aanandhamaya* (the Blissful). The physical body is sustained by food. Hence it is called *sthuula shareera* (the gross body). Next comes the *Suukshma shareera* (subtle body) which is covered by three sheaths of Life-force, Mind and Integral Consciousness. This subtle body is the basis for the pleasures and pains experienced by man. All experiences of man are based on this subtle body.

Next comes *Aanandhamaya Kosha* (the sheath of Bliss). It is the base for the entire Cosmos. The Cosmic Consciousness that is present in the bodily sheath is called "body consciousness." This means that even in the gross body, *Chaithanyam* (consciousness) is present. The consciousness that is present in the *Praanamaya Kosha* (The sheath of the Life Principle) not only indicates the life-principle, but also proclaims the basis of the vital force.

The third is the *Aathmik* Principle, which illumines the mind—*Manomaya Kosha.* The fourth is the consciousness in the *Vijnaanamaya Kosha.* This is the basis for the entire Cosmos. It is called *Chith,* the all-pervading Cosmic Consciousness

Transcending all these is the Pure Divine Self—the Supreme *Purusha.* This is the source of all power. It is the embodiment of the Infinite Will. This is the power that protects the Cosmos. The ancient sages strove to explore the nature of the *Aanandhamaya Kosha* (the sheath of Bliss). They sought to discover how they can experience Bliss.

Maanava means *Aathma*

To begin with, the meaning of the term *Maanava* (man) has to be properly understood. It means *Aathma* (the Self). It is from the *Aathma* that the five basic elements (ether, air, fire, water and the earth) have emerged. Man has brought under his control these five elements. Thereby he has become their master. Failing to comprehend the basic nature of human existence, man today has become a slave of his senses. The *Vedhaantha* has declared that one can know everything if he knows his own reality. To discover who you are, you have to rid yourself of the external vision. All the experiences based on the sense perceptions are external impressions. These are merely reflections of internal responses. To regard these as real and permanent and to ignore the Divine, which is the permanent entity, is the cause of man wasting his life. Hence, man has to utilise the mind to realise his divinity.

The mind is the cause (bestower) of man's joys and sorrows. It is also the means of man's *Mukthi* (liberation). It is the mind which leads man to progress from the human to the Divine and forget the ephemeral world. The very name, *Nara*, for man implies that he is imperishable. This is the *Aathmik* truth of man. Man, therefore, is not the body, but the immortal Self.

Four levels of functioning of the mind

The mind functions at four different levels. The first is Super Mind. The second is Higher Mind. The third is Illuminated Mind. The fourth is Over Mind. Man can comprehend his real human nature only when he understands these four states of the mind.

Super-Mind: An internal enquiry has to be made to understand this. This calls for turning the external vision inward. When this is done, it is realised that the physical body is inert. The mind is a reflecting mirror. The *Buddhi* (Intellect), *Chittha* (Will) and *Ahamkaara* (Ego) are aspects of the mind. All these are subject to change. But they are based on something that is unchanging. The first conclusion to be drawn from the internal enquiry is that there is an unchanging divine entity in man.

From this realisation, one proceeds to the awareness of a Cosmic Divine. This realisation comes out of the recognition that the Divine Consciousness experienced by the individual is also present in all other individuals. This is the Cosmic Power. The all-pervading Divine Power is one and the same. There is no second power. Bodies may be multifarious like electric bulbs. But the energy that makes them shine is one. When this truth is realised, you have the awareness of the Cosmic Divine.

It is not enough for one to realise his true Self. He cannot seek his individual salvation. He must experience the oneness that underlies the multiplicity in creation. Only when that oneness is realised can the true meaning of humanness be understood.

At present, all man's endeavours and enquiries are limited to exploring the physical, the vital and the mental. The journey ends there. Man has proceeded only upto the mind. But he has to go beyond it to the Over-Mind.

How far can the mind take you? It can take you upto the extent comprehending the *Jagath* (physical world). The mind is needed for understanding the variety of physical objects and phenomena in the world. But as long as man confines himself to the powers of the mind he remains as a human being. But, to rise to a higher level, he has to become *Amanaska*—one who transcends the mind. He should progress towards the Super-Mind.

The limitless potencies that man possesses

The Super-Mind is related to the *Suukshma shareera* (subtle body). In the subtle body, the senses, the mind, the intellect, the will, the ego and the physical body are absent and only *Chethana-shakthi* (consciousness) is present. One has to proceed further to the *Kaarana shareera* (the causal body). The Causal body contains the power which can control the body, the senses, the mind, etc.

This means that man possesses within himself all potencies. man's powers are limitless and astonishing. Nothing in the world is beyond his comprehension. Man today appears as a highly knowledgeable and vastly capable being. But these capacities only proclaim his powers over the physical forces of Nature. There is, however, an unseen, unknown, unmanifested infinite power within him. This is the Cosmic Power in man. It is all-pervasive. It is in every human being. Only when one goes by the form, there is an apparent distinction between the microcosm and the macrocosm, like the difference between the air in a balloon and the air in the vast atmosphere outside. But when the balloon bursts, the small air inside becomes one with the infinite air outside.

Human bodies are like the balloon. The infinite potency within each body is regarded as infinitesimally small. But this potency is a part of the universal Cosmic power.

"*Aanoraneeyaan Mahathomaheeyaan*" (minuter than the atom and vaster than the vastest), declares the Upanishath. But the power in both is the same.

However, though the thoughts of the mind, the actions of the body and the role of the *Aathma* as Witness appear as disparate, yet they are all integrally inter-related. The differences are in form, but the bliss that is experienced is one. Hence, the Upanishaths declared the truth of the One in the Many.

Humanness and divinity are same

Humanness is not separate from Divinity. Both are one. So, in the second stage, when you develop a broad vision, you experience the feeling of the oneness of the individual, of the Universe and God. This is called the Divine Universal Form. How do you cognise this? Not by perceiving the myriad diversities among objects, but by recognizing their underlying unity, the recognition of the divine in each of them. This means that human beings are not to be seen as so many innumerable separate entities. The *Chaithanya* (Consciousness) that is in each of them is one and the same Universal Consciousness. It is all-pervading. For example, the air that a man breathes is not exclusive to him. It is the same air that is breathed by others. The air that is all-pervading is inhaled by each according to his needs.

Judging himself by the limitations of his body, man considers himself a weak and powerless being. Once he is conscious of his Divinity, he will realise his boundless potentialities.

Cognition of inner reality

Therefore, the first requisite is for man to realise his divinity. The students have to find out who they are (their inner reality). Modern education, however, attempts to teach everything about the world except what they are. This is sheer ignorance. Along with the stupendous progress of science, there is a corresponding growth in ignorance. Such lopsided growth of science can only result in ignorance of the reality. As long as men are immersed in differences and discord, they are only steeped in ignorance.

Man must go beyond the lower mind to the Over-Mind. This is quite possible. There is nothing that is beyond human capacity if man has confidence in himself. But he is weighed down by the doubt whether he can accomplish anything great with his limited physical abilities. The body is finite, but man is not. When the limited body is placed next to the "I" (*Nenu*, in Telugu), the individual is lost in the limitations of the body forgetting the potentialities of the Self (the "I"). All doubts in man arise from this error. Man has to realise the impermanence of the *dheha* (body) and the immortality of *Dhehi* (the Indwelling Spirit). That Spirit is the Divine.

The human body is called *Kshethra* because the Indwelling Divine is *Kshethrajna* (the Knower of the Field). He is the embodiment of the *Aathma*. Students should understand the nature of the *Kshethrajna*, the Divine Knower, within each of them. Students should have self-confidence. This means that they should get rid of the barrier that separates them from the Self, namely the body-consciousness. Then they will experience the bliss that is beyond all the sheaths enveloping the human body.

Students should realise the Cosmic power that is possessed by each individual. They should not be misled by the limitations of the form. If man did not possess great abilities, how could he have made so many wonderful discoveries?

Spiritual development needed

While man has made astonishing progress in science and technology—in the realms of nuclear energy and electronics—he has been steadily going down in the moral, social and spiritual spheres. You have economic development on one side. On the other, you have divisions of class, caste and creed, language and territory. Unrest among students is growing. It is the animal nature in man that breeds these divisions. There are in man four traits: the animal, the demonic, the human and the divine. Man is developing his intellectual abilities, but not his divine attributes.

Man has to develop faith in himself and in God—this is the secret of greatness. Students should not consider themselves weak and imbecile beings. Rely on

your Conscience and not on the impermanent body
or the fickle mind. Make faith your life-breath.

Aathma is the source of all strength

The *Aathma* (Conscience) is the source of all your
strength. The reality is manifested in you by the "SO-
HAM" that is produced by every breath. This "SO-
HAM" is also known as *Hamsa Gaayathri*. *Hamsa* (the
Swan) is credited with the capacity to separate the milk
from the water with which it is mixed. *Hamsa Gaayathri*
is recited to separate the body-consciousness from the
Aathma.

Gaayathri signifies the mastery over the senses.
Gaayathri has two other names—Saavithri and Sarasvathi.
Saavithri is the master of life. Sarasvathi is the presiding
deity for *Vaak* (speech). The Gaayathri *manthra*, "*Bhur-
Bhuvah-Suvah*," refers to the body—*Bhur*, life—*Bhuvah*
and Awareness—*Suvah*. "*Bhur-Bhuvah-Suvah*" does not
refer to three worlds outside man. All the three are
in him. Hence, man is not an ordinary being. He is
Chaithanya-Svaruupa (the embodiment of the Cosmic
Divine Consciousness).

This jewel of divinity is being bartered away by
man for petty carnal pleasures. This is totally wrong.
If one recognises his godliness, he will be engaged in
godly actions. This transformation must be effected in
human attitudes. Man should transcend the mind and
reach the state of integral—*Chith*. It is total comprehension of humanness. Out of that comprehension
emerges *Aanandha* (Bliss).

All the discord and violence in the world are due
to differences arising from selfishness. This selfishness
should go. This calls for adherence to universal truth,

which is common to all humanity and valid for all time and places.

The ancient sages proclaimed two eternal verities: *"Sathyam Vadha: Dharmam Chara"* (Speak the Truth; Adhere to Righteousness). These were regarded as two eyes for man. Today man has lost these eyes and is helpless. Man has to realise that he has emanated from the Divine *Aathma*.

Students should develop a universal outlook and seek to serve all without regard to race or religion. That is the true purport of education. It must lend to realisation of the Self that is in everyone. Education should lead to elevation of the consciousness. Make use of Summer Course for the purification of your minds so that you may lead selfless lives. For this, there is no other path but the Spiritual.

Discourse at the Institute Auditorium, Brindhaavan on the occasion of the inauguration of the Summer School on 20-5-1993.

ೞ ——————————————————— ೦ಬ

Service without the idea of self is the very first step in the spiritual progress of man.

—BABA

CHAPTER 18

Tame the mind and realise the Self

*E*MBODIMENTS *of love!* To see the lamp that gives light you don't need another lamp. So also no other means of cognition is needed to realise the self-effulgent *Aathma* or Self. The Self is changeless. The *Buddhi* (intellect) has no light of its own but it shines by the effulgence of the *Aathma*. If the intellect is able to apprehend and judge everything in the world, it is due to the power of the Self. *Buddhi* or intellect is based on *Medha shakthi* (intelligence). The power of the intellect is only a reflection of *Aathma Chaithanya* (the effulgence of the *Aathma*).

The mind has two aspects, as doer and experiencer. It is the cause of the sense of attachment and possession. Human action is more evident in the wakeful state

than in the dream state or deep sleep state. In the
deep sleep state, the Super Intellectual Consciousness
is shining and the mind, senses and intellect are
dormant. Just as a red hot iron glows more brilliantly
than fire itself, though the fire is the cause thereof,
the individual intellectual consciousness shines more
because of the Cosmic Consciousness. When the mind
is dormant in the deep sleep state, the Super Mind
becomes active. In this state, man has no desire or
fear or anxiety.

Control the mind and rise higher

Man is bound by the mind and the senses. In the
pursuit of the spiritual path, first of all the mind should
be brought under control. When the mind is steady,
you reach the state of Super-Mind. In this state there
is no room for physical or transient worldly feelings.
As long as the mind is pure, no evil can enter the
heart. When it is polluted with bad feelings, there is
room for evil thoughts to breed.

We have to recognise the fact that human life
depends on the functioning of the mind. As long as
one is governed by the mind one continues to be human.
Once one goes beyond the mind, one can enjoy the
vastness of the limitless expanse of Cosmic Consciousness. Here is an example: Suppose you construct a
spacious house with a number of bed rooms, living
rooms, dining room and bath room. The spacious house
appears divided into a number of small rooms. This
is because of the walls put up for partitioning into
rooms. If the walls are pulled down, the house will
be one vast mansion. Similarly, the body is the Upaadhi
(wall) which limits one's perception to the narrow

confines of the body. Once you get rid of this body consciousness, you will experience the vast expanse of the Universal Cosmic Consciousness which is all-pervasive.

Just as the hands, ears, eyes and legs are all *angas* (limbs or organs) of individual human body, the bodies of all human beings are the limbs of society. Again, society itself is a limb of mankind. And humanity is a limb of *Prakrithi* (Nature) and *Prakrithi* is a limb of Divinity. One should understand this *Anga-Angee-Bhaava*—relationship between Divinity and human beings, in the proper perspective.

Realise that the heart is the seat of Divinity

Though man is endowed with *Buddhi* (intelligence), he is not able to master the senses. One should understand the great significance of human life, which is superior to that of all other species. Because of the body consciousness, man is forgetting his inherent divinity. You study a great deal about *Prakrithi* (Nature) and worldly things, and lead an artificial life, without realising that the heart is the seat of Divinity. If you allow bad feelings to enter the heart, it will be polluted and the Divine will have no place therein.

The whole world today is replete with pollution of not only the individual senses but also the five elements. The air is impure; water is polluted and everything you see or hear or touch is polluted. How can you expect to have peace in the world? *Vedhaantha* teaches that we should go beyond the mind and realise the inner vision to prevent bad feelings entering the heart and polluting the seat of God.

Raama, when questioned by Sage Agastya why he acted like a man, asked him "Am I God?" It is because of the body-consciousness that one does not realise his divinity. The body is just an instrument. We eat to sustain the body. We need food for the protection of the body and clothes for protection from cold and heat. The body is a source of all diseases arising out of *thrishna* (desire). Desire gives rise to *Raaga* and *Dhvesha* (attachment and hatred). There is nothing wrong in having desires for food, shelter and clothing. It is excessive desire that causes attachment and disappointment. Desire should be within limits. It should not become a hidden sickness. The desire to hoard is not there in birds and beasts, but it is rampant only among human beings. Man loses his human quality because of this greed for hoarding for selfish purposes.

Refinement is needed for transformation

How is man to be transformed? Here is an example. If there is a piece of charcoal, it cannot be made white by applying soap. You know that the charcoal came out of wood. The wood when put into fire became charcoal. When the charcoal is put back in the same fire, it burns fully and becomes glowing white. The charcoal was originally wood and when the wood was burnt, it turned into the middle form of charcoal and when it was further burnt, it reached the end form of ash, which is *Vibhuuthi*, representing the end-form of all beings. This teaches the truth that all materials in the world must be refined by fire and reach the final state of *Brahman*. The human body also reaches this end. But the inner reality of man is permanent.

This is the significance of human life. God is "*Sarvabhootha antharaathma*"—the Indweller in all beings, but there is no change in the *Aathma*. Human lives will continue to be generated like the waves of the ocean. But the ocean of Cosmic Consciousness remains unchanged.

The universe is the form of God

Suppose you make am idol of Krishna in silver. All parts of the idol are silver. When you see the form of Krishna in the idol, you are not aware of the silver. When you want to see only the silver out of which the idol is made, the form is out of your view. Similarly when you turn your mind towards God, who is pervading the entire Universe, the mind will be wholly filled with God and you won't see the different forms of the objects in the world. If the mind is directed towards worldly objects, you fail to see the Divinity that pervades all objects. "*Vishvam Vishnu Svaruupam*"— The Universe is the form of God. God is the cause and the Universe is the effect. Failure to understand the cause and the effect results in delusion.

The most precious human life is devalued. A beggar calls himself an *anaatha* (one without anyone to support him), while asking for alms. This is not correct. For everyone, God is the *Naatha* (support). It is only God who is *Anaatha*, because there is no one above Him. Thyaagaraaja considered Raama as his saviour and protector and did not care for the wealth of the world. He considered service at Raama's feet as the greatest treasure. Kabeer was a poor weaver and he used to share his food with others. When the King sent gold and provisions to him through his officials, Kabeer exclaimed: "For whom has the king sent all these?" They said: "The King sent these things to you as you are *anaatha* (helpless)." He replied: "I am not without support. Raama is my *Naatha* (master). You cannot say I have none to support me. It is only Raama who has none to support Him. Give these to Him." Kabeer said *Anaatha* means God. We should understand the correct meanings of words.

Body comes and goes but the *Aathma* is eternal

Embodiments of the Divine! Have faith in *Aathma* alone. The body, mind and intellect are all like the dresses you wear. Do you cry when you change your old clothes to new? Death is a change of dress. Because of the long association you have established with the body, you cry at the time of death. If you consider the relationship as temporary, you won't cry. You must attach yourself only to God and not to anyone or anything in the world. God is permanent friend.

After death, where does the *Aathma* go? This is a question on many people's minds. What happens to the *Aathma* after the body is cast off and how long does it take to be re-born? These are ridiculous questions. This can be explained by an example. If you put on the switch, the bulb burns because of the electric energy flowing through it. When the bulb is removed, nothing happens to the energy which is still there, though bulb is gone. Similarly, the body comes and goes but the *Aathma* is eternal.

Embodiments of the Divine Aathma! You must get rid of all narrow ideas and attitudes. All worldly things are like passing clouds. There is only one that is permanent and changeless. That is *Brahmathathva.* It should be realised through the path of pure Love.

Discourse on the evening of 20-5-1993
at the Sai Ramesh Hall, Brindhaavan.

ꙮ ⸻⸻⸻⸻⸻⸻⸻ ⸻

There are three categories of human beings. There are those who have faith in God, there are those who have no faith in God, and and there are those who are indifferent. For instance, in a bush there is a flower, its fragrance goads those who have faith in God to search for its source. These can be termed as Aasthikas or believers. Then there are those who enjoy the fragrance but do not bother to question about the source—these can be termed as the believing non-believers. There are yet others who are neither looking for the flower nor perceiving its fragrance. They may be termed as non-believers. We presume that the non-believers are those who have no faith in God, but in fact it is not true. There can be no one who has no faith in himself. All people who have faith in themsleves are believers.

—BABA

CHAPTER 19

Man, mind and the Cosmos

*E*MBODIMENTS *of Divine Love!* The gross body is formed by the combination of *Pancha Mahaabhuuthas* (five basic elements) and the operation of *Karma* (past deeds). This body is the cause of both pleasure and pain.

> *Only he is truly a man*
> *Who knows that by which*
> *Everything else is known,*
> *And without knowing which*
> *All else is not worth knowing,*
> *He is the knower of the Supreme Truth.*

In human life, what every one should try to understand is the truth relating to the *Sthuula, Suukshma, Kaarana* and *Mahaakaarana* (Gross, the Subtle, the Causal and the Super causal) bodies. Only then can man understand the phenomena in the world. He will then comprehend the nature of man, of the world and the relationship between God and man.

Subtle body is associated with *Maaya*

The physical body is inert. It is formed by the aggregation of physical constituents. The body is composed of elements like iron, water, phosphorus, calcium, lead, etc. Hence, the gross body is described as inert matter.

The *Suukshma shareera* (subtle body) is *Maaya svaruupa* (illusory form). In the dream state, the mind not only creates itself but also experiences pleasure and pains, worries and fears. In the subtle body, these illusory creations of the mind are experienced. These experiences are felt to be real only at the moment. *Maaya* is that mental state in which what does not exist appears to exist and what exists is not perceived as real. All the experiences in the dream state are seen in the waking state as unreal. The mansions witnessed in dreams vanish when the eyes open.

What is real and true must be that which exists in the waking, the dream and the deep sleep sates. Truth is that which is true and unchanging at all times— past, present and the future. Hence the subtle body is associated with *Maaya*.

Then there is the *Kaarana shareera* (Causal body). It is only an image or reflection. It is the image of the *Mahaakaarana* (Super-Causal body). The *Mahakaarana* represents the Supreme Principle. It is as a reflection of the Supreme—*Parathathva*—that the causal, subtle and gross bodies function. It follows from this that all these aspects are contained in the human being. The mind, the Super-Mind, the Higher Mind, and the Illuminated Mind are all present in these bodies.

In the waking state, the mind functions in response to the sensory organs by seeing, listening, talking, etc. The mind is bound by the limitation of time and space.

How the Super-Mind is active in dream state

In the dream state the mind creates its own world. It is related to time alone. For example, you get into the train to night, and reach Bombay the day after tomorrow. In this you see the mind at work in respect of four things: the reason (for travel), the actual journey, the arrival at the destination and completion, of your duty. How did you go? You went by train. How long did the journey take? Thirty-six hours. What was your destination? Bombay. What was the reason for your journey? Some job to be done in an office. Time, action, and result—all these are involved in the operation of the mind.

At night you had a dream. In the dream, you reached Bombay and saw various things there. You were pleased. But in this dream, none of the four things, experienced in the waking state were present—neither time, nor movement, nor objective, nor any consummation. In the dream, how did you travel, how much time did it take, for what purpose and what was the outcome? None of these things happened. All that took place in the dream was over in five minutes. This is the mystery and the marvel of what happens in the realm of the mind. All that happens in the dream state, the experiences and events, occurs in fleeting moments.

What is experienced in a life of forty years is covered in two minutes in the dream state. In those forty years, you have completed your education, got married, had a son, educated him and sent him abroad. The entire panorama of these events appear in your dream in a few minutes. But what you experience in a dream vanishes in a moment in the waking state. What is active in the dream state is the Super-Mind. It is more powerful than the ordinary mind, because it encompasses in a brief moment all that happens in space and time over long distances and periods.

Higher Mind functions in the deep sleep state

Next, you have the Higher Mind. This functions in the *sushupthi* (deep sleep state). In this state, there is no thought or worry. The mind is absent. The senses are not functioning. There are no experiences of any kind. But on waking from deep sleep, the individual experiences *Aanandha*. He declares that he felt extremely happy in sound sleep. This state confers a sense of bliss without any experience. This bliss is beyond the mind and the senses. In the deep sleep state, there is life, but no mind. Only bliss remains. In deep sleep, there is no pleasure or pain, because there is no consciousness of the phenomenal world. You are conscious of the world and experience pleasure and pain only when the mind is active.

Because in the deep sleep state the ordinary mind is not present, the consciousness in that state is attributed to the Higher Mind. This is associated with the *Kaarana shareera* (Causal Body). Here you have the cause. But there is the Doer, there is action and there is a reason for action. The relationship between cause and effect accounts for all happenings in the world. The Divine is the cause and the Cosmos is the effect.

Divine Causal Principle is called Illuminated Mind

Who is this cause? Is it the Divine, who is *Mahaakaarana* (the prime cause)? This Divine Causal Principle underlies all that happens in the universe. This Principle is termed the Illuminated Mind. This is the Power that illumines everything in the world. To experience this cosmic principle, we need a divine form. That is the Super Divine Self. It is called *Purushathva*. This is a primary attribute of the Divine.

Above the mind, the Super-mind, the Higher Mind and the Illuminated Mind is the Over-Mind. *Purushathva* is the over-Mind. It is Divinity.

It is from this *Purushathva* that the sense of 'I-ness' emanates. This 'I-ness' is present in all beings, from the highest to the lowest. It is the index of the *Purushathva* (cosmic consciousness). Why is man called *Purusha?* The human body is called *Puram* (a city), as he dwells in the body he is called *Purusha*. All bodies are the same, irrespective of differences in sex. The three states of consciousness are common to all. The effects of qualities *(Sathva, Rajas, Thamas)* are the same for all. In sorrow, one grieves, whether man or woman. Hunger and anger have the same effects on both men and women. The intensity of the experience may vary from person to person. The manner in which it is experienced may also vary. One may grieve in secret, while another may make a show of it. Such differences are relative to the individuals concerned. But the experiencing body is a common factor.

In every body, the *Mahaa Purusha* Principle (the Super Divinity) is present. The entire cosmos is a reflection of the gross, subtle and causal bodies. The *Kaaraka* (primal Doer) is the Supreme Lord. The cosmos is the effect (creation).

This relationship can be recognised in the daily life of every individual. There are *Pancha bhuthas* (five basic elements), *Pancha koshas* (five sheaths), *Panchendhriyas* (five sense organs), *Pancha praanas* (five vital airs), the mind, the *Buddhi* (intellect) the *chittha* (will) and the *Ahamkaara* (Ego). All these together make up twenty four principles. The Supreme who pervades all these twenty four entities is the *Mahaa Purusha* (the Supreme Person), the twenty fifth principle. Thus, the human body is made up of these twenty five constituents. Similarly, the entire universe is made up of these twenty five constituents.

All differences are the handiwork of *Maaya*

There is no difference between the *dheha* and *dhesa* (body and the world). But, when one looks at the external world with the physical vision, numerous differences appear. All these differences are the handiwork of the delusive power of *Maaya*. Not recognizing the mystery relating to this delusive power, man falls a prey to many difficulties.

Maaya envelops man in its multifarious coils. The cosmos is made up of the twenty five constituents. All is subject to delusion. In the waking state, you see, you hear and you experience many things. In sleep, you are steeped in a dream. In that state, what happens to your experiences in the waking state?

Everything is forgotten. You consider the experiences in the dream state as real. This lasts only till you wake up. Then you dismiss the dreams as of no account. What is the truth? The experiences of the waking state or the experiences in dreams? The former is a day-dream, the latter is a night-dream. Both are dreams.

Once, the Emperor Janaka, a great *Jnaani* and *Yogi*, devoid of body-consciousness, was having a colloquy with his ministers after dinner at night. He fell into deep sleep. Some time later, he got up and started putting the questions: "Is that true or is this true?" (that is, whether what he experienced in the dream was true or whether his experience in the waking state was true).

The Self is present in all the three states

Nobody could give the answer. Seeing the agitated state of mind of the Emperor, the ministers tried to find an answer, but no one came forward to solve the riddle posed by the Emperor. "Is that true or is this true?" At last, the sage Vashishta was called and he, after *yogic* meditation, gave the reply to the emperor's question. "Your Majesty! Neither that is true nor is this true. You are the only reality. You experienced certain things in your dream and some in the waking state. In the waking state, there was no dream. In the dream, there was no waking state. But you were present both in the dream and the waking states. Therefore, you are the truth. You were the experiencer in both the states!"

This means that the Self is present in all the states of every human being. It also means that the Self exists in the past, the present and the future. Humanness is thus associated with Divinity and is no ordinary existence. All the sacred pronouncements in the *Vedhas* and the *Upanishaths* apply to man.

The Divine is described as possessing eight forms of wealth. In fact, man is endowed with all these *Ashtaishvarya* (eight forms   of wealth)—*Nirgunam, Niranjanam, Sanaathanam, Nikethanam, Nithya Shuddha, Buddha, Muktha* and *Nirmala Svaruupinam* (beyond qualities, untainted, eternal, ever-abiding, ever pure, intelligent, liberated and immaculate). Out of a sense of weakness, man assumes that these attributes relate only to the Divine and not to him. This feeling should be totally eschewed.

An individual, through considerable effort, acquires many kinds of knowledge. Wherefrom has this knowledge come? How did he acquire it? At the time of birth he was totally ignorant. But by *Shraddha* (diligent endeavour) anything could be acquired.

Think of the society beyond your family

Man today is preoccupied only with the concerns relating to himself and his family. Immersed in selfishness, he does not think of the society beyond his family. But what would happen to him and his family if society was not there?

All man's desires are centred on his own welfare, even when he appears to desire the welfare of the world. But, in fact his welfare is bound up with the well-being of the world. Hence, one should proceed from the 'I,' to the family, to the society and to the world at large. All the world's problems arise out of the obsession with selfish interests and lack of concern for the well-being of society. If every individual strives for the welfare of society, all these problems will cease to exist. Millennia ago, the Vedhas declared: "Lokaasamasthaas-sukhino Bhavanthu!" (Let all the people of the world be happy).

When men get rid of the narrow egoistic feelings born out of ignorance, they will experience the Divine, as declared by the Vedhic seers. The Vedhas summoned human beings to strive together in unity for achieving the highest goals of life. The essence of the Vedhas is summed up in one phrase, the sense of Ekaathmabhaava (spiritual unity of all human beings). This is the realisation of the Divine. This is true Adhvaitha (Non-dualism).

Unity in spiritual oneness of all beings

Declarations like "Aham Brahmaasmi" and "Taththvam-Asi" are cited as pronouncements proclaiming non-dualism. But this is not correct. These statements themselves refer to two entities—Aham and Brahma; Tath and Thvam ('I' and the Absolute; That and You). The recognition that the one and same Aathma dwells in all beings is true Adhvaitha. The bulbs may be of different sizes, colours and wattage, but they are illumined by the same electrical energy.

It is because the doctrine of human unity based on the spiritual oneness of all beings, is not propagated in the right manner that we have today so many divisions, giving rise to conflicts. Differences between people professing different faiths are not due to differences in the teachings of the different religions but in the mental attitudes of those belonging to these faiths.

All religions teach the
same good ideals.
Understanding them, men should
learn to live in harmony.

Those who preach hatred on the basis of religion are verily men with perverted minds. The broad vision of Bhaaratheeya culture, the infinite sacredness of Bhaarath, the unfathomable faith in unity—all these proclaimed the glory of the Divine and upheld the fundamental oneness of humanity. Today, because unity has been lost, humanness has reached its nadir. Morality and integrity have disappeared. This is the progress humanity has made!

This is not progress. What we should seek is spiritual progress, progress in righteousness and morality. People today talk about saving the world and safeguarding their nation. There is no need to protect the world or the nation. If you safeguard *Sathya* and *Dharma* (Truth and Righteousness), the nation and the world will be automatically protected. This is the profound message of the ancients: "Speak the Truth; follow Righteousness."

Recognise the Omnipresence of the Divine

The Divine is the basis of everything in the cosmos. The integral relationship between the Divine and the Universe should be properly understood.

Through many lives people have tended to identify themselves with their bodies and pursue wrongful practices. The Omnipresence of the Divine—from a piece of stone to a mighty emperor should be recognized. Man should be grateful for the innumerable benefits provided by the Divine. Raamakrishna Paramahamsa was an illiterate person. But he achieved world wide fame by his pursuit of Truth and his realisation of the Divine. Self-realisation is the goal for every human being. This is the message of the Bhaagavatha.

Today almost every person is wedded to untruth. Once a year they perform *Sathyanaaraayana Puuja*. But every moment should be employed in the worship of *Sathyanaaraayana* (the Lord of Truth). This calls for unity in thought, word and deed, which is the form of Truth.

Transcend the feeling of smallness

Men think that to reach the spiritual height is an arduous adventure. Svaami assures you that this is not so. The spiritual journey is much easier than the worldly struggle in which men are engaged. Men should aim at reaching the Supreme state instead of carrying on their wrangles upto the Supreme Court. Man has all the divine potencies for realising the Divine Self. His consciousness can comprehend the cosmos, even as a mirror can reflect the firmament. The heart is a mirror in which one can see the entire universe. Realise from this moment that man is the embodiment of the Divine. Transcend the feeling of smallness. As you think, so you become. Therefore, divinise yourselves by constant reminder of your inherent divinity.

Discourse at Summer School in
Brindhaavan, on 21-5-1993.

CHAPTER 20

Beyond the Mind

What can the evil forces of Kali do
To the man whose heart is filled with compassion,
Whose words are immersed in love,
And whose body is dedicated to the service of others?

Knowledge of all the shaastras and Vedhas
Will not serve to remove the curtain of the mind
Which stands between the individual and God.

This curtain makes it appear
That God and man are separate
Though both are one.

Only when the mind is subdued
Will God and man, Nature and God,
The Cause and the Effect become one.

EMBODIMENTS of Divine Love! The mind is responsible for differences in opinions, likes and dislikes, and diversity in attitudes. The world is perceived through the mind. The world is permeated by the mind. Without the mind there can be no world and no attachments and hatred, no joy and sorrow.

It is because of hatred and attachment that man today is plunged in misery. As the mind is the root cause of all this, man has to go beyond the natural infirmities of the mind to the over-mind to be able to recognise Divinity.

In the three states of waking, dream and deep sleep, man is bound by the mind. When man transcends these three states by developing his Inner Vision, he can progress from the human to the Divine.

The seed and the tree are not different things

There is a Sanskrit saying: *"Yaddhrishyam thannasyam"* (That which is seen is subject to extinction). *"Yathpindam thath Brahmaandam"* (what is in the microcosm is in the macrocosm) is another saying. All that appears in the microcosm are miniature replica of the macrocosm. It is like the tree that is latent in the seed. The seed and the tree are not different things. When the tree emerges, the seed disappears (becomes formless). In both the form and the formless, the principle of *Sath* (Being) exists as one and the same. When one looks at the seed, the tree is not visible. But all that are seen in the tree, the branches, the leaves, the flowers and the fruits, were immanent in the seed. When you enquire into the divinity inherent in man, this profound and sacred reality can be recognised.

As long as man sees only with his external vision, he can experience only the external. When man develops the internal vision and experiences the Divinity within, the cosmos will appear as a reflection of the Divine. This is called realization of the Cosmic Divine. What is the difference between the Cosmic Divine and the Inner Divine? There is no difference between the two. But when it is experienced by the individual, it is described as Inner Divine. When the individual experience is extended to the entire universe, it is called Cosmic Divine. The Individual Self and *Paramaathma* (the Omni-Self) are one, like the rind of a fruit and the juice inside.

The differences one notices in the world arise not from the nature of creation but from the perspective from which one looks at the world. Man's view of the world has to change. This cannot be done by intellectual argument. When the mind is subdued, the oneness of the *Jeevi* (Individual) and the Divine will be experienced.

Beautify your heart by good qualities

From the time he wakes up, till he goes to sleep, man looks at everything externally. He hardly spends a few moments to develop his inner vision. All the external objects can only confer momentary pleasure. Pursuing these pleasures, man wastes his precious and sacred life. He can never achieve peace in this way.

Man devotes considerable time and energy to decorating his home, expecting to derive joy from it. But how long can this last? What he should seek to beautify is his heart. This is not visible to anyone, but the beauty of a pure heart is beyond description. What is it that lends beauty to the heart? The heart is beautified by qualities such as love, forbearance and compassion. These qualities confer enduring bliss on man. Such a man's words and actions are sweet. He is worthy of adoration. Every man should aim at becoming such an ideal human being.

What does adoration of the Lord mean? It is not mere offering of worship with the paraphernalia of rituals. It is an attempt to merge in the Divine, experiencing the bliss of oneness with the Divine, recognising unity in diversity and the Divinity that is present in all beings.

Triple pollution that affect the eyes, ears and tongue

Nature will not give real bliss as long as it is viewed from a physical and worldly point of view. The pleasure to be derived from any object in the world depends on the condition in which it is enjoyed. For instance, a mango will be tasteless if it is tender, sour if it is half-ripe and sweet when it is fully ripe. Likewise Nature is a sweet fruit. But if it is seen from purely sensory point of view, it will give only bitter taste. But when it is viewed as a manifestation of the Divine, its unique sweetness will be apparent.

Thoughts influence the vision, which, in its turn, affects the mind. Thoughts assume good and bad forms. Good thoughts, good speech and good actions make a man truly human. This is the message of the three monkeys pictured as one with closed eyes, another with closed ears and the third with a closed mouth—"See no evil, hear no evil, speak no evil."

Today the entire environment is polluted by evil things which offend the eyes, the ears and the tongue.

Everyone should free himself from this three-fold pollution. The mind has to be turned towards God.

Proceed from the mind to the Over-mind

To enjoy the fragrance of the sandalwood, it has to be rubbed on the grinding stone vigorously. Likewise, to experience the great fragrance emanating from Nature, its unity with the Divine has to be realised. For this, it is necessary to transcend the limitations of the ordinary mind and proceed to the Super-Mind, the Higher-Mind, the Illuminated Mind and the Over-Mind.

It should not be presumed that this is a difficult task. In fact it is quite easy. For instance, people feel that adhering to truth is difficult. Actually it is uttering untruth that creates difficult problems. All kinds of plans have to be made to cover up a lie. But to stick to the facts as they are is easy. Men should realise that it is easy to be good. It is going astray that causes difficulties. One cannot always avoid committing a wrong. But one should learn the lesson from it and avoid repeating it. That is *saadhana.*

When it is admitted that God is in all beings, one should strengthen that conviction and act on that basis. On the contrary, men who profess to believe in God, do not live up to their belief because of their attachment to useless trifles. Here is an illustration from the life of Shri Raamakrishna Paramahamsa.

Shri Raamakrishna Paramahamsa used to ecstatically enjoy himself in the worship of the Goddess in the temple built by Raani Raashmani. One night thieves broke into the temple and carried away all the jewels on the idol of Krishna in the temple. With a view

to carrying on his regular priestly duties, he went to
Raani Raashmani's nephew, Mathuranaath, and told him,
"Sir, thieves have stolen all the jewels on the idol."
Mathuranaath was angry and proceeded with Raamakrishna to the temple. Losing his temper and balance
of mind, he burst out in anger: "Oh Krishna! Are you
not ashamed of yourself? If you are unable to protect
your jewels on your own idol, how are you going to
protect the whole world? Were you paralysed when the
thieves were carrying away the jewels? Or were you
asleep? This is a disgrace to your Divinity."

Do not rebuke God, change your vision

Hearing these words, Shri Raamakrishna said:
"Mathuranaath! Shut up your mouth! For the sake of
your petty jewels and trinkets, is this the way you
should berate God? When the Goddess of all wealth,
Lakshmi, is the Consort of the Lord, why do you get
so agitated over the loss of a few trivial ornaments?
The Lord can have no such petty feelings. You are feeling
so much for the action of a few thieves who loved
some jewels and came to the Lord to get them. It is
because of your love for jewels that you are getting
distressed so much. But the Lord has no desires. He
is ready to give Himself away. God is prepared to offer
Himself. Such a One, will he be worried about this
petty loss? Hence, change your vision. Don't comment
on God." At these words Mathuranaath felt ashamed
of himself.

Then, Raamakrishna sat near the idol of Shri Krishna
and prayed: "Oh Krishna! As long as one is caught
up in the coils of the world, he will speak like an
intoxicated man. Only when he gets immersed in God

will he become oblivious to himself. Therefore, do not let me get intoxicated. Confer on me the boon of self-forgetfulness." This is what is meant by the saying: "The knower of the *Brahman* becomes *Brahman* himself." When one experiences the Divine, he sees the Divine in everything.

When does man experience the pure Divine Self? It is in the *Thureeya* state—the fourth state of consciousness beyond the waking, dream and deep sleep states. This is the state of the Over-Mind. In that state man is one with the Divine. He has no attributes. Therefore, He is all-pervading.

Nature is bound by the five qualities of sound, touch, form, taste and smell (these are the qualities of space, air, fire, water and earth—the five basic elements). With the loss of each quality, starting from smell, a process of expansion takes place. Finally, we have *Akaasha* (ether or space) which has only one quality, sound, and is all-pervading. That being the case, how much more pervasive must be the Lord, who has no attributes.

The mind perpetually seeks comfort

If man asks the question, "I am posing this query to the entire world. I have nothing to do with the world. Am I the Truth or not?," the answer that he is the Truth will be evident in a few words. We see before our eyes many persons dying, being cremated or buried after death. In spite of this, everyone has a desire, "I must live for ever." What is the inner meaning of this desire? You are eternal and the idea of immortality arises in you because of this. The body is impermanent, but you are eternal. This truth has to be properly grasped. Whatever one may see, one always declares to himself, "I must live, I must live," and does not say, "I too must pass away one day." Even if this idea occurs, it is followed by the desire to live a little longer. Even a hundred-year old ailing man tells the doctor: "Please give the injection gently and don't cause any pain." The mind perpetually seeks comfort.

Truth, Bliss, Beauty are forms of the Divine

Truth, Bliss, Beauty are forms of the Divine. They are also known as *Sathyam, Shivam, Sundharam.* These represent the true form of man. *Shivam* is that which has no death. *Sathyam* is that which is not subject to change (on account of time, place or circumstance). *Sundharam* (Beauty) is the form of the Divine. Vishnu is described as *Alankara Priyah* (a lover of beauty). Man is described as *Bhojana priyah* (a lover of food). What is this food? This gross body flourishes on food. But it is bound to perish some day. But the subtle body, made up of *Praana* (the Life-Force), *Manaa* (the mind) and *Vijnaana* (intelligence) lasts longer. But, for how long? Only as long as the mind lasts. When the mind is absent, what happens? This state is described as *Sushupthi* (deep sleep state). In this state, there is only the *Kaarana shareera* (causal body). There is no mind. This is a state of bliss.

Hence, it is essential to understand the functioning of the mind. Man and mind are not separate. To treat the mind as something apart and becoming subject to it is wrong. It has to be treated as a servant as long as the body-mind consciousness remains. Then the mind obeys you. Today man follows the dictates of the mind.

Everyone should acquire the Divine Will Power

Dear students! It is not easy to subdue the mind immediately. But you must begin to bring it under control. When the mind desires something, you must immediately set the *Buddhi* (intellect) at work. Why? So that the intellect may give you the proper advice. The mind has to be taught the lesson: "Oh Mind! Don't play your petty pranks. Examine your desire, using the power of discrimination to find out whether it is good or bad, right or wrong. Do not wish to acquire whatever you desire." When you try to teach the mind in this manner, it loses its potency (the keenness to acquire what it wants).

This *Vijnaana* is full of intelligence and common sense. It is called Divine Intellectual Will. The Divine Will Power has to be acquired by everyone. Only then, they can realise their true human nature. It is through this Will Power that the Cosmic Divine nature of the universe can be recognised.

This Cosmic Power has to be seen with the eyes, experienced mentally, practised through the body and made an integral part of one's being. Do not speculate whether this is possible or not. If one has the determination anything is possible. If an ant has determination it can travel any distance. But, even an eagle, if it has no will to fly, will be confined to the ground. Resolve to accomplish what you want to with a firm determination.

Develop the feeling, "I and God are one." This should not be purely a verbal exercise. You must realise the implications of the *manthra* you recite such as *"Soham"* (I am He) and live up to it. That is true concentration.

Most students do not listen attentively to the discourses. How can they ever practise the teaching? The eyes are turned towards Svaami, but the ears do not absorb Svaami's words. How can such persons put into practice Svaami's teachings? A few may benefit from these discourses. Even if one or two practise the teachings, that is good enough!

Four steps to experience ineffable bliss

Listen carefully. Ruminate over whatever you have heard. Put into practice whatever you have absorbed. This is the meaning of the Upanishathic injunction: "*Shravanam* (listen), *mananam* (ruminate), *Nidhidhyaasanam* (practise)." Just as there is no meaning in preparing delicious food unless it is consumed and digested, it is useless to listen to discourses unless you put into practice what you have learnt. Only then can the bliss of learning be experienced. Metaphysical lectures alone will not transform the mind. What is learnt must be put into practice. This is the real *Vedhaantha* you have to learn today. This is the spirituality that is vital for you. The Lord's name on your lips, thoughts of God in your mind, seeing the Lord with your eyes and meditating on the Lord with love—these four will give you ineffable bliss. Strive to experience this bliss.

Discourse in the Sai Ramesh Mandap,
Brindhaavan, on 22-5-1993.

CHAPTER 21

Thought waves make up the Cosmos

God has endowed mankind
  With the great weapon of the Mind.
Only the one who subjugates the mind
  can achieve victories on earth.
We cannot imagine anyone who is a salve of
  the mind and has attained happiness or peace.

*E*MBODIMENTS *of Love!* Human existence can become meaningful only when man, at the very outset, recognises the nature of the mind and bases his actions on that understanding. The mind is extremely powerful. It runs at great speed. It is subtler than the sky and even more subtle than electricity. When such a mind is turned to bad purposes, a man becomes a prey to all kinds of sorrow.

The mind can run faster than light. Just as you are able to hear a broadcast of music from a radio station in Delhi simultaneously in Whitefield, the mind also operates like radio waves. Thought waves emanating from the mind have also got properties of radio waves. There is no end to the waves arising from the ocean of the mind.

The power of thought is immense. Thoughts outlast the human body. Thought waves radiate very much like heat waves, radio waves and light waves. The thought waves are the cause of man's joy or sorrow, health or disease, birth or death. The potency of these waves has to be understood by man and his conduct has to be based on this awareness.

The whole cosmos is made up of thought waves; hence, the scripture declares: "The mind is at the root of the cosmos." There is no place, or form or action wherein the mind is absent. Hence, all thoughts of man should be turned in the right direction.

Our fortune is linked to our thoughts

When good thoughts, good feelings and good intentions are developed, the mind becomes pure. Only when the mind is pure, can the action be pure and the fruits thereof be pure.

Today we sow the seed of thought—*karma*—and reap the fruit of action. From the seed of *karma* arises *svabhaava* (the fruit of behaviour). Out of the seed of behaviour comes the fruit of character. The seed of character yields the fruit of *adhrishtam* (fortune). Thus, from thought to fortune, the chain of human progress can be perceived. Our good and bad luck are thus linked to our thoughts. The mind immerses man in impenetrable darkness through bad thoughts. The same mind can lift man to sublime heights by good thoughts. Thus, thoughts are supremely important for man. They constitute his very life-breath. Without understanding this truth, man allows evil tendencies like anger, envy, hatred and conceit to fill his mind and thereby courts disaster.

A man seeking to harm others nourishes many evil thoughts in his mind. But these thoughts cause him ten times the harm they do to others. He is not aware of this truth. Consequently, he indulges in abuse of others and in doing harm to them. But there are no "others," but only manifestations of the Divine. Not realising the divinity in others, man tries to harm them. But whoever wields the sword against others, will perish by the sword. The harm which he does to others will be the undoing of himself. Whoever abuses others, will also be the target of abuse by others. As are the thoughts, so is the outcome. The entire human existence is based upon thoughts and their results.

Face is the index of the mind

Man perpetually tries to conceal his faults like the ostrich which buries its head in the sand hoping that thereby the hunter will not see it. In fact, the ostrich becomes an easy target for the hunter. Likewise, a man filled with ego and wickedness imagines that his thoughts are not known to anyone else. But a man's mind is like a gramophone record. His good and bad thoughts are reflected in his face, though he does not notice it. But any outside observer can observe it well. The face of a man filled with evil thoughts appears like that of a man with pimples. The face becomes like a board indicating what goes on in the mind.

As thoughts lead to actions, man's behaviour, speech and conduct affect the tendencies of the mind and give rise to good or bad impulses. Man imagines that no one can know his thoughts. While entertaining evil thoughts about others, he acts as if he rejoices in their company. But in fact, he is not deceiving others, but deceiving himself. He is only nourishing evil thoughts and degrading himself.

The natural state of a man's heart is pure. But by letting in the poisonous snakes in the form of evil thoughts, he is inviting trouble.

How can a man have peace in his home if there is a snake in it? Bad thoughts in the mind are worse than poisonous reptiles in the house. Absolutely no room should be given for bad thoughts.

Good company leads to the Divine

By our thoughts we can even cure the ills of others. When the friendship of good persons is acquired through good thoughts, the union of the good leads to the realisation of the Divine.

One's thoughts determine the kind of people with whom one associates. A drunkard seeks the company of drunkards, a thief joins the company of thieves, a lawyer with lawyers, and so on. So, good-intentioned persons should associate only with like-minded persons. If they get into the company of evil-minded persons, even their good thoughts may get polluted.

Men do not realise today the prodigious powers of the mind. The five elements, the five life-breaths, the five sense organs, the five sheaths are all based on the mind. It is because the immense power of the mind is not recognised, human life is ruined. By belittling the mind, man is dehumanising himself and behaving either like an animal or as a demon. When man broadens his mental vision, he can realise his Divinity.

If the nation has to improve and progress, if you want to experience the Divine that pervades the cosmos, you have to cultivate good thoughts. Do not treat thoughts as trifles. A giant banyan tree grows out of a small seed. There is a saying in Thelugu that even a small serpent has to be beaten with a long stick. In the same manner, even a small bad thought has to be rigorously eschewed.

*Discourse to the Summer School
at Brindhaavan on 23-5-1993.*

I do not recommend the giving up of Karma, for it is not possible. What is generally meant by Karma-Sanyaas is the giving up of rites and rituals prescribed by the Scripture.

—BABA

CHAPTER 22

From the Mind to the Over-Mind

Can life be redeemed merely
by performing Japa?
Only when the mind is subdued,
can man become sublime.

THE mind proclaims its astonishing uniqueness to the world by its capacity to express feelings, recognise forms, appreciate the beauty of colour, enjoy different smells, as well as its power of thought. As the world is permeated by these qualities of the mind, these five qualities are all-pervasive. The mind is highly powerful. Once the powers of the mind are understood, the nature of the whole world can be comprehended. When you taste a single drop of sea-water, you know the taste of all the water in the ocean. The drop and the ocean are the same. Likewise, the mind is the world and the world is the mind.

In this vast world, there are today more than 500 crores of human beings. There may be differences among them in name and form and in their food and recreation habits. But when you view them from the physical point of view, all human beings are one. In every human body, there are four forms, which can be understood through proper *Tathva* (enquiry). In this enquiry into truth, *Tath* refers to *Paramaathma* (the Omni-Self). The Omni-Self is infinite and immeasurable.

To understand the infinite *Paramaathma* you have to pursue one of the innumerable paths. *Vedhaantha* laid stress on nine of these paths: *Shravanam* (listening), *Keerthanam* (singing the glories of God), *Vishnuh naama smaranam* (remembering the names of the Lord), *Vandhanam* (offering salutations), *Archanam* (ritual worship), *Paadha sevanam* (Service to the Lotus feet of the Lord), *Dhaasyam* (service), *Saakhyam* (friendship) and *Aathma-Nivedanam* (total surrender). All these nine paths of devotion have been prescribed to enable man to experience their varied novelty.

Constituents of physical and subtle bodies

To begin with, there is the physical body. It is visible to the eye. The body is made up of twenty five constituents: five *Karmendhriyas* (organs of action), five *Jnaanedhriyas* (sense organs), *pancha-praanas* (five life-breaths), *pancha Thanmaathras* (five sensory faculties). In addition, there are four inner instruments: the mind, the will, the ego, and the *Anthahkarana* (Inner Motivator). All these total twenty four. When these are associated with the Life-Force, you have altogether 25 constituents. As these twenty five constituents have emanated from the cosmos, the embodied being is called *Vishva*. The physical body is cosmic in form. It is not something that is individualistic. The human state is a manifestation of the collective.

The second body is *Suukshma dheham* (the subtle one). This is made up of seventeen constituents: the five sensory faculties, the five senses and the five vital airs. Together with the mind and the intellect, they make up seventeen constituents. As these constituents have the quality of *Thejas* (luminescence), the subtle body is called *Thaijasa*. The results of man's good and bad actions are experienced by this subtle body. All the pleasant and unpleasant happiness in the world are experienced by the subtle body. This body is also *Yaathana* (experiential) body because it is a prey to various experiences.

States of awareness and forgetfulness

The third is the *Kaarana shareera* (causal body). It is made up of only two constituents: *Chittha* (will power) and *Prajna* (Constant Integrated Awareness). Because of its association with *Prajna*, this body is called *Prajnaanam* or *Praajna*.

The fourth one is *Mahaakaarana* (the Over-Mind). This is self-luminous and effulgent in its original form. This is called *"Uniki,"* (a Being that is self-knowing). Because of its capacity for self-knowledge, it is also called *"Eruka"* (Awareness). As against Awareness, there is its opposite, forgetfulness. The physical, subtle and causal bodies belong to the latter (of forgetfulness). The three states of *Jaagrath* (waking),

Svapna (dream) and *Sushupthi* (deep sleep) also belong to the state of forgetfulness (or non-awareness of the true Self).

Hence, the true form is Awareness. Awareness is the subtle base. Forgetfulness is gross. But in both the subtle Awareness and the gross Forgetfulness there is a Divinity that is present equally. This is described in metaphysics in a different way. The *Jeevaathma* is present always in all the three states of Consciousness and in Awareness as well as Forgetfulness as the Inner Being.

Matter and energy are inter-related

In every *padhaartha* (object) in the world, the *Paraartha* (transcendental) is immanent. The *padhaartha* is perceptible. The *paraartha* is present in it as energy. Although *padhaartha* (matter) and *Paraartha* (Energy) appear to us as two different entities, their unity constitutes the Divine principle immanent in the cosmos. Energy is the subtle base, matter is its gross expression. They are inextricably inter-related. The Geetha has described this relationship as the one between *Kshethra* (the Field) and *Kshethrajna* (the Knower of the Field). The whole of Nature is *Kshethra*. The *Kshethrajna* is the One who pervades the whole of Nature and animates it. Without the *Kshethrajna* (the Knower), the *Kshethra* cannot exist. Without the *Kshethra,* the *Kshethrajna* cannot be perceived. In the Bhagavath Geetha, Krishna declares: "Know me also as the Knower in the *kshethra.*"

In this context, it should be realised that it is by the power of the mind that creation, sustenance and dissolution take place in the cosmos. This truth is expressed in the *Brahma Suthra* as: "*Thath Jalaan.*" "From That everything is born, is sustained by it and merges in it." *Thath* (That) is also called *Akshara Purusha* (the indestructible Supreme person).

Kshara and *Akshara* contain the secret of life

Akshara in common parlance means that which is indestructible. *Kshara* means that which is liable to change. The secret of life is contained in the terms *Kshara* and *Akshara.* The body is subject to decay. The *Aathma* (Self) is indestructible. The word *Akshara* contains both the indestructible and the perishable. "A" refers to the *Aathma,* which is indestructible. *Kshara* is the perishable body. *Akshara* represents the unified form of the perishable body and the imperishable Self. "A" also signifies that which is *Anantham* (Infinite) and *Amritham* (Immortal). *Kshara* is that which is impermanent and unreal.

From the *Akshara* emerges the effulgent Divine, which is a combination of both *Paramaathma* (the Omni-Self) and *Prakrithi* (Nature). The Divine is immanent in Nature. The One is present in both. This was what Prahlaadha proclaimed when he told his father, Hiranyakashipu, "Do not have any doubts that He (God) is here and not there." *Prakrithi* is not inert. It is by the union of Nature and the Divine that humanness acquires its effulgence.

Here is a match-box in my hand. The match-box does not burn my hand. I keep it in this towel. The towel is not burnt. We know that there are match-sticks in the box. When you strike the match-stick, a flame bursts forth. This flame will cause a burn if we hold it in our hand. It can set fire to a towel. Where does the fire lie? In the match stick or the coating outside the match-box? It is in both. But only when the match-stick and the outer coating are brought together does the flame emerge. Likewise, there is divinity in the mind and in the heart. But only when the mind and the heart unite does the radiance of Divinity shine.

When the match-stick is dipped in water, you cannot produce fire by striking it, because the fire-producing element in it loses its power. Likewise, when the mind is immersed in the waters of sensuous desires, it loses its power to radiate the Divine effulgence. When will it recover this power? When it is rid of its dampness by going through the drying process of *Vairaagya* (detachment). It is only when this detachment grows in one that he can experience the bliss of oneness with the Divine.

Be aware of your true essence

As long as man is immersed in sensuous pursuits, he cannot experience the effulgence of his true nature. When man cultivates detachment by realizing the transience of sensory pleasures, then he begins to be aware of his true essence. All forms of ritualistic worship are of no use because they are rooted in duality. Man has to outgrow this state and realise his oneness with the Divine.

Man is continually seeking to have a vision of the Divine. But he fails to realise that the Divine is present everywhere in the cosmos. Failure to see the Divine in the visible universe is a mark of ignorance. Everything in the phenomenal universe is pervaded by God. When you see Nature, you see only its worldly aspect. When you mind is centred on God, you see the Divine in everything. The fault lies, therefore, in your *dhrishti* (outlook) and not in *srishti* (creation). Transform your perspective.

Therefore, from the outset, you have to view everything as a manifestation of the Divine. The difficulty in recognising the truth about the Divine was expressed by the Saint Surdas when he said, "Oh, Krishna! How can I recognise you? You are subtler than the atom and vaster than the vastest. You are present in the eighty-four lakhs of species in the universe, permeating everything in the cosmos, from a blade of grass to the vastest thing in creation. How can I recognise your infinite form?" The great ones experienced God in this infinite form, recognising that the Divine was present even in the wicked and the evil-minded.

Waves are essentially the same as the ocean

The infinite number of human beings in the world are like the waves of the ocean. The waves may differ in form. But however innumerably the waves, each of them is essentially the same as the ocean. From the ocean of *Sath-Chith-Aanandha* (Being-Awareness-Bliss), endless waves of human beings arise. Each of them has the attributes of *Sath-Chith-Aanandha,* the Divine. You may be a drop in the ocean of *Sath-Chith-Aanandha.* But the difference is only in quantity (size) and not in quality. The divinity present in man and the divinity in God are one and the same, just as bulbs may vary but the current that makes them shine is the same. The differences in luminosity are related to the wattage of the bulbs and not to the current that flows in them. This applies equally to the differences among

human beings. When a person is filled with narrow
feelings, he appears inferior to one who is more broad-
minded and good-hearted. A man may consider himself ignorant, foolish or stupid. But this is utterly
wrong. He is, in fact, not ignorant or foolish. He is
intelligent, well-intentioned and wise. All that he
needs is a change in attitude to experience these inherent capacities. You have to make the divine effulgence
in your heart shine.

Broaden your mind and your vision

People often recommend that one should enlarge
his heart. But enlargement of the heart will compel
you to go to a cardiologist! What you have to do
is to broaden your mind, your vision. The heart,
meaning not the physical heart but the spiritual heart,
is inherently broad. It is one with cosmic consciousness. There is no need to broaden it. Only a broad
mind is needed to recognise the vastness of the spiritual
heart. Narrow-mindedness should go. Narrow ideas
of "me" and "mine" should be totally given up in
all forms.

On the contrary, starting from the "I", you should
go on expanding your consciousness to embrace your
family, your village, your nation and the entire world.
Then your divinity will shine forth in all its brilliance.
This is described as having the vision of one's own
true universal Self. This is called the *Mahaa-
purushathva* (Infinite Divine). You have to become this
Infinite Divine. You are Divine even now. But this
is only a temporary phase as a result of your devotion.
What you should aim at is the Infinite Divine that
is unchanging. This divinity is within you. You do

not need to acquire it from outside, from anyone else. It is inherent in you. Strive to realise it. When can you realise it? When you have got rid of the consciousness of the waking, dream and deep sleep states, then you can recognise the *Mahaakaarana* state (the state of the Super Causal Consciousness).

You have to transcend the gross, the subtle and the causal bodies and realise the Super Causal body. By this process you proceed from the Super-mind, the Higher Mind and the Illuminated Mind to the Divine, which is called the Over-Mind. This is the state beyond the mind; it is called *Amanaska* (where the mind is absent). It has also been described as the state of *Vidheha* (where the body consciousness is absent). The mind is associated with the body. The world is associated with the mind. And the world is bound up with pleasure and pain. All these are sources more of bondage than of Bliss. Bliss can be experienced only through the Over-Mind.

Four kinds of offerings to reach the Over-Mind

How is one to reach the Over-Mind? *Vedhaantha* prescribed the offering of four things as the means: *Pathram, Pushpam, Phalam, Thoyam* (a leaf, a flower, a fruit or water). The Lord is not secured by offerings of wealth or by flaunting one's power or position. The proper significance of the four kinds of offerings mentioned in the scripture should be understood. Out of the selfish desire to secure Krishna entirely for herself, Sathyabhama made an offering of Krishna to sage Naaradha and tried to buy Him back by offering all her wealth and jewels to be weighed against Krishna. But all of them did not equal Krishna's weight. Then

Rukmini was brought and she taught a wise lesson to Sathyabhama regarding the power of devotion. Something, however small, has to be offered to the Lord to secure his grace. This is evident from the experiences of Dhraupadhi and Kuchela. This is also the rationale for the Bhaaratheeya practice of taking some flower or fruit as offering to the Lord when one visits a temple.

In reality, the mere name of the Lord is equivalent to the form of the Lord. When Rukmini invoked the name of Krishna, that was enough to balance the two sides of the scales, in one of which Krishna was seated. Narada said that something more should be offered to lift the scale in which the offering was being made to him. Rukmini then placed a *thulasi* leaf above the jewels and prayed: "If it is true that an offering of a leaf, a flower, a fruit or water by a devotee will win the favour of the Lord, Oh Krishna, submit yourself to this *thulasi* leaf." The scale in which the *thulasi* leaf was placed, uttering the name of Krishna, went down immediately.

The body, the heart, the mind and the tears of joy

What is the inner significance of the reference to the four kinds of offerings? *Pathram* refers not to some kind of leaf which is subject to withering. Your body is the leaf that has to be offered. *Pushpam* refers to the flower of your heart. *Phalam* refers to the fruit of your mind. And *Thoyam* signifies the tears of joy flowing from the devotee's eyes. These are to be offered to God.

When one offers these things to the Lord, he enters the state of the Over-Mind. This devotion, moreover, should not be a part-time exercise. It should be present all the time, through weal or woe, pleasure or pain. "*Sathatham Yoginah,*" declares the Geetha. The *yogis* are in constant communion with God. To be *yogis* in the morning, *bhogis* (lovers of food) at noon and *rogis* (victims of disease) in the evening are the ways of men today.

The true devotee is immersed in the Lord all the time and performs all actions as offerings to the Lord. Any action you do, as a teacher or a student or an employee, when you do it in the name of the Lord, it becomes a pious offering. This is the easiest way to sublimate the mind. When you consider your body as gift from God, you will not do any sinful act. When you consider your wealth as a gift from God you will not misuse it. You will make the right use of it. Likewise, when you regard all your talents as endowed by God, you will use them in the service of the Divine.

The four-fold programme on ceiling of desires

In the Sathya Sai Organization, a fourfold programme of ceiling on desires has been laid down. This enjoins on everyone not to waste food, money, time and energy. Avoiding waste of these four forms of gifts from God is spiritual *saadhana*. It is the means to Self-realisation.

Spirituality consists in forgetting worldly concerns and immersing oneself in God. This means sanctifying every action in life, whether it be talking or walking or anything else. Reading and writing are also forms of meditation, because they call for concentration. Everything in life can become a form of meditation.

Avoid doing anything in a hurry. It is not difficult to attain the state of the Over-Mind if one has the determination to realise it. Crores of rupees are being spent on exploring space. But very little effort is made to explore the heart within one's self.

When everyone tries to act according to the dictates of his conscience, he will realise the sublime consciousness within him. There are two basic elements in man, the head and the heart. When these two are put to right use, the hands will act in the right way.

Discourse to the Summer School
at Brindhaavan on 24-5-1993.

***

Bhakthi and Jnaana are like the pair of bullocks for the cart; both have to pull in unison. Each must keep pace with the other and help to drag weight quicker. Jnaana has to help the increase of Bhakthi; Bhakthi has to contribute to the growth of Jnaana.

—BABA

CHAPTER 23

Follow the intellect : not the mind

O foolish man, why do you seek God outside
        like the ignorant musk deer?
Like the fragrance in a flower,
God is right inside you,
        if you look with insight.
God is in many; nay, man himself is God.
But strangely and foolishly man searches
        for God in the outside world.
However just like the ash that
        covers the fire on the charcoal,
Desire and hatred envelop this divinity in man.
Even as the fire is revealed
        when the ash is blown off,
The Aathma will reveal itself to man
        when he gets rid of desire and hatred.

*E*MBODIMENTS *of love!* One and the same man plays different roles in his family and society as the husband of his wife, the father of his children, the child of his parents, the boss of his employee or vice versa, depending on physical relationship, mental attitudes and inclinations, or other circumstances. Love is showered on the daughter but not on the daughter-in-law. The son-in-law does not enjoy the same affection as the son. One does not have the same attachment for one's mother as for one's wife. What is the reason for such differences based on temporary bodily relationships, giving rise to all kinds of attractions and aversions, likes and dislikes, joys and sorrows? It is because man's mind is subject to five types of *Kleshas* (distortions or complexes)

The five types of mental complexes

Avidhya klesha (Ignorance Complex): Man becomes a prey to several afflictions due to narrow, deluded feelings such as, "I am the body," "I am a *Jeeva*," and "I am separate and different from God." This is called *Avidhya Klesham* (Ignorance Complex), which demeans the status of man and results in many kinds of sorrows.

Abhinivesa klesha (Attachment complex): The mind is the abode of all desires, sorrows, likes, dislikes, attachment and aversions. In spite of knowing that the mind is the culprit, which causes attachment to *Samsaara* (trans migratory existence and attendant miseries), man is unable to detach himself from his mind or otherwise control its vagaries and thereby to escape from sorrows and suffering. This is termed as Attachment Complex.

Asthitha Klesha (Vacillation Complex): The world is full of various *vishayas* (sense objects) which entice the weak-minded persons who go on flirting from one sense object to another, not realising that these *Vishayas* (sense objects) will ultimately turn out to be *Visham* (poison) which deprives them of all sense of discrimination and dispassion. As a result of this men are plunged in endless suffering throughout their lives. This is termed as *Asthitha Klesha* (the Complex caused by mental unsteadiness).

Lobha Klesha (Greed Complex): Labouring under the delusion that the goal of life is to acquire gold, wealth, vehicles, mansions and the like, man toils ceaselessly from dawn to dusk, to acquire and hoard such possessions beyond his needs. In the process he foregoes even food and sleep, thereby endangering his health. In spite of knowing that all such possessions are temporary, he pollutes his mind by excessive greed and falls a victim to untold suffering and sorrow. This is known as the *Lobha Klesha* (Greed Complex).

Dhvesha Klesha (Hate Complex): For his own selfish ends, man gets trapped in a maze of unending desires of various kinds. And when his desires are not fulfilled, he unreasonably blames it all on other men as well as on God Himself and thus he develops hatred against both man and God. Hence this is designated as *Dhvesha Klesha* (Hate Complex).

All these complexes are nothing but mental aberrations which are injurious to man himself. Having become a victim of such aberrations, man forgets his real *Aathmik* nature and falls a prey to all kinds of sorrow and misery. In this world we find very few

people who are always blissful. A large majority of
people are found to be swinging between joy and
sorrow. There are some others who are always sad and
depressed and have never tasted bliss even once. There
again, are some others, who are not bothered about
anything and who lead a sort of mechanical life like
animals. What is the reason for such a state of affairs?
It is not due to *Prakrithi* but due to the different ways
in which man is influenced by his own mind.

Four categories of human beings

Based on their mental predisposition, human
beings may be classified under four categories as
follows:-

Dheva-maanava (**Godly man**): "*Brahma Nishttha
Ratho Dhevah,*" it is said. This means: He is a Godly
person, who rejoices in communication with *Brahman,*
and is ever established in *Brahman,* dedicating all actions
to God, looking upon all things as His manifestations
and joyfully experiencing all forms as reflections of
the Divine. The Godly man finds self-fulfillment in
his life.

Maanava-maanava (**The human man**): "*Sathya
Dharma Ratho Marthyah*"—He alone is a man who takes
delight in truth and righteousness having faith in the
scriptural injunction, "*Sathyam Vadha, Dharmam Chara*"
(Speak the truth and practise righteousness). He
conducts his life according to the twin principles of
truth and right conduct. He considers duty or responsibility as more important than rights or privileges. He
is endowed with virtues such as kindness, compassion,
generosity, charity and forbearance. Thus, the human-
man leads the peaceful life of a house-holder.

Maanava-dhaanava (**Demonic man**): *"Madhyapaana ratho Dhaanavah"* (A demon is one who takes pleasure in drinking intoxicating liquors). The demonic man spends his time in such *Thaamasik* activities as eating, drinking, sleeping, etc. He is concerned solely with his own selfish interests and enjoyments, and never with the happiness of others. Kindness and compassion are alien to him. Not even a trace of discrimination and dispassion could be found in him. It is his nature to deride, abuse and hurt others. What is worse, the very sight of great and holy men will arouse in him feelings of jealousy and hatred. A person whose mind is filled with such evil thoughts and feelings is called a "demonic man."

Maanava-pashu (**The animal man**): This type of man wastes his life in seeking only sensual pleasures from birth to death. In this respect he is worse than beasts, because the latter are at least governed by instinct while there is no consideration of reason and season for the human brute who has no control over his ever-growing evil qualities.

Discipline the mind to achieve the goal

The mind is at the root of all such perversities. If the mind is properly understood and disciplined and is applied to get rid of wicked qualities based on selfishness, it will lead to a purposeful and fruitful life. It is basically owing to selfish thoughts that one fails to achieve the goal of human life.

We should first of all have firm faith in the inherent divinity of man. On the one hand, there is the manifested world, which attracts the attention of our body and senses and also entices our mind, and on the other hand there is the unmanifested divinity, which is the substratum of the manifested universe. The two are only aspects of one and the same divine principle of *Sath-Chith-Aanandha* (Being-Awareness-Bliss). Since all is *Sath-Chith-Aanandha*, the *Upanishaths* have declared: "*Puurnamadhah, Puurnamidham* etc.," meaning that both the unmanifest and the manifest aspects are fully divine. Although man's essential and true nature is *Sath-Chith-Aanandha* (Being-Awareness-Bliss), he is perpetually haunted by all sorts of problems, difficulties and sorrows. What is the reason? It is because he follows the mind and not the *Buddhi* (intellect).

Follow the guidance of the intellect

To live as *maanava-maanava* (human man) is only a mediocre life. Man's aim should be to live as a *Maanava-Dheva* (Godly-man). But man today is leading the life of an animal because of desires and hatred only. Non-fulfilment of one's desire results in hatred. The true nature of man is neither joy nor sorrow, but it is *Sath-Chith-Aanandha* (Being-Awareness-Bliss) that transcends both joy and sorrow, which are transient. Hence man should endeavour to experience this *Sath-Chith-Aanandha*. Living in this vast universe, you should try to cultivate correspondingly broad feelings. But, misguided by the mind, people are harbouring narrow feelings and thus making their lives miserable. The solution to this is to follow the guidance of the intellect, eschewing the vagaries of the mind.

> *The foolish man who relies on his mind*
> *will degrade himself,*
> *By becoming worse than a brute.*

> While the wise person who follows the
> guidance of his Buddhi
> Will become Pashupathi.

Why is there this importance for the intellect? Because the sense organs are superior to the body, the mind is superior to the sense organs and the intellect is superior to the mind. The *Aathma* (the Self) is superior to the intellect. Thus it can be seen that the intellect is the nearest of all to the Self and hence it has the advantage of receiving the maximum potency and effulgence from the Self. Therefore, man should utilise his intellect to understand and experience the Self and lead a blissful life.

Man owes to God all his achievements

From birth to death, man is spending his time and energy for the sake of food and sleep. Is this an achievement befitting the status of man? Some may boast about their scholarship or their pilgrimages or about the worship and rituals performed by them and about the high offices held by them. To think high of themselves based on such achievements is a sin.

Only when people recognise whole-heartedly that they owe all such achievements to God's grace, they would be true to their salt. Man is degrading himself into the state of a demon by thinking one thing, saying another thing and doing quite a different thing, violating the much-needed harmony among these three activities.

Once Aadhi Shankaraachaarya reached the holy city of Kaasi (Benaras) after the successful completion of his *Digvijaya Yaathra* (country-wide campaign) of philosophical debates. There, while having *dharshan* of the presiding deity of the place, Vishvanaath, he offered the following prayer: "O Lord! I have come to you for the expiation of my sins." How strange?

Aadhi Shankara explains his three "sins"

Aadhi Shankaraachaarya had sanctified his short span of life by studying all the scriptures of the land as well as writing many volumes of brilliant expositions and profound commentaries on the *Vedha,* the *Upanishaths* and other texts. Also he had conducted his life on the lines laid down in the scriptures. Because of his glorious achievements, he is acclaimed as the very incarnation of Lord Shiva. It may, therefore, seem strange and even paradoxical that a great person of his standing should have prayed like that. What, then, were the sins committed by him? He himself gave the answer as follows:

"O Lord Shankara! My first sin is that in spite of my knowing (and also teaching others) that God is beyond mind and speech, I have tried to describe you through the several *sthothras* (hymns) composed by me. This betrays lack of conformity between my thought and my word."

"Next, having been convinced of the scriptural savings that God pervades and permeates everything in the manifested universe, I have been preaching this truth to one and all. Nevertheless, I have come to Benaras to have your *dharshan.* This shows that my thoughts, words and deeds are at variance with one another. This is my second offence."

"Thirdly, I have firm belief in the teachings of the scripture that one and the same *Aathma* (Self) is immanent in all beings and there is no difference

between the so-called *Jeevaathma* (Individual Soul) and
the *Paramaathma* (Over-Soul). While I have been
proclaiming this truth in all my discourses, I have now
come here to stand before you as if we two are separate
and different from each other. This is my third lapse.
Hence I pray that I may be absolved of all these three
sins, of which I am guilty."

The true meaning of "sin"

From the above episode in the illustrious life of
Shankaraachaarya, we have to learn an important lesson.
The popular notion is that indulging in activities like
accusing, abusing or physically hurting others alone are
to be considered as sin. But contrary to this notion,
thinking one thing, saying another thing, and doing
quite a different thing, constitute a sin which is
committed by most people. Only when man gives up
this kind of sin and ensures harmony and unity in his
thought, word and deed, can he be considered *Puurna
Maanava* (a perfect man). This is why the *Upanishaths*
have declared that a *Mahaathma* (great-souled person)
is one who practises purity and unity of thought,
word and deed, whereas he whose thoughts, words
and deeds are at variance with one another, is a
Dhuraathma (wicked one). In this connection, the mind
plays a crucial role, and it can either elevate a man
to the greatest heights or degrade him to the lowest
depth. We should be master and not slaves of our
mind. Proper mastery over the mind is the challenging
task confronting mankind today.

Man should develop high and noble ideals and
feelings in all spheres of life—physical, moral,
religious and spiritual. He must not be content with

sensual pleasures which are temporary and leave a trail of misery. It is the mind that is responsible either for one's upliftment or downfall. One should not hastily rush into action, based on the whimsical dictates of the mind. It is only after considering whether the action is good or bad, right or wrong, that a person with a disciplined mind acts. Such a man will ultimately reach the goal of self-realisation.

Discourse to the Summer School
at Brindhaavan on 25-5-1993.

ॐ ─────────────────── ॐ

A cleansed heart is the most appropriate altar. In that fragrant bower the Lord will establish Himself. At that instant another incident too will happen: the group of six vices that had infested the place will quit without so much as a farewell. When these vices quit, the wicked retinue of evil tendencies and vulgar attitudes which thrive on them will also break camp and disappear, without even leaving their addresses! Then man will shine in his pristine splendour of Truth and Love, and finally succeed in merging with the Supreme.
—BABA

CHAPTER 24

Essence of the *Shad-Dharshanas*

THE *Shad-Dharshanas* are six great works (Philosophical systems) that shed light on Indian culture, which many consider to be based on blind belief. Explaining the *Vedhas* explicitly, they share with the world the wisdom contained therein.

The six texts are based on (a) The *Vedha* (b) Non-belief and (c) Inner Vision. They explain incidents and events that pertain to all the three times of past, present and future. They have taught man how to do away with suffering, restlessness etc., and lead a good life by removing the dirt in him. They explicitly state that the *Vedhas*, the *Vedhaantha* and the knower of *Vedhas* are all one and the same. They explain the nature of the mind which is responsible for all intelligence, intellect and discrimination. These six great *Dharshanas* (texts) are: (a) *Nyaaya* (b) *Vaisheshika*

(c) *Saankhya* (d) *Yoga* (e) *Puurva-Meemaamsa* and (f) *Utthara Meemaamsa.*

Nyaaya Dharshana forms the life for other *dharshanas*

Nyaaya Dharshana was given by Sage Gauthama and hence it is also called *Gauthama Shaasthra.* This forms the life for the remaining five *Dharshanas.* We have measures to judge the quantity and volume of material in the world. Even in respect of Divinity, a measure must be available by which the proof may be obtained. *Vedhas* speak of four kinds of proofs. They are (1) *Prathyaksha* (direct perception), (2) *Anumaana* (inference), (3) *Upamaana* (comparison) and (4) *Shabdha* (sound).

Prathyaksha pramaana: This is called direct proof, as it is perceived by the sense organs. These organs are only instruments. The mind enters them and helps them to function. There are some limitations on the senses like disease and imperfection, that make proof obtained by this method to be infirm. For example, a normal eye can see all colours, a jaundiced eye sees everything as yellow. Though the *laddu* is sweet, the tongue of a malaria patient classifies it as bitter. Here, there are two points of view. From the point of view of the matter it is sweet. But from the point of view of the senses it is bitter. It can be concluded, therefore, direct proof is not complete evidence for real justice.

Padhaartha and paraartha: Students must remember that the findings of ancient Indian sages were based on extensive investigations that went beyond the four regions of mind and even the Over-mind. They were the expositions of saints who had the vision of the Divinity.

Many scientists today are anti-God and are proud that they have discovered something our ancient sages could not. How wrong! Out ancient seers concluded that all these findings of today pertain to the Low-mind and are associated with *Padhaartha* (matter). Their findings were based on the study of the Over- mind, associated with the *Paraartha* (Supreme Source) and were hence of a highly elevated nature. Before the shining splendour of these, today's investigations and discoveries look like glow worms.

Investigation of the heart is the real proof

Any enquiry made with machines is subject to errors just like the machine itself. It is the investigation of the heart that will vouch as real proof.

These four methods of obtaining proof is very important because all religions attach great importance to justice. It was said of Mohammed the Prophet, that when his son committed a sin, he was awarded the 100 strokes by whip prescribed by the religion for that particular mistake. When he died after 50 strokes, the Prophet ordered that the remaining 50 be carried out on his son's grave!

Anumaana pramaana: This is based on doubt and inference. One sees cranes in the distance, for example, and infers that water could be available there. Similarly, one infers about fire by seeing the smoke. from the *Svabhaava* (natural traits), one makes out about the *Svaruupa* (the real form).

Upamaana pramaana: This kind of testimony is based on comparison. It enables us to understand many things that cannot be otherwise easily understood, by comparing them to some others that can be. By studying the *Praathibhasika* (apparent reality) and the *Vyaavahaarika* (empirical reality), one can infer about the *Paaramaarthika* (transcendental). For example, by studying the foam (empirical reality) that originates from the waves (apparent reality), one can understand the reality of the Ocean (transcendental reality). This is possible because both the foam and the waves originate from the Ocean, and mirror its character in them. This is the example cited for all beings emanating from the Ocean of Divinity as waves.

Shabdha pramaana is the ultimate proof

Shabdha pramaana: It is the proof garnered on the basis of sound. It is considered to be the ultimate proof. It is based on the testimony of the sound that the *Vedhas, Vedaangas, Upanishaths* and the Bhagavath Geetha came into existence, But, to be able to perceive this testimony, one must be properly attuned and extremely careful. It needs one to travel beyond the mind and the senses. At this stage of *Samaana chittha* (mental equanimity), sound becomes the very form of God. The eight forms of God are *Shabdha Brahma mayee* (sound), *Charaachara mayee* (All pervasiveness), *Paraathpara mayee* (Transcendental nature), *Vaang mayee* (speech), *Nithyaanandha mayee* (blissful), *Jyothir mayee* (Effulgence), *Maaya mayee* (illusion) and *Shree mayee* (prosperity).

Another significance in this is that God is most pleased with sound in the form of *Saama gaana* (songs in praise of God). It is said that Lord Vishnu once told Naaradha that He would always instal Himself wherever his devotees sang his glory with a full and devoted heart. This is the actual sound—the songs that contain the glory of the Lord.

In this way, *Nyaaya Dharshana* lays down the four methods of gathering proof.

Students must listen to sounds that are Divine in nature. *Nyaaya Dharshana* declares that it is the human conscience that is the best judge. Conscience is beyond the mind, it is the vibration of life.

Words originate in the mind. But, when it comes to the tongue (body) it appears different under different situations. When it goes beyond the mind, the word becomes Truth itself. *Vedhas* call this truth as *Bhur.* It is the radiation. In the materialization of body, this truth is all-pervasive and is the vibration of that truth which is the conscience. Hence from Radiation comes Vibration; from Vibration comes Materialization.

The *Vedhas* and their form

It is said that the word is itself *Rig Vedha.* It is all effulgent. The mind is the *Yajur Vedha* and life is itself *Saama Vedha.* Life gives breath. From this breath comes the song. Hence *Saama Vedha* is the form of life itself. The *Yajur Vedha* is the form of the *Manthras* that originate in the mind. The three *Vedhas* hence collectively state that God who is the effulgent One (as stated by *Rig Vedha)* must be prayed to and worshipped with the *Manthras* (as stated in *Yajur Vedha)* and pleased by sweet songs that are most endearing to Him (as said in the *Saama Vedha).* God is most pleased by songs alone and not by words or speeches.

Once you understand and follow the six *Dharshanas,* you need not do any other *saadhana.* Without understanding such lofty ideas, Indians are today groping in ignorance. Our ancient truths are eternal. You must know that they are based upon investigations of a kind unattained or unattainable in the world today.

Vaisheshika dharshana speaks about speciality of atoms

Sages and seers, in a state of deep dedication understood and grasped the spiritual reality in all matter. They hence gave little importance to the kind of secular education seen today. They understood that the same five elements within the human body constituted the tree, mountain and the entire creation. Only the forms differed.

The saints propounded that matter is constituted of atoms, but each atom was unique in itself. The difference between two atoms is the *Vishesha* (speciality) and the *Vaisheshika Dharshana* (that which brings out the speciality) speaks about this speciality.

Matter and nature are reality: Matter is unchangeable. It is only the form that changes; for example, the mud and water are creation of God; they are matter. The pot made out of mud and water may assume various shapes. It may break and splinter but the mud and water remain. Hence matter being unchangeable, is reality.

Nature consists of the five elements that are unchangeable. For example, sound is of different kinds, but the Primordial Sound, *Aum* is unchanging. All the *Sapthasvaras*—Sa, Ri, Ga, Ma, Pa, Da, Ni— are *Vikaaras* of the *Omkaara* (the different forms of the Primordial Sound). Matter and Nature are hence both unchanging.

Equality of men and women: This is another truth propounded by the *Vaisheshika Dharshana*. Men and women differ only in gender and one is not weaker than the other. Just as woman cannot work without man's help, man also cannot function without woman's help. Basing its *aadhaara* (proof) on the world, this *Dharshana* also states that society is in trouble when it does not accept this equality and attempts to diversify the essential unity in both men and women.

Do good to the society: When man constantly asks for happiness, he expects the society to give it to him. He asks for peace and expects the world to give him peace. How is it possible? If he asks himself the question what he has done for the good of the society, there is no answer. If he asks himself the question what he has done to promote peace in the world, there is no answer. Only if one does good to the society and strives to promote peace in the world, can he expect good from the society and peace from world. This is another *Vishesha* (speciality) expressed in the *Vaisheshika Dharshana.*

Inherent unity of all humans

This *Dharshana* explains there is enormous power in the microcosm that man can harness by learning with discretion. It is this kind of study that explains the differences in the past, present, future and also the truth that remains the same in all the three times.

The *Shukla Yajur Vedha* has made an exhaustive study of unity in diversity. The same shows up in the *Vaisheshika Dharshana,* which states "All are birds of the same house (family); all men are children of the same mother; all are flowers of the same creeper; all are citizens of the same nation."

1. The first statement is: "All are the birds of the same house." The house is the body. It is like a nest

that restricts the bird. The bird remains in the nest till it acquires wings. It then leaves its nest and flies away to freedom. In the same way, with the wings of *Antharjnaana* (Wisdom), man can develop detachment and fly away to liberation. This much is common in all men.

2. The second statement explains "All are children of the same mother." This mother is 'Mother Earth.' All of us are born from earth, as we are composed of mind. A newly born baby is bathed and made to sleep in the cradle. But yet, in the baby's hand can be found mud, after a few hours. This is ample proof that man's body is made of mud.

3. The third statement is: "Flowers of the same creeper." This creeper is the heart. The flower is the sweetness of the heart-to-heart relationship that each man has with another. All hearts are thus inter-related.

4. The fourth statement is: "All are citizens of the same nation." We are all members of the human race. Ours is a nation of men and not animals or rocks. We form the human society. Just as the waves originate from the ocean, all the different forms come from the *Sath-Chith-Aanandha.*

Vaisheshika appeals not to fight over petty matters

With these explanations, the *Vaisheshika Dharshana* points out the essential unity among all men. Thus the *Vaisheshika* appeals to them not to fight over petty matters.

Nimitthaadhaara and *Muulaadhaara:* There is nothing good or bad in creation. But, as long as body consciousness exists, one has to experience both. It is said:

For one who lacks intelligence and wisdom,
detachment becomes a burden.
For one who lacks knowledge, the body becomes a
burden.
For one who lacks love, the mind becomes a burden.

Man must develop discrimination to be free from all these burdens. It enables him to understand the Truth or the basis of everything. What is this truth? One must know two things: The *Nimitthaadhaara* (instrumental) and the *Muulaadhaara* (basis). *Muulaadhaara* is the basis on which the *Nimitthadara* (instrumental) builds something. Example: Mud and water are the *Muulaadhaara*—the basis. The potter becomes the *Nimitthaadhaara,* who uses them and makes pots of different shapes and sizes.

Man must control senses to the extent possible

The child Prahlaadha told his father Hiranyakashipu "O father! you have earned victory over all the three worlds, but are a slave to your senses." Such a one who knows not himself and is a slave to his senses, has no authority at all. He who succumbs to the enemies within, can never defeat the foes without.

Man must control his senses to the extent possible. Otherwise, he will suffer grief. Man must not commit the blunder of resigning everything to his fate. With enquiry and determination, one can achieve anything. But today, man is becoming a slave to the mind. Man is the master of mind. He alone is a real man who understands the reality—that the microcosm is in the macrocosm and the macrocosm is in the microcosm.

Saankhya dharshana is related to numbers

It was Sage Kapila who gave to the world this philosophical text. *Saankhya Dharshana* is also called Kapala. Elucidating that only a person with sense control is true man, it states that it is impossible otherwise for man to live in this physical frame with infinite powers.

At sight, this *Dharshana* appears to refute the statements in the *Nyaaya* and *Vaisheshika Dharshanas*. It argues that nature is a combination of numbers— *Saankhya* (and hence the name)—and is full of conflicting forces. It explains how to reach God with the help of numbers.

Divine exists in this Nature like oil in the oil seeds and fragrance in the flowers. Like the seeds and the flowers, Nature is just the external form of the Divine. This truth is called *Saankhya* or *Thathvam*. It is the power of enquiry that shows the Truth.

Yet another testimony to this cause-effect theory was also placed forward by *Saankhya Dharshana*. Creation can only be made by a combination of two forces. These two forces are God and Nature.

This *Dharshana* says that Nature is composed of twenty-four aspects—the five organs of knowledge, the five organs of action, the five senses, the five life breaths, *Manas* (mind), *Buddhi* (intellect), *Chittha* (reflective mind) and *Ahamkaara* (ego). Each one appears as a conflicting, unique force. For example: where there is fire, there can be no water. But yet the *Saankhya dharshana* splits these conflicting forces into just three subheads to facilitate an easy understanding—that of the *Jeeva* (individual), *Prakrithi* (nature) and *Paramaathma* (creator). But the *Saankhya* does not stop with the Creator. It says that: "When, to the 24 numbers is added the Self, the number becomes 25. While the 24 numbers are matter, the 25th is the Self—the Creator. The process of evolution of the human soul begins with all the 24 numbers of matter, crosses the 25th (Self) as well and finally merges in the Shiva aspect—the 26th.

While the 'Self' forms a part of the human being in the heart, it is also in the Nature. He is only a noble one who can see the two-in-one aspect of the Self being within as well as in the Nature. Man is like a bridge between the visible Nature and the invisible all-pervasive Divinity. He is hence called *madhyama*—the middle one. What we consider as invisible is what is actually guiding the consequences contrary to our belief.

Mind is a white paper on which is recorded the life-records of several births of ours. It is called the *Chittha*. He who is hidden in this and does the recording is called Chithraguptha—the hidden recorder. This power is also called the *Prajna Shakthi*—the Radiation. This Radiation vibrates the *Life force* (Vibration) that helps this body to be alive and function—Materialization.

What is *Moksha*?

It is not something that needs to be specially earned. The *Saankhya Dharshana* explicitly states that actually, no special effort need be made to attain liberation. When man realises his true form, he is liberated. When man destroys all the desires in him, he is liberated—*Moha Kshaya* is *Moksha*. In terms of numbers, the *Dharshanas* explain that as long as man identifies with 24 numbers and the *Purusha* (Self) aspect, he can never realise that he is the truth. It is only when he travels beyond, to the Super-mind that he can fathom the Truth. That is the Divine mind. It is sacred, and, from this stage, one can step on to the Illuminated-mind from where is visible only the Higher-mind and nothing else.

When the roof is removed, one can see the sky from where he is sitting. Similarly when the roof of the Lower-mind is removed, one can see the Higher-mind, and finally the Over-mind. In this way, by showing the numbers, this text helps in guiding man from Nature to God.

Start the process now to reach the goal of life

Yet another fact elucidated in the *Saankhya Dharshana* is the relation between man and *Aathma*. *Aathma* can never be obtained by investigations of the secular kind. It is natural and all-pervading, whether the body is present or not. For example, though one cannot see the electricity flowing through the wires, the moment a bulb is connected to a socket attached to the wire, the bulb glows, proving the presence of electricity. Similarly, the *Aathma* stays permanently. Only the body comes and goes.

Saint Thyaagaraaja sang that however high a bird flies, it will have to come down and rest on a tree at some time. Similarly man has to submit to Divinity one day whatever be his reservations. That is the goal of life. Instead of realizing it at some later stage of life it is better to do it now and start the process.

This *Dharshana* states that it is a demonic quality to forget God. Man must remove the demonic quality, develop the human quality and reach divinity. Just as one blows off the ash to see the latent fire, one must blow away the ashes of bad qualities on the self with the air of *Naamasmarana*. Just as one removes the moss on the water with the hands to reveal crystal clear water, man must remove the moss of sensual pleasures with the hands of good-acts. *Naamasmarana* is the best way prescribed for the *Kali* age to attain liberation.

When man submits to illusion, man himself becomes illusion. This illusion is an aspect of the 25th number. When we understand the secret between the illusion and Divinity, we ourselves become the 26th aspect—Divinity. One cannot gather all the five organs of action and knowledge, and the five senses together. But exercising control and following some limits, Divinity maybe realised. A scrupulous adherence to discipline is essential.

In England, it was discovered that when a farmer fed and milked the cows at erratic times due to some tensions in the family, the quality of milk was much poorer than what was originally obtained when feeding and milking was done on a strict schedule. That is the importance of sticking to discipline in life.

Nature does not deceive

Man must never neglect anything however small. Tiny termites may destroy an entire block of wood.

The *Nyaaya dharshana* states the differences between two atoms. But the *Saankhya dharshana* states that the entire creation is in the microcosm an atomic structure. So why talk of a separate atomic structure? God is this microcosm. That is the significance of the *Vedhic* statement: *"Anoraneeyaan Mahatho Maheeyaan"* (Smaller than the smallest, mightier than the mightiest).

Pathanjali's eight-fold *yoga*

Sage Pathanjali has prescribed eight kinds of *Yoga* in his text for man to enjoy health and happiness. These eight are *Yama, Niyama, Aasana, Pranaayaama, Prathyaahaara, Dhaarana, Dhyaana* and *Samaadhi*. It states explicitly that *Yoga* is not just for the ochre clad monks, renunciates in the forest and celibates. Modern investigations show that in today's machine age, it is the ordinary man who actually needs *Yoga*.

Man struggles the whole day to feed and foster his family. This exertion and motive makes him restless and robs him of his sleep. He then resorts to artificial means to induce sleep and rest to the body, like taking sleeping pills or taking intoxicating drinks. This artificial induction has disastrous side effects and combined with the lack of rest, causes heart diseases, blood pressure, etc. Research has hence concluded that *Yoga* is ideally suited for all these problems.

The sacred texts were all born in India. But due to the rise of blind beliefs that are consequences of modern education and civilization, Indians show scant interest or belief in these works of brilliance. It is the misfortune of Indians that today, these sacred texts are much more fostered and believed abroad, who were quick to realise their importance. They investigated and understood that due to lack of rest, the body weakens. This causes the breathing process to speed up. This in turn spoils the lungs. As the blood circulation also speeds up, a stage arrives when blood pressure sets in. Medicine cannot cure it completely and hence *Yoga* is prescribed.

This was a finding, supported by researchers at the International University in America and some others at the University of Hawaii. Some of these researchers even reversed their views on *Yoga* after they saw the results of their studies.

A healthy mind and body is essential

It was shown that the bliss and vitality enjoyed after two hours of sleep, could be got by just twelve minutes of *Yoga*. Though man can adjust without food, he cannot do the same without sleep and rest. Lack of sleep is a common problem in several countries, including India. This extracts a heavy toll on one's health. To achieve the four goals of life—*Dharma, Artha, Kaama* and *Moksha*—a healthy mind and body is essential.

In old Mexico, an experiment conducted on the inmates of a prison showed amazing results. While previously the inmates were all restless and sick, after the practice of *Yoga*, within two months, they were all hale and healthy.

Yet other investigations resulted in inducing addicts of drugs, smoking, drinking, etc. to give up their habit. It is currently estimated that about 3 to 4 lakh students abroad practice *Yoga*.

In India, the birth-place of *Yoga*, there is not much progress or interest. Devaki was said to have lamented that though she had suffered the birth pangs, it was given to Yashodha to enjoy and foster the Baby Krishna. In the same way, though Patanjali gave up his life to experience and share this great *Yoga* in India, it has only fallen on barren soil. The main cause for this is the lack of *Shraddha* (Interest) and *Bhakthi* (faith) in not only *Yoga* but also in all the scriptures.

Importance of discipline

Pathanjali prescribes some major disciplines as pre-requisites for deriving the benefits of *yoga*, notably with respect to diet. The food taken is to be both *Mitha* and *Hitha*, (limited and nutritious). Since food and water are only medicines to cure the ailment of hunger and thirst, they should be taken in that spirit. Taste should not be the yardstick to eat food, for it is only to protect the body that one eats, after all.

Foreigners realised this and found that by reducing chilies, salt, tamarind etc. from their diet and by eating limitedly, they could stay healthy. Pathanjali states that excess food weakens the nerves, causing blood pressure problems. Man becomes prone to excitement easily.

Lack of health among men also causes agitations and restlessness in society. In Germany, a research conducted on monkeys showed that the primates, when practised sitting silent for 3 to 4 hours daily, soon became very intelligent, developed their memory and were highly enthusiastic—in some cases, even more than man!

A similar experiment on a student considered a dullard and roguish, showed that with the help of *Yoga*, in just a few months, the boy became one of the most intelligent and well-behaved boys. Encouraged, even the boy's 70-year-old father took to *Yoga*. Soon his body was functioning with the vitality of a 50-year-old man!

The importance of *Praanaayaama*: This *Yoga* consists of three parts, each to be done one after the other. It starts with *Puuraka*, then *Kumbhaka* and finishes with *Rechaka*.

Puuraka: This is the inhalation of breath. One must note carefully the time taken for this process, the duration of time can be justified as per the capacity of the person. Care must be taken to see that gasping and such kinds of exhaustion must not occur during the process.

Kumbhaka: The breath taken in must be retained for the same duration as it had taken for the inhaling process.

Rechaka: Once thus retained, it must be exhaled in the same time limit as that taken for inhaling and retention.

Caution to be exercised while doing *Praanaayaama*

While doing *Praanaayaama*, one must not concentrate or aim to hold the breath for as long as possible. One must instead concentrate on assuring that all the three processes take the same amount of time. Otherwise, this process spoils the lungs. Doing the same under an inexperienced teacher also can prove to be disastrous.

The next step is to breathe in through the right nostril alone. This is the Ida. One must then retain the breath at the *Sushumna* (between the eye-brows) for the same time duration as that taken for inhaling, then release the breath through the left nostril only, again taking same time. This last step is *Pingala*.

The *Yoga Dharshana* combines with the *Nyaaya* and *Vaisheshika Dharshanas* in many of its contents. Through the *Nyaaya Dharshana*, one understands that a proper decision ought to be made regarding the measure to be appropriately selected for the *Yoga*. This is evident in the way caution is advised in limiting the time factor during the *Praanaayaama,* taking into consideration the individual capacity.

These good thoughts are Divine thoughts and *Yoga* prescribes a process called *Angaarpanam* as the method to achieve this end. *Angararpanam* means to offer all of one's limbs and organs to the Lord. It does not mean to cut them off and place them at the Lord's feet. It means to use these limbs and organs only in actions that will please God. This is where, the importance of discrimination is stressed in *Yoga.*

When such *Angaarpanam* is done, real *Aanandha* results. Bliss is related to the heart. When used in pursuit of sensual pleasures, only happiness results. This is called *Santhosha,* as it means *some + thosha* = limited happiness. This *Santhosha* is related to the head, the centre of responsibility. One must hence take care to think well, contemplate on the thought and then put it into action. This is the real 3 HV's—the values of Head, Heart and Hands. It is the unity of thought, word and deed.

Dhaarana can be done without doing *Praanaayaama*

Students must cultivate tolerance to the extent possible. Though difficult at first, it will become second nature to you with constant practice, as stated in the Bhagawath Geetha. Even if students find *Praanaayaama* difficult, they can still do *Dhaarana.* It is the single-pointed concentration of some chosen object. It is not very difficult. If practised well, it leads us on to *Dhyaana* (meditation) easily. It is said that with the power of *Yoga,* one can control anything, including the evil from entering the mind through the senses, in any form. Senses are like doors to houses, where only authorised personnel may enter. *Yoga* helps strengthen this guard.

This absolves us of animal qualities like ego, restlessness, fickleness, anger, jealousy etc.

In the first place, if you see God in each form, within three days you can feel the Divine feelings latent in you beginning to develop. Otherwise, even 30 generations of *saadhana* will be of no use.

Puurva meemaamsa and Utthara meemaamsa

Sage Jaimini's concentrated and persistent life-long efforts resulted in this work. *Meemaamsa* means enquiry. It is called *Puurva* because it was in existence even before the *Vedhas*.

The *Puurva Meemaamsa* deals with the regulations and methodologies of devotion and wisdom. Both are related to the *Karma kaanda* (the field of action). It traces the route to realising *Brahman* as first starting with *Karma*, then on to *Dharma* and finally to *Brahma*. This is mentioned as *Karma Jignaasu, Dharma Jignaasu,* and finally *Brahma Jignaasu*.

Karma Jignaasu: It pertains to all the actions performed by man. Even breathing and blood circulation are described as a kind of *Karma*. In terms of worldly explanations, it may be compared to the mixing together of ingredients like salt, tamarind, chilli, etc. to prepare chutney. Just as the ingredients must be mixed in correct proportions, the actions in daily life must also be in ideal proportions.

Dharma Jignaasu: This may be compared to the tasting of the chutney made. Tasting brings out any defects in it. This may hence be compared to the identification of defects.

Brahma Jignaasu: Having identified the lapse, rectifying it is the *Brahma Jignaasu* state. It may be said that experiencing worldly life is the *Karma Jignaasu;* Understanding that there is no permanent joy obtainable from this world is the *Dharma Jignaasu* and introducing this bliss into daily life through introspection is the *Brahma Jignaasu.*

Man is unable to absolve himself of all worries and anxieties despite worshipping all the deities. This is because he has forgotten moral and ethical living methods and takes the body to be the real self. When questioned as to one's identity, he introduces himself by his name first. When asked for more details, he gives his profession next. When probed still further, he names his country. But man is not the name or the profession or the country. He is the *Aathma.* The correct answer is "I am *Aathma.*" One may assume an alias; one may change his profession or even migrate abroad in search of better living. But, his true self is changeless.

Shivam without Aathma becomes shavam

When a person keeps saying "I" and "Mine," "I" actually is related to the *Aathma;* "Mine" is related to the body—*Dhehi* and *Dheham.* It is only when all the organs and limbs combine together that a body results. Similarly, the *Aathma* is a combination of Mind, Intellect and *Samskaara.* It is the *Aathma* that enters and prompts, the organs and limbs to operate. A body with *Aathma* in it is hence called *Shivam* (auspicious). When the *Aathma* leaves the body, all organs and limbs come to a stand-still. The body becomes inert. Hence such a body is called *Shavam* (dead-body).

Aathma is a combination of Mind, Intellect and *Samskaaras* (tendencies). The mind thinks, reflects and forms thoughts based on the promptings of *Aathma.*

The intellect, endowed with the triple power of discrimination, analyzing and deciding also functions due to *Aathma*.

Samskaara means elevating culture and is the basis of rebirth. Our present actions become seeds of *samskaara* that decide the fruit in the next life. It is hence advised that doing good and constant contemplation of God, will enable one to be peaceful at the end of one's life. This can surely be achieved by constant practice, as is stated in the Bhagavath Geetha. Good actions lead to good *samskaaras*, that confers a good birth.

Selective adherence to *Karma kaanda*

Jaimini investigates the paradox that though the body is temporary, why emphasis is laid on our *Karma* (bodily action). This, he concluded, was necessary to purify the mind. Hence the body must enter into actions. But today, people take from this *Karma kaanda* whatever part is useful to them and discard the others. A story is said about a lazy celibate, who came to a house to beg for alms. The kind lady, though it was an odd time, did not want to break a family tradition. She requested the celibate to have his bath and ablutions at the river nearby, while she cooked something for him. The lazy person answered that "Lord Govindha's name is itself a hearty bath." The wise lady saw through the fake *saadhu* (mendicant) and countered: "Very well then! The same Govindha's name will also be your food."

It is because of this kind of selective adherence to *Karma kaanda*, that man has become so impure.

People argue that Nature is a natural entity, in the sense that, no one has created it. Matter and energy need someone to combine them. Oil, wick and container may be present. But it needs someone to strike a match and light the lamp. Though the subject and intelligence are present, a teacher is needed to impart a proper guidance for being educated. Jaimini states that good education must impart good habits, ideals, truth, responsibility and discipline besides intellectual knowledge.

Puurva meemaamsa deals with anger control

To achieve all these, Jaimini advises purity. Without this inner purity, Divinity is a distant illusion. Clouds arise from the sun and cover the sun itself. But, it is a temporary effect. Man must also have patience to wipe away the ignorance that covers his self. Patience is another virtue mentioned in the *Puurva Meemaamsa*.

Method to control anger: The text advocates a very logical method to counter obstacles. For example when grief strikes, it advises that one must think of joyful incidents. This gives joy. It also conducts enquiries into the fields of *Ajnaana-Prajnaana.*

Control of anger and overcoming the obstacles in daily life, is also dealt with. The *Puurva Meemaamsa* states that one must slowly analyze the situation when angry. By the time a conclusion is reached, tempers cool down considerably. One may also do any one of the following to control temper: (1) drink a glass of cold water; (2) see the mirror, where your distorted features will repulse you enough to cool you down; (3) walk fast and alone. This speeds up your circulation that draws away anger; (4) open a tap and watch your pitch of song with that of the falling water. In all these attempts, the time and attention definitely help cool tempers.

Do not give in to excitement

One must try to involve *Utthara Meemaamsa* into practice as well, to the extent possible.

Man must not give in to excitement. Arjuna was highly perturbed when Krishna was leaving to make peace with Kauravas, as a last ditch attempt. He entreated that a war was best suited as the Kauravas would not concede the demands of the Pandavas. But, the same Arjuna collapsed at the sight of his grandfather, teachers, cousins, relatives and friends lined up to do battle. He did not want to live with their blood on his hands.

Hence students must stay calm and composed. You need not become excited to acquire something. If it is destined to reach you, it shall be delivered to you wherever you are. You must remember meanwhile to concentrate on protecting your righteousness; which in turn will protect you. *"Dharmo Rakshathi Rakshithah,"* it is said. Hence, while following your daily routines, contemplate always on God. Wherever you are, whatever you do, do it with divine feelings.

A summary of discourses from 27-5-1993 to 31-5-1993, to the students of Summer School in Indian Culture and Spirituality at Brindhaavan.

CHAPTER 25

Jealousy—the root cause of evil

THE main purpose of human life is to realise one's true identity. It is only when you recognise the sacredness of human life that you can realise the Divine. It is sheer ignorance to consider man as made up of merely the body, mind and sense, which are only *upaadhis* (instruments). To identify yourself with the body is as absurd as to consider yourself as the house in which you dwell or the car in which you travel. It is essential to realise the truth of your divine identity through the instruments of the body, mind and intellect. The Inner Self of Divinity is referred to by several synonyms such as *Dhrishta* (Seer), *Chith* (Awareness), *Chaithanya* (Consciousness), *Sath-Chith-Aanandha* (Existence, Knowledge and Bliss) and so on. It is *Paripuurnam* (complete or whole) and *Sthiram* (permanent). You may enquire whether the Inner Self is the subtle, causal or super-causal body, whether it is *Bhakthi* (devotion) or *Jnaana* (wisdom), whether it is inert or awareness, whether it is *Hiranyagarbha* (cosmic mind or womb) or *Vishvam* (cosmos), whether it is *Pinda* (microcosm) or *Brahmaanda* (macrocosm), whether it is the beginning, the middle or the end. The answer is in the negative. All these are related to duality, while the true Self is non-dual. *"Ekameva Adhvitheeyam"* (There is only one and no second at all).

However, when you perceive the principles of *Pramedhya, Prameya* and *Pramaana,* you can understand this Supreme Principle. *Pramedhya* is reflected in the individual awareness. *Prameya* is that which is reflected in *Prakrithi* (Nature). *Pramaana* is the nature of *Chittha* (the mind intellect principle). These constitute the triple aspects of seer, seen and the act of seeing.

How to realise the sacred Inner Self

The question is how to realise the sacred Inner Self. Even in worldly things, Divinity is present. We see endless waves emanating from the vast ocean. Though the ocean is one, the waves are innumerable and apparently not of the same form. But all the waves contain the essence of the ocean and its quality, whether they are big or small. Similarly, though there are infinite forms of beings in the world, each of them contains the essence of Divinity within. The same Divinity is everywhere. This Divinity existed in the past, is in the present and will continue to be there in the future. It is, therefore, beyond the three categories of time and is eternal.

Every human being is a combination of *Brahma thathva* and *Jeeva thathva* (Omni Self and individual Self).

The waves in the ocean are caused by the wind blowing over it. Similarly, *Maaya* (illusory power) causes the diversity of names and forms in the world. The original basic entity, *Sath-chith-aanandha*, is the only one that exists and all the variety of beings in the world are all like the waves of the ocean. This *Sath-chith-aanandha* is termed as *Asthi, Bhaathi* and *Priyam*, which are changeless, while name and form will always be changing. This phenomenal world is called *Jagath*, which implies it is "coming" and "going." The only one that is ever-present is the collective form of Divinity. Human life emerged from the Divine, is sustained by the Divine and merges in the Divine.

Birth and death go together

Though the body is transient, it is given only to do *Dharma* (righteous deeds) and reach   the goal. *"Shareeram Aadhyam khalu Dharma-Saadhanam"* (The body is essential for realising *Dharma*). Birth and death go together. Death follows birth like a shadow. One cannot say when,   where and how death will occur. It may be in childhood, youth or old age, in a house or outside, in a town, or a forest, on the ground, in water or in the sky. One should realise that death is natural phenomenon and avoid worrying about it.

Since you are provided with the faculty of discrimination, you should use it in the right way and not with selfish motives. When you use it for collective benefit, with social awareness, it is very beneficial. It is because man is using his intellect for selfish purposes, he is not happy. If it is used for the common benefit of all, one can enjoy real happiness.

Sujnaana, Vijnaana and Prajnaana

Raavana was a most powerful king, fully accomplished in all the arts, with mastery of the *Vedhas*. He had performed a severe penance. But, because he used all his talents for his selfish purposes, he met with an ignominious death. He was warned by his wife Mandodhari, who was a paragon of virtue, standing for *Sujnaana* (right knowledge), that he was not following the righteous path as he had stealthily kidnapped Seetha, wife of Raama. She questioned him whether he would keep quiet if his wife had been kidnapped. She thus taught *Sujnaana* (beneficial wisdom). But Raavana ignored her advice.

His brother, Vibheeshana, tried to teach him *Vijnaana* (discriminatory wisdom) by telling him that he was not using his *Buddhi* (intellect) in the right way and was doing a reprehensible act which was unbecoming of an emperor like him. Raavana ignored this too.

Later, Hanuman advised him in terms of *Prajnaana* (Supreme Wisdom). He told Raavana that in spite of his *Vidhya* (vast scholarship and knowledge), he had failed to recognise the *Aathma* as the reality of an individual and with body consciousness he was indulging in a despicable act, losing control over his senses and mind. He had brought Seetha, the Mother of the Universe, with a base motive.

Raavana paid no heed to the three types of advice and as a result courted disaster. The life of one who acts out of selfish motives is in the hands of others, while the one with a pure heart and selfless motive, seeking the welfare of the world, has his life in his own hands. Raama was an example of this. A really virtuous human being will see divinity in himself and also in others. Human life is nothing but a reflection of Divinity. It is ignorance to consider God as living elsewhere in a remote place. When you are yourself the embodiment of Divinity, of what avail is it to seek the Divine elsewhere? You are the Supreme *Brahman.* Forgetting the truth of man's inherent Divinity, worrying themselves about what is happening somewhere, people lose their moorings. These worries are not natural, but acquired from outside. All have to realise that death is the end of everyone who is born. Birth is what is important. When the meaning of birth is realised, one transcends birth and death *(Janma-raahityam).* Therefore, in human life, one should understand this *Para thathva* (transcendental truth) and seek to realise the Divine. That is the main task of the aspirant.

Jealousy is the cardinal evil

However, many kinds of aberrations are appearing in human life. The root of all the evils arising in the world can be traced to the operations of "One hand." When something untoward happens, people try to attribute it to some foreign "hand" or to the hand of some religious sect. These are meaningless speculations or wild conjectures. They are exercises in untruth.

There is a "hand" indeed. But what is that hand? It is the hand of *Asuuya* (jealousy). This is a dire malady which has entered all spheres of life in the world today. There is a remedy even for the dreaded disease of cancer. But there is no way of curing the malaise of jealousy. The final end is the only cure for it.

Today the malady of jealousy has invaded every field of activity. As a result, such gruesome events occur from time to time. There are three offsprings for *Asuuya*

(Jealousy). They are *Dhvesha, Krodha* and *Lobha* (hatred, anger and greed). There are three children begotten by *Anasuuya* (The one who is totally free from jealousy). They are: Brahma, Vishnu and Maheshvara, symbolising *Sahana* (forbearance), *Prema* (Love) and *Saanubhoothi* (compassion). This is the difference between *Asuuya* and *Anasuuya.* The former gives birth to demonic qualities. The latter begets Divine qualities. The demonic qualities produced by *Asuuya* (Jealousy) result in the destruction of the discriminating power and lead men to have no sense of what is temporary and what is permanent. Consequently they pursue evil ways.

Asuuya is the reason for June incidents

We often ask what is the reason for a particular action or event. There is no need to search for reasons. Just as hunger arises out of digestion, jealousy arises out of the disappearance of noble motives. The jealous man cannot bear the sight of a noble person or of one who is handsome and attractive. He cannot bear to look at one who is getting a good name or who has secured an eminent position. This jealousy has "no reason or season." Those afflicted with this malady begin to entertain many evil thoughts.

In the world today, Sai's name and achievements are getting known the world over. To counteract this and to diminish it by some means or other, envious persons are resorting to certain types of propaganda. These propaganda campaigns will not affect My reputation in any manner. My purity is the root cause of the glory of My name. It is not due to any publicity or propaganda. My all-pervading selfless love is the cause. No one can affect this pure love. I have no ill-will towards anybody. Svaami has done no harm to anyone. How can anyone harm Svaami? It is impossible.

"All activities of Sai are utterly selfless"

These happenings should be attributed to jealousy. Devotees should not be perturbed by such events. Those who have true and firm faith will not be shaken in any way by these happenings. You have listened to the speeches of Goldstein, Sinclair and Haksar. What has impelled them to make these declarations? It is their firm faith. Although they are living in far off places, they are sustained by their firm faith. For those consumed by envy, only the false is apparent. They cannot have even a glimpse of truth.

So, whatever may happen, this *Sathya* will remain unmoved. Adhere, therefore, to truth. Observe purity in life, embark on a life of selfless service. Believe it or not, there is not a trace of selfishness in Me. No one is qualified to point a finger at My purity. How can anyone recognise the grandeur of My divine purity? Only an intelligent person can recognise another's intelligence. How can a fool recognise intelligence?

My goodness is the cause of My invulnerable purity. It is not that I want to glorify Myself. It is because the time has come when I have to speak out.

All activities of Sai are utterly selfless and aimed at the well-being of the whole world. You are aware that we built the Super Speciality Hospital. In this Hospital, we have given a fresh lease of life to many mothers and fathers and many children were enabled to enjoy the love of their parents. Who could do this? What great good fortune is it that this small, obscure

village has found a notable place on the world map?
This is a source of jealousy.

Nobody can fully comprehend the significance of
Sathya Sai's actions, whether small or big. Human beings
cannot accomplish such things. Only those who do not
choose to come here, see and find out the truth about
what is being done here, and derive joy from that
experience, are preaching all kinds of things to the
world, sitting in their air-conditioned rooms. Are these
persons qualified to preach to the world? People whose
minds are polluted should be ashamed to claim that
they are striving for the welfare of the world. Let them
enter the social arena, do good deeds and engage
themselves in selfless activities. Only then can the truth
be understood.

On the contrary, if one is filled with envy, his
words and preachings will be meaningless. Truth is
the life of the spoken word. A word without truth
is lifeless.

Sanctity of Sathya Sai Central Trust

All the propaganda that is being done is false. It
is a form of cheap publicity. Do not be affected in any
way by such publicity. Adhere to your truth and your
purity.

There are some other matters on which I have to
speak because of the large gathering here and what
you may have read in the media. Fire cannot burn our
Sathya Sai Central Trust. It is such a sacred trust. We
alone know with what sacred concern we are spending
every naya paisa. The world cannot know this. For the
past twenty years, the members of the Central Trust
have been rendering selfless service. When they have

to go to Madras. Delhi or other places, they travel at their own expense, pay their hotel bills and do not draw a single paisa from the Central Trust. In the case of other trusts, the members submit their bills even for their conveyance charges. The Sathya Sai Central Trust members are using the funds in such an utterly sacred manner. Reports have been published that the trust members are after power and position. They are not interested in office. They have not lacked positions in life. They have come out of love for Svaami, and not for any position.

Pure manner in whichTrust Funds are handled

You must also note how the funds of the Trust are drawn from banks. During the past 20 years not once have we drawn any cash from the bank. All payments are made only by cheques. Our Institute teachers are paid their salaries not by cheques but by the amounts beings credited to their accounts from month to month. The accounts are being maintained in this strict manner. It is because the funds are handled in this pure manner that we have not sought or have had any need to solicit donations.

This body is now 67 years old. Not once have I stretched My hand to seek any donation. What is the reason? When we are engaged in sacred task, there is no need to seek funds. Our purity will bring in funds of its own accord. There is a dearth of men of integrity. Where there are such persons there is no problem at all in securing funds.

I do not misspend even a single *naya paisa* of Trust money. Nor is there any room in our Trust for anyone else to draw money. Every cheque has to be signed by two persons. On every cheque, nobody can sign without My signature on it.

It is a sin to level charges against the Trust

There are reports that some crores of Trust funds in cash have been swallowed by some persons. This is totally false. We do not handle cash at all. If anybody offers cash, we see to it that the money is given to the bank manager in the presence of a Trust official in the residence of the donor himself. Therefore, no one can point an accusing finger at the way our trusts are managed. In these circumstances, it is a sin to level such charges against our Central Trust.

In the whole world, you cannot find any Trust that is being managed in this pure manner. That is why our institutions are growing ceaselessly. Not now alone, but as long as the sun and moon last, there is no danger to our institutions.

This propaganda stems from the frustration born of jealousy. In the peaceful atmosphere that was pervading here, such propaganda has caused pertur-bation. This is highly sinful. It is not good to indulge in such acts. Do good if you can, but if not, remain silent. You will be rendering help if you don't do any harm. But it is not good to do harm.

Some may ask why Svaami had so far refrained from answering the traducers. For everything there is a right moment. The Kauravas, for instance, were harassing the Paandavas in many ways, insulting and humiliating them. The Kauravas were well aware of the Paandavas' divine potencies. Each of the Paandava brothers was a man of great prowess. But they did not make use of their strength. They bore their troubles in silence. The Kauravas attribute this silence to cowardice and weakness. But this was not so. No one can realise the strength that underlies forbearance. Likewise. The Sathya Sai Trust chose to maintain forbearance. This forbearance represents courage, strength, truth and non-violence.

Our students are like pure refined gold

And, now, about our students; you may compare them with anybody, you cannot find anyone like them anywhere. It is now 28 days since the events of June 6th happened. Our students have been offering prayers every day, observing fasts, and thinking day and night, without food or drink, as to how they can remove the stain that has been caused by this episode. They are in anguish and distress.

Are there not likely to be a few stones in a bag of rice? In an big group there may be a few black sheep. On account of a few miscreants, it is an outrage to blacken the entire body of students. Our students are like pure refined gold. They are prepared to do anything for Svaami's sake.

You have all listened to the song sung by a young lad at the beginning of the function. He sang; "We are ready to offer our lives to you Bhagavaan." It is not proper to blame all for the crimes of a few. We have to put up with this situation for some time. Have patience. When you go to sleep at night, one or two mosquitoes may bite you. The next day you use Flit to get rid of all mosquitoes. It is because of the association of other mosquitoes with the troublesome one that they also get killed. Hence the advice.

"Thyaja durjana Samsargam" (Give up association with wicked persons). Never get into bad company. You must gain good company. You have to put up with calumny. A good man becomes a victim of calumny even if he is remote from bad people, just as a moth damages all kind of cloth, whether it is ordinary cloth or valuable silk, because it cannot discriminate between what is useless and what is precious. So also an envious person does harm to good and bad people alike.

"Whatever I say is for your good"

By forbearance, good people will achieve their objectives in due course. Hence, do not worry about what has happened. Such things happen in the world from time to time. There is one other matter about which I have not spoken to any one so far.

There are many devotees who ask why, when such things were impending, Svaami did not warn Raadhakrishna or try to save him. I am explaining the matter from the spiritual aspect and not from the mundane viewpoint.

Both of us took our meals at 7.00 p.m. Raadhakrishna was sitting in the ground floor. Svaami told him: "Raadhakrishna, let us go upstairs. Don't sit here." "Svaami, if I go there, I cannot get sleep at 7 0' clock itself," said Raadhakrishna. Svaami asked him: "If you cannot sleep, what are you going to do here? You can do in upstairs what you intend to do here. I don't ask you to go to sleep. Get up immediately. Come, come," I insisted repeatedly.

See how things happen. Death overtakes one, in whatever way you attempt to circumvent it. At last Svaami assumed an angry tone and rebuked him:

"Your misfortune is your stubbornness." I pretended as if I was very angry with him. He felt pained. Svaami retired upstairs. He reflected for some time. He had been with Svaami for 22 years. He knew that whatever I said was for his good. He went to the kitchen and brought a tumbler of buttermilk. He came smilingly. "Svaami, you have been angry with me. Please drink this buttermilk and calm down." "Raadhakrishna! It is not anger, I have said everything for your good." said Svaami. Raadhakrishna said, "Svaami has perhaps some doubts that I may go out somewhere and talk to others." I replied, "If I have such doubts, will I keep you with me? Not at all. There are no doubts. I am saying this for your good."

And then I said: "I am not used to drinking buttermilk at night. Why have you brought it for the first time to night?" He replied: "I felt like giving buttermilk to Svaami tonight and hence I brought it." "It is good that you got this idea. I shall take it, but, on one condition. I shall take the buttermilk as desired by you, but you must give me your word that after going down to place the tumbler in the kitchen, you will return upstairs." He said: "I will certainly return."

I do not take buttermilk at all. I took a little quantity and told him, "I have taken buttermilk to please you." He had a pure heart. He asked me: "Svaami! Can I drink the rest of the buttermilk? I said: "Why throw it away? You may drink it." He drank it there itself. Svaami said: "But put back the tumbler and come up." He went down. He had given his word. But, he had perhaps the doubt that if he remained downstairs Svaami might call him. This kind of stubbornness is one of the traits of young people.

They will not listen to the words of elders. If only they listen to their words, no danger will befall them. Apprehending that if he remained downstairs I might call him, he placed the tumbler in the kitchen and went to his sister's house. The messenger of death dogged him at 10.00 p.m. This is how it has happened. Whatever I say is for the good of others.

I say only sacred things and nothing that is unholy. Whether you believe or not, I may tell you that all the time I only think of what good I can do to better the lot of the people. Svaami never thinks about Himself.

The three 'desires' of Svaami

After the Summer Course was over, Indulal Shah, V. Srinivasan and others came to Me with plans for various projects to be carried out in the next three years. Each year they wanted to carry out one project. I told them: "You should not do anything for Me. You may do anything you desire for the sake of the people, the society and the poor." I told Srinivasan: "I have three desires."

Even I have some desires, not for My sake. "Today, middle class farmers are experiencing difficulties in cultivating their fields. Owners of five or six acres are not able to get labourers to work on their farms and do not have cattle for ploughing the fields. Therefore, you get 70 tractors to be presented to small farmers on My Seventieth birthday in 1995." Action followed right in the wake of my words. The Escorts people were immediately contacted on the phone and the tractors were brought for the selection of those that would be suitable for small farmers. As Svaami was offering the tractors free to small farmers, the Escorts people offered a concession in price: Orders were placed immediately for 70 tractors.

Srinivasan asked what was Svaami's second wish. Svaami said that young people were going about in Puttaparthi without any occupation and taking to bad ways. Some useful work should be provided for them. The Super Speciality Hospital is far from the township. Even the Post Office is at a great distance. Many people are having difficulty in going to these places. To provide employment to these unemployed youth and provide an essential amenity for the public, Svaami suggested that 70 autorikshaws may be provided to the un- employed. "If these young men are given these vehicles, it would please me," I said. Orders have been placed for these autorikshaws.

Svaami's thoughts are devoted to the good of others

The third wish was this: There are a number of women belonging to good families, who have no independent means to sustain themselves and are not in a position to take up jobs outside. I felt that such women should be taught tailoring and given a sewing machine so that they can earn some income indepen- dently. Immediately 70 sewing machines have been purchased.

A fourth wish: Marriage should be performed for 70 poor couples without regard to caste or creed. The marriage should be such that they should feel happier beyond all their previous experiences in life. It is not enough to give them wedding clothes and the *Mangala-suuthram.* The *Mangala-suuthram* should be attached to a gold chain. In addition, to enable them to lead a life of ideal householders, each couple should be provided with a home.

In this manner, all My thoughts are devoted to promoting the good of others. Is any Government or wealthy person thinking along these lines? None at all.

Jealousy rears its head in envious folks

When such sacred things are being done, jealousy rears its head in some persons. This is the outcome of their sins. These envious folk will not do anything good themselves, nor will they allow others to do good. This is not a human quality. A true human being should be filled with large-hearted sentiments.

The truth can be known only when one comes and sees what is being done here. Instead, if men whose hearts are filled with the poison of envy indulge in all kinds of slander from remote places, it can be described only as demonic conduct and not that of a human being. Nowhere in the world can you see the kind of work that is being carried on here. Is Free Education offered elsewhere in outside India on the lines offered here? One has to spend atleast Rs. 20000/- to get a child admitted in the Ist Standard. Here, from kinder-garden to post-graduate studies, education is totally free.

As for heart surgery cases, in hospitals outside, no patient will be admitted unless Rs. 4 to 5 lakhs are deposited in advance. In our Hospital, we are spending one crore of rupees a month (Rs. 10 million). Which Government or millionaire is doing such a thing? There are some such persons who spend 10 lakhs of rupees in a Hospital with the hope of earning Rs. 10 crores.

They are making it a business. Here, we are not charging anything. There is no place for business here. It is not proper that such good and sacred work should be misrepresented.

"I am in the heart of devotees as well as the wicked"

Sai's heart is as wide as the sky. Even the sky may have its limits. Sai's heart is boundless. Some say Sai is in the hands of some persons. Yes, I am indeed bound; bound by the devotees as well as by the wicked. In my view, I have more love for the wicked than for the good. The good devotees remember Me only occasionally. But the wicked remember Me all the twenty four hours. I am thus in the hearts of the devotees as well as the wicked. I cannot be caught in the grip of anyone.

In regard to every matter, my thoughts are always sublime and exemplary. You must note that Svaami's life is in His own hands and not in those of anyone else. If I will it, I can live for as long as I please. I can also terminate it at will. It is my will that decides and not any other person. The reason is My purity, selflessness and divinity. What other testimony is called for? The life of the pure hearted is in their own hands and not in those of others.

Embodiments of the Divine Aathma! Today is Gurupuurnima. Who is a *Guru?* Truth is the Preceptor for the whole world. Uphold truth with steady mind and a pure and selfless heart. That truth will be your protector, your armour and your unfailing companion. There is no *Dharma* higher than Truth. *Dharma* protects its protector. If you protect *Dharma,* that *Dharma* will protect you.

Therefore, without being cowed down or shaken by these incidents, you must go forward with faith and fortitude. Keep truth as your ideal. Fill your hearts with purity and love all and hate none. Then Divinity will manifest itself in you.

An inspiring and reassuring discourse to a vast gathering of devotees from all parts of the world, who had assembled in the Puurnachandhra Auditorium on Gurupuurnima Day, 3-7-1993.

ಐ━━━━━━━━━━━━━━━━━━━━━ ೮ೞ

Your devotion to God is best expressed by achieving the control of the senses. For the senses rush towards the temporary and the tawdry; and they foul the heart. I require from each of you no other gift, no more valuable offering than the heart I have endowed you with. Give Me that heart, as pure as when I gave it to you, full of the nectar of Love I filled it with.

—*BABA*

CHAPTER 26

The Divine and destiny

The Goddess of Wealth flourishes at the tip of the tongue.
Friends and kinsfolk grow from the tip of the tongue;
Bondage and realisation emanate from the tongue;
The tip of the tongue makes death certain.

*E*MBODIMENTS *of the Divine Aathma!* Speech constitutes the wealth of the world. Speech promotes friendship and kinship. It is speech that lends sweetness and affection to all relationship. Speech, again, leads the way to death.

Speech is endowed with immense power. The power and potentialities of speech represent the Divine feelings of man. Hence, one has to be very vigilant in speech.

The mysteries of creation are marvellous. When two persons meet at any time or place, the differences between them are patent. Their forms and manners differ. They differ in their cleverness and intelligence. Their opinions also vary. Without understanding what underlies these differences, the materialist thinkers emphasize the differences. Today, growing numbers of intellectuals, ignoring the unity that underlies the diversity, propagate the cult of differences. The good persons who realise the unity behind the apparent diversity are dwindling in numbers from day to day. This is highly unfortunate.

Lay stress on unifying factors than differences

Man's foremost task is to recognise the unity that underlies the multiplicity. If one enquires into the matter with a pure and unselfish mind, one will see what is common to all beings. Birth and death are common to all men. Hunger and thirst are experienced by every person. These are truths that apply to all persons, whether they are destitutes or millionaires, whether they are scholars or ignorant men.

Every human being has a body and a Spirit. Consequently everyone enjoys a certain degree of freedom. This is described as "Free Will." Not comprehending the nature of this freedom, men tend to stress the differences rather than the unifying factors.

Man is a combination of two kinds of traits. One is the animal nature. The other is divinity. Swayed by evil qualities like lust, anger, greed, delusion, conceit and egoism (the six enemies of man), he degrades himself to the level of the animal. On the other side is the one who makes right use of the good qualities conferred by God such as intelligence, wisdom and virtue, pursues the path of truth and righteousness, engages himself in divine activities and ultimately realise the Divine. Man can choose either the path that leads him to animality or to Divinity because the potentialities are common. What is important is the path one chooses. "As the thoughts, so the outcome." The mind determines the goal one pursues. Hence it is essential to divert the mind on the right path and realise the true nobility of human existence. If you have a knife, you can use it for slicing vegetables and preparing a good meal. The same knife can be used for taking away another person's life, behaving in a demonic manner and ceasing to be human.

State of the mind depends on nature of thoughts

Thus, the same mind is responsible for either animal or divine behaviour. In *Vedhaanthic* parlance, this is stated as: "The mind is the cause of human bondage or liberation." The state of the mind depends on the nature of the thoughts with which it is filled, even as the smell of a paper depends on what is wrapped up in it, flowers, fish or potato chips. When the mind is used properly, man achieves fulfilment.

Men perceive the world in terms of diversity. But, as the scripture declares: "There is only the One. The wise call It by many names." People experience heat and cold, joy and sorrow, darkness and light, profit and loss. All these are opposite aspects of the same thing and not two different things. For instance, darkness helps one to enjoy light. If there were no darkness, light would have no value. Darkness is absence of light. Light is absence of darkness. Darkness lends value to light. Sorrow contributes to the value of happiness. Likewise, censure has its value. It enhances the value of praise. Censure is the stepping stone to praise. The two are inter-dependent.

For all the experiences in the world relating to pleasure and pain, joy and sorrow, the cause is one. All the troubles one experiences are stepping-stones to happiness. This is the essence of *Vedhaantha*.

Hence, for man, the proper spiritual *saadhana* consists in cultivating equal-mindedness, without succumbing to grief or getting elated over a happy event. In daily life, people experience all kinds of happiness and distress. The scripture declares: "Treat joy and sorrow, profit and loss alike."

Peace, Truth and the Self

Embodiments of Divine Love! What is the purpose of your joining the *aashram*? What is its inner meaning? You have come to lead a peaceful, sacred and blissful life dedicated to the Divine. This peace does not lie in the external world. Peace is your very form. Truth is equally so. It is folly to think that you have to search for Truth somewhere. To know one's Self is Truth. To experience the Self within is Peace. Peacelessness is caused by involvement in external experiences, ignoring the Self within.

All things, good and bad, in the world are related to man's actions. Your well-being is based ion your conduct. Your wealth is dependent on your actions. You will secure peace and prosperity when your conduct is good. This calls for *Sahana* (forbearance). The Upanishathic prayer says: "Let us have forbearance towards each other. Let us rejoice together. Let us all strive together." Forbearance is a potent instrument. Dharmaja (the eldest of the Paandavas) was able to score many victories with the *asthra* (weapon) of forbearance. Forbearance is not a sign of weakness or cowardice. No other weapon has the power of forbearance. It should not be used only as an individual instrument. It has to be experienced collectively also. That is the reason why the scripture has commended collective forbearance at the very outset of the spiritual quest. What is its inner meaning? "Let us live and move in harmony. Let us grow together. Let us cherish the wisdom that we have acquired together. Let us live in complete harmony without any misunderstanding." Therefore, do not have any misunderstanding amongst you. All of you should live in amity as the children of one mother.

Human effort is necessary to enjoy God's grace

God is all-powerful. But, at the same time human effort is also necessary. Without it, man cannot enjoy the benefit of God's grace. It is only when you have both Divine grace and human endeavour that you can experience bliss, just as you can enjoy the breeze of a fan only when you have both a fan and the electrical energy to operate it.

In the great drama of cosmic life, the Cosmic Director, God, is also an actor. The Cosmic play is governed by certain rules and regulations. Because He is the Almighty, God cannot behave in an arbitrary manner. His actions have to be in accordance with His role in the cosmic play. There are certain rules as to how one should act according to the time, the place and the circumstances. He cannot behave according to His whims just because He is all-powerful. For instance, the officer who lays down the rules for controlling traffic cannot disobey them on the ground that he is their author. Likewise, the Creator has to conform to the rules laid down by Him for creation.

Every place is a temple for God

Not recognizing this truth, men, who are involved in worldly ways, ask questions as to why in certain situations God did not use his limitless powers to avert certain untoward events. These arise out of a narrow conception of things, without understanding how the Divine operates. They are concerned only about themselves and their interests. They ask: "Here is a sacred temple. How could something unholy occur in such a place?" They see things from a narrow perspective. They do not realise that for God the entire universe is His temple. So, whatever happens anywhere, happens in God's temple. The Cosmos is the form of God (Vishnu). God is immanent everywhere in the cosmos. When a temple is constructed on a piece of land, if becomes a temple. if it is knocked down, it becomes mere land again. For God, every place is a temple. "His feet and hands, his mouth and eyes and His ears are everywhere. Encompassing all, He remains pervading everything." (Stanza from the Geetha).

When things are seen with this broad perspective, it will be recognized that anything can happen to anyone at any place or any time. No one is competent to determine where a certain thing should take place. Life may end in a town, in water or in a forest. Each one's life will end in the place, the manner and at the time prescribed for him. This is inescapable. This is according to the operation of Nature's law based on the pairs of opposites in life—the concept of *dhvandhva* (duality).

There is a continual conflict between these opposites (pleasure and pain, birth and death, etc.)

Krishna's role as envoy of the Paandavas

By way of illustration, here is an episode from the Mahaabhaaratha. Krishna was all-powerful. He was aware that peace parleys with the Kauravas would be of no avail because of their stubbornness. He knew that war was unavoidable. But, in the context of worldly affairs and having regard to public opinion, he had to make an effort to promote peace. Consequently, he went as an envoy of the Paandavas, made a vain effort to convince the Kauravas to accept a peaceful settlement, acted as if his peace mission had failed and told the Paandavas that war was inevitable. All these were scenes in his play.

It is asked, when Dhraupadhi was being humiliated in various ways, when Dhuryodhana was unabashedly behaving in a wicked manner in pursuance of his evil intentions, why did not Krishna intervene to prevent them? Why did not Krishna destroy the wicked Dhuryodhana? The reason is the time had not yet come for it. Bheema was the destined instrument for slaying Dhuryodhana. Dhuryodhana had to meet with his death at the hands of Bheema and not of Krishna. Krishna was waiting for the appropriate time.

Therefore, whatever has to happen, how, at what time and in what manner, has been predetermined and the mere fact that I am nearby will not serve to alter them.

In Duryodhana's audience hall, Sishupala was hurling abuses at Krishna. But Krishna waited. The appropriate time had to come. Only when the cause, the time and the necessary action are in fruitful combination will the event happen. Krishna was patient till the time was ripe. When the moment for action came, Krishna put an end to Sishupala.

The Lord observes His rules and regulations

The Lord always adheres to His laws, the rules and regulations laid down by Him. Man does not always abide by the rules when he faces trouble. But, whatever the situation, the Lord observes His rules and regulations. Therefore, no one can determine what limits and laws govern the Lord's actions.

Jesus Christ declared: "I am the Son of God." But when he was crucified, God did not come to his rescue. Christ even cried out in anguish: "Oh Father, Why are you not coming to save me?" But the Lord acts having regard to the time, place and the circumstances. He accords to each person the honour and esteem that is due to him. Christ became a glorious figure in the moment of his crucifixion.

Thus by a certain action, in a certain context, a person achieves name and fame. For instance, Abhimanyu pleaded with his mother to be allowed to fight his way through the maze Padhmavyuuha, organised by the Kauravas. The mother tried to dissuade him in all possible ways.

In the last resort, she told him: "The maze is a dreadful trap. The great Bhishma is commanding the enemy's hosts. Neither your father Arjuna, nor your uncle Krishna is near. Your wife is enceinte. It is not proper in these circumstances for you to embark on this perilous adventure." She spoke all this as a mother.

But Abhimanyu had to speak out from the son's point of view. "Oh Mother, is it right for you to ask a lion's cub to refrain from attacking a herd of petty animals? You should have ordered me to go and fight them like a warrior and return victorious. Instead, is it not infamous if I am asked to keep away from the fight?" Saying so, he left for the battlefield.

Abhimanyu could not refrain from going to the battlefield. No warrior can fail to respond to the challenge for a fight. Death is preferable to the infamy of cowardice. Recognizing the validity of Abhimanyu's reasoning, his mother permitted him to go. "Son! You may go. May all the goddesses protect you even as they blessed their sons when they set out to fight the demons. Above all, let Shri Raama be your protector." All these blessings did not save Abhimanyu.

The Lord is a witness to all happenings

Abhimanyu was destined to die in the *Padhmavyuuha* (the Lotus Maze). Could the blessings save him? Because he died in the *Padhmavyuuha* he found a place in the Paradise reserved for heroes. Such fame is not got by dying in an accident or from a disease or old age. For every kind of fame, there is a specific form of death.

Death however, is born together with birth. And death must come in the way it is bound to come. The Lord, however, is a witness to all happenings. In some instances, He gives prior indications and warnings. When these are heeded, the person concerned gets sanctified. When one disregards them, he forfeits his sanctity. One, therefore, should do his duty. The Lord's heart is boundless. He is concerned about the collective well-being of all.

Man, however, tends to have a narrow and limited perspective. A narrow outlook can lead only to a limited result. God makes no distinction between one group and another. He loves all equally. He blesses all. He wishes good for every one. "Let the whole world be happy" is His benediction. Whatever people's desires are, they will be fulfilled by God only according to their deserts. One cannot go to the Ganga with a small tumbler and hope to get more than a tumblerful of Ganga water. But when one acts according to the Lord's command, the capacity of the container may get enlarged.

In the Mahaabhaaratha, Krishna wished to avoid the charge that he had done nothing to prevent the great battle. Hence, he chose to go as an ambassador of peace to the Kauravas, though Arjuna expostulated with him in strong terms that there was no use in having peace parleys with the wicked Kauravas.

Overcoming calumny manifests glory of the Divine

The noble and the pure have been subject to calumny in all ages. From ancient times to the present, the evil minded have assailed the high-souled men who have sought to serve their fellowmen. Such untoward events happen from time to time. Only when these attacks are faced and overcome does the glory of the Divine become manifest. No great man has ever achieved eminence without overcoming abuse and calumny, trials and tribulations. Gold acquires greater brilliance by being heated in the crucible. Likewise a diamond becomes more brilliant when it is cut to produce more facets.

Trials and tests are stepping stones to fame for good people.

Devotees should develop firm faith

The world is steeped in trouble because of the divisible forces which have broken up human society on various irrational grounds. Devotees should develop unwavering faith, disregarding whatever happens in the world. Those who have pure and unselfish hearts will remain unshaken in their faith like an iron ball which remains unmoved even in a storm. But those who are swayed by mundane desires will waver like a dried leaf blown by a slight breeze. Let your devotion be firm. It is good for you.

Consider for a moment where you are and for what purpose you have come here. You have come to this *aashram* (hermitage) to fill your hearts with sacred thoughts. Not the *aashramites* alone, but everyone has to develop fraternal feelings and eschew hatred altogether. You have to develop equal-mindedness and face all situations in life with equanimity and fortitude. Anger, hatred, ostentation and pride are animal qualities. Love, kindness, forbearance, compassion and sacrifice are natural human qualities. Spirituality does not consist merely in offering worship, doing *bhajans*. It calls for the elimination of the animal qualities in man and striving for the realisation of oneness with the Divine. *"Adhveshtaa sarva bhuuthaanaam"* said Narasimhan in his speech earlier. Bear no ill-will towards anybody.

The means to prolong or shorten one's life lie in one's own hands. Your life-span is prolonged when you are full of joy, when you are calm and filled with pure thoughts. When you are filled with envy, anger, hatred and conceit your life-span gets shortened. The envious man gets no sleep at all. Sleeplessness ruins the health even more than lack of food. Envy torments a man all the time. These troubles lead to shortening one's life. As for hatred, the man filled with it cannot even bear the sight of his enemy. He suffers from hallucinations which consume his body and spirit.

True devotees should always be smiling

Anger is the cause of destroying the divine potencies in man. Hatred ruins a man's circulatory system. Envy drives the man crazy by depriving him of his sleep. In that condition he cannot relish his food. Thus, these three evil qualities—hatred, envy and anger—are wasting diseases. When you consider yourselves as devotees of God you should get rid of these three evil qualities.

Lead peaceful and pure lives. To call yourselves devotees but to look with envy at others is totally unbecoming. True devotees should always be smiling. Exude joy always. That joy will manifest itself when you experience your oneness with the Divine within you. If you are unhappy, it is because you have not experienced the Divine.

Don't worry about what has happened, what is happening or what is to come. Let things happen in their due course. You have, however, to learn lessons from what has happened. *"Thasmaath Jaagratha! Jaagratha!"* (Therefore, be vigilant, be vigilant). In many matters people tend to be careless. Troubles occur from time to time to warn us to be on our guard. Recognise the truth that whatever happens is for your good. Realise that even what seems to be bad is for your good. Even calumny is a precursor of greater renown. Alongside of censure, praise also grows, as in the digging of a pit, when a mound rises by its side. Look up to the good name that is in store for you. Do not bother about the trifles that happen. Nor should you blame others or revile at them. Be vigilant and foster your good nature. Share your goodness with those around you and experience the joy that results from such sharing.

A good man sees good even in what is bad

Our young students are tender hearted. As Sainath, (a student who spoke earlier) said, the students have been resorting to *paaraayanas* (reciting scriptures), fasting, prayer and other such practices by way of atonement for what they regard as their lapses. They are a prey to all kinds of apprehensions and fancies. They should not bother about what is past or what is likely in the future. They must concentrate on the present, which is a product of the past and the parent of the future. Live in the present and be happy. Entertain only happy thoughts. Behave like brothers.

Keep way from bad company. Even a noble and a generous hearted warrior like Karna suffered grievously because of his association with the evil-minded Shakuni, the wicked Dhuryodhana and the malicious Dhussaasana.

You must cultivate good company. How do you decide who is good and who is bad? Think over the matter deeply. The one who sees the bad in what is good is a bad man. The one who sees good even in what is bad is a good man. Therefore seek the company of the good alone.

Man, it is said, is a combination of Truth and Righteousness. Truth is God. Righteousness is Divine. Verily there is no greater Righteousness than adherence to Truth. We must live in the mansion of Peace, whose foundation is Truth, whose walls are Righteousness and whose roof is Love.

Act according to promprings of your conscience

Dear Students! You are yourselves the exemplars of your pure hearts and unselfish lives. You are feeling sad because of the feeling that a slur has been cast on the good name of the Institute students. Don't give any thought to this. When you are free from blame why should you worry? In a bag of rice there many be a few grains of paddy. You should not feel that because of the misbehaviour of a few, the taint affects all students. Act on the conviction that no blame attaches to any of you. Act according to the promptings of your conscience. That will lead you to Divinity.

Carry on the *Saadhana* which you have taken up. You are bound to earn a good name and bring credit to your parents. Even the Institute will be vindicated. As youth, your journey is long. You must stick to the path of Truth and lead ideal lives.

Devotees also should conduct themselves with fortitude. Fear sin. Show gratitude to the Divine. When you have fear of sin and love of God, you are bound to observe morality in society. Carry on your activities with zeal and faith.

Svaami will return soon to Prashaanthi Nilayam and fill you all with joy and enthusiasm. Never cease to meditate on God. Cultivate a spirit of broad-mindedness. Devotees, men and women, tend to magnify trifles. Avoid commenting on others. Love all, greet everyone with a smiling face, eschew harsh language. A soft answer turneth away wrath.

Recognise first of all that the Divine is in every one. Understanding others is the key to adjustment.

Discourse in Prashaanthi Mandhir on 21-7-1993.

In all lands the true sense of values has to be restored, and faith in the divinity of man has to be implanted. This is the work for which I have come. The world has to be saved from the consequences of limited knowledge, and from the blinding pride that precedes a fall.

—BABA

CHAPTER 27

Inscrutable are the ways of the Lord

"Kleem Krishnaaya, Govindhaaya, Gopeejana-
vallabhaaya Svaaha!" Kleem means the earth.
Krishnaaya means water. Govindhaaya means
fire. Gopeejana-vallabhaaya refers to air. Svaaha
refers to ether. Krishna's name encompasses the
five elements: earth, water, fire, air and ether.
This signifies that the Cosmos is permeated by
the Divine.

*E*MBODIMENTS *of Divine Love!* "The Cosmos is under the sway of the Divine. God is subject to the sway of Truth. Truth is subject to the *Uthama* (noble one). The Noble one is the embodiment of the Divine" explains a Sanskrith *shloka* (verse).

It is not easy for all to recognise the truth about the Divine. Only the person who can comprehend the inner meaning can recognise the nature of the Divine. The Divine, which has both an internal and external significance, cannot be understood by exercising the imagination alone.

Every person born on earth should recognise his inherent divinity and make his life meaningful by leading a Godly life. This is the primary goal of life. Only that person has redeemed his life who recognises every moment, the Divine in every atom and in every cell and who inspires in others this consciousness about the Divine. It is not enough to secure a vision of the Divine. One has not only to lead a Godly life himself but help others to live likewise. This is the supreme purpose of human existence.

Man does not devote any thought as to how he should make his life meaningful. The human heart is the seat of the Divine. Every devotee should adore the Lord seated in the heart. The spiritual aspirant should fill his heart with divine feelings and lead a life of fulfilment.

The Chathaka bird and gopikas

You have the example of the Chaathaka bird. It is in continuous search of pure rain-drops falling from clouds. There is no lack of water on the earth. But the Chaathaka bird desires only the pure unsullied rain drops falling from a cloud and will go through any amount of trouble to secure them. It has no use for any other kind of water associated with the earth. Likewise, the true *saadhaka*, devotee or disciple, will only desire to secure the nectarine love of the Lord and for its sake will be prepared to go through any trouble or sacrifice.

The *Gopikas* exemplified such deep devotion in their love for the Lord. They offered all they had in the service of the Lord and performed every act as an offering to the Divine. The term "Gopi" is derived from the word "Gup". The term "go" means the *Vedhas*. It has another meaning, "the earth." It also refers to the cow. The *Gopikas* used to chant the *Vedhas*. They protected the cows. They sanctified the earth. Not understanding this sublime aspect of their nature, people have misrepresented them in various ways, regarding them as ordinary women, Even their devotion was misconstrued because of the failure to understand the true nature of their love for the Lord. On account of their narrow-mindedness, these critics could not grasp the deep significance of the *Gopikas'* devotion.

God is the master of eight-petalled *Hridhaya Kamala*

In every human being, there are what are known as the *Shatchakras* (the six centres of life energy). Among them, two are important. One is the *Hridhaya Chakra*—the *Chakra* relating to the heart. The other is the *Sahasraara Chakra*—the *Chakra* relaitng to the head. The *Hridhaya Chakra* is described in *Vedhaanthik* parlance as *Hridhaya Kamala* (the Lotus of the Heart). This "lotus" has eight petals. Every petal is called *Prakrithi* (Nature). All the eight petals are under the sway of the Lord. This means that God is the *Adhipathi* (master) of the eight petals. Because Krishna is the *Pathi* (husband) of these eight petals, he is said to have eight "Queens," according to the scriptural text. Those who did not understand the esoteric meaning of all this, described

Krishna as having eight queens and as having sported with 16000 *Gopikas*. The real meaning of the reference to Krishna's "eight queens" is that he is the Lord of the lotus of the human heart. As such, he holds sway over the heart. When this is rightly understood, the supreme greatness of the Divine will be apparent.

The symbolic attributes of the Divine

God is called in His Cosmic form as Vishnu, who permeates everything in the cosmos. God is the cause and the cosmos is the effect. You must try to understand the various attributes of the Lord. Vishnu is depicted as having a conch in one hand and a wheel in another. In a third hand he carries a mace and in the fourth a lotus. What is the esoteric significance of all this? The conch is a symbol of Sound. Hence, God is described as the embodiment of Sound. The *Chakra* (wheel) symbolises *Kaalachakra* (the Wheel of Time). The Lord is the master of Time and Sound. The mace signifies strength or power. This means that the Lord holds in his hand the strength of all beings. The lotus in the Lord's hand is a symbol of the heart. This means that the Lord holds in His hand the hearts of all beings. Because the symbolism of these attributes of the Divine was not properly explained by the commentators on the scriptures, a great deal of misunderstanding and confusion came to prevail in later years.

As regards the *Sahasraara Chakra* in the head of the human body, it is a thousand-petalled lotus, each petal having sixteen *Kalaas* (phases). There are thus 16000 *kalaas* in the *Sahasraara*. These phases were symbolically described as the wives of the Lord. The inner meaning of these expressions should be properly understood.

Going only by the superficial and literal meaning of these terms, the nature of the Divine is misconstrued and misinterpreted.

The Lord confers freedom

It is necessary to get at the inner meaning of what is said in the Raamaayana, the Bhaagavatha or the Bible or any other scriptural text. The good is liable to be misunderstood and construed in perverse ways. There is need for protecting carefully what is good and sacred. A beautiful parrot is kept in a cage. No one bothers to safeguard the crow. Likewise, the wicked are without restraint. Only the good are subject to restraints, ordeals, tests and difficulties.

Krishna was born on *Ashtami* (the eighth day of the Lunar month). From the moment of birth, He was subject to troubles. But whoever cherished the name of the Lord in the heart was free from bondage. Vasudeva was a prisoner. But the moment Dhevaki placed the infant Krishna on her husband's head, he became free. The moment the Lord touched his head, Vasudeva's fetters dropped away. As long as he carried Krishna on his head and till he deposited the child in Repalle, he was free. He placed the child in Yasoda's house. Then he returned to his prison and became bound as before. What is the meaning of this episode? As long as Divine thoughts fill our minds, there is no bondage. But when you give up the Lord, you get bound in every way.

There are deep inner meanings for the actions of the Lord. Kamsa tried every conceivable means to kill Krishna. But the Lord is beyond the grasp of anyone. Small-minded persons, consumed by hatred and jealousy,

may entertain such designs. But these evil plans only
recoil on the plotters and can cause no harm to God.
They will only enhance His glory.

The foes of Krishna

There were reasons for Kamsa's hatred. An ethereal
voice had declared that Kamsa would meet with his
death at the hands of the eighth child of Dhevaki. Out
of the selfish desire to save his own life, Kamsa sought
to do away with Krishna by various means. All his
efforts were of no avail. Kamsa carried out a slaughter
of the children in Repalle in the hope of killing Krishna.
Krishna eluded his grasp. A man's intellect turns crazy
when he is facing destruction. Because of his wicked
actions, Kamsa came to a disastrous end.

This, however, is not the end of the story. Two other
wicked men, Sishupala and Dhanthavkra, rose against
Krishna. After these two had been slain by Krishna,
Jaraasandha came forward. Many demons in human
form sought to eliminate Krishna. They all failed utterly.
They brought disaster upon themselves. Thus, from aeon
to aeon, the Divine is confronted with such hostile elements. Happiness cannot be got without going through
difficulties. Fame is the product of blame.

Such incidents happen in the life of every *Avathaar*
and in every age. They serve to promote the greatness
of the *Avathaar* and not to tarnish it.

Is it possible for any ordinary individual to make
his appearance simultaneously in numerous different
places? If it is stated that the same person appeared
simultaneously in the homes of 16000 *Gopikas*, not only
will people today disbelieve in it, but many will ridicule
it. But this is the reaction of petty, unthinking people,

who have no spirit of enquiry. If one enquires into the truth, it will be seen that even in modern times such a phenomenon is taking place. The broadcast of music programme from Delhi is heard in millions of homes in its completeness, all at the same time in a myriad different places. A person speaking on T.V. can be seen in a million homes. If a man made *yanthra* (contrivance) can have such a far-reaching power, why should it not be possible for the power of *manthra* to reach millions simultaneously?

How God's grace operates

The image of Krishna could appear in the hearts of the *Gopis*, though they were far away from Him. What is necessary is to purify the heart. The image of the Divine will not be reflected in an impure heart. There is no limit to the power of the Divine. Only the small-minded have limited power. God alone knows to whom, in what circumstances, at what time, to what extent and in what form His grace should be showered.

For example, take the case of Dhraupadhi. In his vast audience-hall Dhuryodhana was inflicting humiliation on Dhraupadhi. Unknown and unseen by anyone, Krishna was giving to Dhraupadhi an endless number of saris. How are ordinary persons likely to view the situation? They might ask: "How is Krishna tolerating this kind of disrobing of Dhraupadhi? Why does he not reduce Dhuryodhana to ashes that very moment? Why does He not put an end to his life? When the devotees are in agony, should the Divine merely look on?" The ignorant may tend to react in this fashion.

But the Divine, who is the embodiment of peace, love and truth, has to take note of *Kaarana, Kaarya* and *Karthavya* (the cause, the remedy and the task to be done). In the great cosmic drama, the Lord is also an actor. The time should be ripe for the role He has to play in a particular sequence of events. His action should be appropriate to His role. He cannot act otherwise.

God's role in the great cosmic drama

For instance, if Krishna decided to kill Dhuryodhana at the moment of Draupadi's humiliation, He would be going against His role in the play. He has to play His specific part. Krishna knew that Dhuryodhana's end lay in the hands of Bheema and not in His. It would be against his *dharma* if he did what Bheema had to do. Bheema alone should slay Dhuryodhana with his mace. This is the law of creation. Krishna waited for the ordained event.

Likewise, in various situations, the Lord remains as a witness. Is the Lord powerless or is the devotee's prayer ineffective? This sort of doubt arose once in the mind of saint Thyaagaraaja. Thyaagaraaja's elder brother subjected him to many ordeals. Resenting the action of Thyaagaraaja in rejecting the treasures sent by the ruler of Thanjavur to the saint, the elder brother cast into the river the idols of Raama and others worshipped by him. Thyaagaraaja made a frantic search for the missing idols. Although a great devotee, Thyaagaraaja felt frustrated. He asked the Lord, "Oh Raama! why are you subjecting me to these difficulties? Is it because my devotion has weakened? Or has your power declined?" Thyaagaraaja felt that his devotion had not diminished. So Raama's power must have weakened. But, pondering over it further, he realised that Raama's strength remained undiminished. He began to sing a song in praise of Raama's prowess. "Without Raama's power, could a monkey have been able to cross the ocean? Or would the Goddess of wealth have chosen to be his consort? Or Lakshmana serve him? Or the supremely intelligent Bharatha revel in beholding him and worshipping him?" Thyaagaraaja ecstatically extolled the infinite prowess of Raama and blamed his own ignorance for having doubts about Raama.

Many devotees, out of their worldly pre-occupations and narrow-mindedness, tend to develop doubts about the Lord. The Lord, however, always remains at the same supreme level. He is not elated by praise or depressed by censure. The Lord is unchanging.

Lord's concern for the well-being of the world

The Divine, therefore, has to be viewed from a wide perspective. Whatever the Lord does is for the well-being of the world. His sole concern is the welfare of the world.

It was this which made Bhaarath declare from ancient times, "Let all the world's people be happy." From early times Bhaarath held forth great ideals to all other countries in the realms of ethics and spirituality. With the passage of time, faith in these ideals has waned. Man today is plagued by scepticism. He is racked by doubts. The combination of these two is the cause of all troubles.

In the Mahaabhaaratha, Shakuni represents *Anumaana* (doubt). Karna symbolises *Avishvaasam* (lack of faith). When these two come together, *Asuuya* (envy) in the form of Dhuryodhana emerges. Envy is accompanied by wickedness in the form of Dhussaasana. When the

four came together, the fate of the Kauravas was
sealed. The Kauravas represent bad thoughts, bad
intentions, bad actions and bad attachments.

Krishna clearly foresaw the fate of the Kauravas
long before the Kurukshethra war. He told Arjuna: "Get
up. Be prepared for war. Justice will prevail. Selfishness
will suffer disaster. This is the *Dharma* of every age.
The parents of these wicked ones will have none of
their children left to offer them the last rites. That is
the decree of fate." Krishna concluded His call to Arjuna
with the declaration that there has to be a downpour
of arrows to ensure world peace after the wicked Karna,
Shakuni and others had been destroyed in the fires of
hate stirred up by them.

Over the ages, the wicked have behaved in the
manner of the Kauravas and have met with the fate
they deserved. There is no escape for anyone from the
consequences of his actions. Death may come at any
time, in any place, in any form. No one can tell time
or manner of anyone's death. It is pre-ordained. There
is no meaning in analyzing the pros and cons of such
happenings. Even good devotees sometimes develop
doubts and argue over trifles.

How anger reduces one's strength

Once Krishna set out to kill Jaraasandha. But
whenever Jaraasandha came out of his city to fight
Krishna, the latter would flee from the battlefield. Was
Krishna afraid of Jaraasandha? Not at all. But Krishna
wanted to find out the appropriate means of slaying
Jaraasandha. Krishna had a strategy. Each time Krishna
went to challenge Jaraasandha, he would get enraged.
He would come out to pursue Krishna. Krishna would

go on retreating. By repeating these tactics several times, Jaraasandha was made to expend his strength in futile rage.

A man's strength is considerably reduced by his anger. A man's life-span is cut to pieces by the shears of envy, anger and hatred. Envy is the main cause of shortening a man's life; when a man gets angry, his whole body trembles. His blood gets heated. It takes three months for the blood to get cool again. One moment of anger may consume the energy got from six months of eating. This is the way anger debilitates a person. By systematically weakening Jaraasandha in this way, ultimately Krishna managed to slay him.

The Lord is not visible to the non-believer

Consider the cases of Hrianyaaksha and Hiranyakashipu. They were not ordinary men. They were the incarnations of Jaya and Vijaya, the divine guards at the gate of the Lord's mansion (in Vaikunta). Hiranyakashipu developed bitter hatred towards Vishnu as the slayer of his brother, Hiranyaaksha. He searched for Vishnu in every conceivable place—in the ocean, deep in the earth and in the sky—but could not find Him. Had Vishnu run away from Hiranyakashipu out of fear? No. He was omnipresent. But He could not proclaim it Himself. He made Hiranyakashipu's son Prahlaadha declare it. He asked Prahlaadha: "You simpleton! You go on praising Hari. Where is that Hari? Show him to me. I have explored every particle of the Universe. I have not found him. Hence I am the Lord whom you should worship." Prahlaadha replied: "How can I worship the enemy of Hari? Hari is everywhere." "Can you show Him?" asked his father. "Certainly," replied Prahlaadha. "Is he in that pillar?" "Yes, he is," said Prahlaadha. The Lord came out of the pillar to confirm his devotee's faith. Prahlaadha had affirmed the omnipresence of the Lord and the Lord testified to the truth of his belief. The Lord is not visible to the non-believer.

Lord observes the rules of the Cosmic game

Whether the Lord makes his presence felt in certain situations or not should not be judged by narrow human considerations. The Lord will reveal His powers only at the appropriate moment, when the time is ripe. Just as a fruit takes time to ripen, God also bides his time. It is improper to speculate on the nature of the Divine's actions. Even the omnipotent and omniscient Lord has to respect the time factor. He has to observe the rules of the Cosmic game. He cannot violate His own rules and regulations even as a traffic authority cannot transgress the traffic rules made by him.

For instance, God has endowed a lamp with the power to shed light and the wind with the power to blow out the lamp. When a lamp is exposed to the wind, the Lord will not direct the wind not to blow out the lamp. Everything in creation has to act according to the laws of its existence. The five elements are governed by laws which they have to observe.

The Bhaagavatha relates many episodes which give rise to questions. The answers to these questions may vary according to the understanding of the persons concerned. But no one can fully comprehended the ways of the Lord. Whatever is destined to happen must happen. No one is competent to ask of God why he has not prevented something. God alone can decide this matter.

Few can account for the actions of the Lord. For five thousand years, men have been exploring every kind of phenomena in this Universe. But no one has been able to unravel the mystery of the Divine. God is all-powerful, all-knowing and all-pervasive. But whatever happens in the Universe is governed by cosmic laws. Their working cannot be easily understood. That is why a devotee said: "Is it possible, Oh Krishna, to recognise your mystery? You are subtler than the atom and vaster than the vastest thing in creation. You are present in the 84 lakhs of species in the Universe and permeate every place in the cosmos. You are present in the good as well as the wicked and make them play their respective roles. You are in the accuser and in the accused. How can anyone understand your Divine mystery?"

When men declare their belief in the idea that God is one, irrespective of differences in names, they should act upto their belief by developing equal-mindedness towards everyone. This is the cardinal principle of Bhaaratheeya culture: to treat joy and sorrow, loss and gain with equal serenity.

Submitting to God's will leads to bliss

Realise that it is not possible to comprehend fully the ways of the Divine. Strengthen your faith in God, carry out the Lord's injunctions, experience the bliss derived therefrom and redeem your lives. Do not indulge in futile speculation or controversy. All are aspects of the Divine. Whatever happens is for your good. Fill your hearts with this conviction. Consider everything as coming from God for your good. God knows what is good for you even as a loving mother knows what a child needs. No one can expect to receive whatever he prays for, because in his ignorance he may ask for what is not good for him. The wise man will not seek anything from God, but leave everything to God.

Chaithanya's firm faith in the will of the Divine

Chaithanya exemplified this quality of unquestioning faith in the will of the Divine. When he was going about in his native village Navadhweep, chanting the name of Krishna, some envious persons attacked him and took away the cymbals from his hands. Chaithanya accepted the loss as a sign of grace from Krishna and continued singing, using his hands for clapping. He said: "Oh Lord! I am using these hands you have given to me for clapping, while singing your praise. I can do without the cymbals." The miscreants then bound his hands to prevent him from clapping. Chaithanya exclaimed: "Lord! I shall keep the rhythm of my chanting with my voice. Your love will be my tune. I know no *yoga*. I have done no penance. I do not care for the treasures of the world. My greatest and only wealth is your love. Confer this wealth on me."

Of what avail are *japa* and penance without the love of the Lord? They are like preparing an excellent food in an untinned vessel. The entire food gets poisoned. Likewise, one may practise the nine forms of devotion, but without love of God in the heart, they are useless. Chaithanya declared. "Oh Lord! I want your love alone and nothing else."

At his birth, the name given to Chaithanya was Gauraanga, because of his fair complexion. But as he was always chanting the name "Krishna, Krishna," he got the popular name "Krishna Chaithanya" (one who was immersed in Krishna consciousness). The moment he repeated Krishna's name he used to lose his consciousness.

In this manner, there are many great ones who have the names given to them at birth and the names by which they get known later on. The lives of these great ones should be regarded as ideals for the rest of mankind.

Strive continually to develop Divine Love

Embodiments of Divine Love! It is not enough if you merely celebrate this day as a festive occasion because it is Krishna's birthday. Krishna was the very embodiment of love. He attracted every one by His love. He melted the hearts of one and all. He made the lives of many meaningful. Love was at the root of all He did.

All must strive continually to develop love. In earlier ages, men had fear of sin. The Lord's command was: Fear sin, love the Lord. Unfortunately, today in the *Kali Yuga* (the present age of discord), people love sin and abhor God. Why should anyone fear God? Those, who ought to be afraid to commit sin, are having fear of God. Instead of loving God, people are loving sin. This is the reversal of what ought to prevail. People are leading lives opposed to what is proper.

The Chaathaka bird will not shrink from being near a cloud to catch the fresh raindrops even if there are dreadful thunder and blinding lightning. It prays constantly for the pure unsullied raindrops. This is the attitude *saadhakas* should cultivate today. They must be prepared to face any kind of censure, criticism, trouble or obstacle. They should adhere to their goal regardless of anything. The *Gopikas* exemplified this type of devotion. They had no fear of any threats or abuse. They were totally unaffected.

Love God and fear none

Hence, stick to your truth. Love God and fear none. Only the guilty need fear. Why fear when you are innocent? Without any fear in your hearts, meditate on God. This is the royal road to the Divine in the *Kali Yuga*.

There is no protector like the Divine. This was demonstrated in the case of Dhraupadhi, when none of her valiant husbands or others came to her rescue and Krishna alone saved her from humiliation.

The Lord alone is the saviour of the helpless and the forlorn. Do not waver in your faith in the Lord in any circumstance. Go ahead with your tasks with faith and determination.

God tests people in many ways. They are intended only to promote your spiritual progress. None can affect God in any way. Why lose your faith in Him? They are signs of weakness. Give no room for such unfortunate doubts. Strengthen your faith and realise God by your devotion.

Discourse in the Sai Ramesh Mandap, Brindhaavan on 10-8-1993, Gokulaashtami Day.

CHAPTER 28

Bhaarath : then and now

What greater misfortune can there be
Than the failure of Bhaaratheeyas to know
The unique greatness and sacredness
Of Bhaarath's ancient culture?

*E*MBODIMENTS *of Divine Aathma!* In ancient times, the spiritual culture of Bhaarath spread the message of peace and harmony to various countries in the world. Then, as well as now, the Aryan tradition has proclaimed to the world the benediction: *"Lokaas-samasthaas-sukhino bhavanthoo!"* (Let all the world be happy!). This tradition was upheld even at the sacrifice of their lives by the ancient kings, the savants and the noble women of the land.

Today the rulers as well as the citizens are caught up in worldly concerns and are forgetting this great cultural heritage. In the sphere of the physical and the material, man has achieved many significant victories. But he has not made the slightest progress in the fields of morality, spirituality and wisdom. What is the reason? It is the deep-rooted selfishness in human beings.

Reign of selfishness in today's world

All of man's thoughts, desires and actions are saturated with selfishness. Man today has become a puppet in the hands of selfishness. Whatever object one desires, he does not seek it for its own sake. When he loves anyone, it is not for that person's sake. He loves the other for selfish reasons.

Those who have not understood the sacredness of Bhaaratheeya culture cannot realise the sacred nature of love. The ancient Bhaaratheeyas were votaries of truth and practioners of righteousness. They stood for justice. Today the people have forgotten this legacy. This is the calamitous influence of Time. It is only when, spiritually and morally, the character of the nation is developed will Bhaaratheeya culture come into its own.

Our youth today are unable to appreciate the value of this ancient culture because its values are not being properly propagated among the people. With the waning of the hold of this culture on the people, humanness itself is being undermined. If human values are not upheld, of what use is the human birth? As a human being, a man should manifest human values.

Moreover, human beings can realise their inherent divinity only when they recognise the unity that underlies the apparent diversity. There are today many intellectuals who propagate divisive tendencies, but there are very few good men engaged in promoting unity.

All men belong to one human family

Despite differences in names and forms, in food habits and in speech, all men belong to one human family, of which God is the Father. Not realising this truth, men are victims of divisive forces.

Every man has to develop the divine faculties in him. God is the embodiment of Love. Love is His nature. Such sacred love is in every man. Even as God is manifesting to the world His selfless love, every man should manifest his unselfish love to everyone. Man is not apart from God. The Lord has declared in the Geetha: "Every human being in the world is a fragment of My Eternal Self." This implied that man is not an aspect of Nature or of the physical elements. He is Divine in spirit. This is the repeated declaration of the Lord.

The ancient sages described this Divine Love as *Aathmavaan*, implying that Love is the form of the Divine. This is called *Svashakthi*, meaning the power of the *Aathma*. Today people are oblivious to this *Aathmik* power. Relying on the strength of physical and the material world, men are forgetting the boundless power of the *Aathma*. The physical body is perishable. Only *Dhehi* (the indwelling Spirit) is Divine.

Today, there is great need for propagating the doctrine of Love. Divine love is beyond comprehension by the mind or description by words. Love is the very form of *Brahman* (the Absolute). When men forget love, are they not forgetting the Divine Itself?

People speak about freedom, calling it *Svechcha*. What is this *Svechcha?* Knowledge of *Brahman* is *Svechcha.* It is Absolute Bliss—*Brahmaanandham.* Instead of seeking this kind of spiritual freedom, people today are going after freedom in worldly terms. In the place of the pure, sacred, eternal Divine Love, men are lost in transient and momentary attachments.

Need for people to cultivate good thoughts

The Divine cannot be realised through wealth, scholarship or by any other means except love. This sacred love is being fragmented in many ways out of worldly attachments and is being treated as a trivial thing. This is the manner in which people today reject truth and welcome falsehood and go afar to consume alcoholic drinks while refusing wholesome milk and curds offered to them at their doorstep. It is the bad feelings within them which make them behave in this way. Hence, there is great need for people to cultivate good thoughts and good feelings.

Love can be promoted only by the grace of God's love. The world has no dearth of wealthy men, intelligent men, or powerful men, but there are few spiritually realised persons. What is it that great emperors like Harishchandhra, Nala and Raama took with them when they left the world? What is in store for the men of wealth and power today? What is it that they will take with them? Nothing. God alone is the eternal truth that will accompany the lover of God.

Bhaaratheeyas got their freedom in 1947, but did not achieve unity. True education consists in teaching people to live in peace and harmony with a feeling of common fellowship. Life today is riddled with differences and discord. Hatred reigns everywhere. Of what use is our *Svathanthram* (freedom)? *Sva-than-thram* really means freedom of the Spirit *(Sva)*. It is not related to the physical. People speak about "Independence."

What is this Independence? It was meant to convey the idea that freedom means not depending on any outsider. But are we really self-reliant today? We are dependent on many in several respects. How can we claim we are independent when we are dependent on others? There is only one difference between the old British days and now. In those days we used to accuse the white men of oppressing the coloured natives. Today the natives are oppressing the native population. Did we achieve freedom only to inflict suffering on ourselves through our own men? Is it to besmirch our culture that we got our freedom?

Spiritual freedom is the true freedom

We must certainly safeguard our freedom. But essentially that freedom is spiritual freedom. Any other kind of freedom is not freedom at all.

Youth today have no sense of patriotism. In the pre-independence days, many young men made great sacrifices for the sake of freedom. This was because the leaders of those days also made great sacrifices for freedom and inspired the youth to do likewise. However, leaders today talk in one way and act in another way. They deliver lectures on Bhaaratheeya nationalism. The moment they get down from the stage, they talk about caste and creed and promote divisions among the people. How, then, can youth develop a genuine feeling of nationalism? The result is there is hardly any sense of national love and pride among the young people.

Dear students! Whatever anyone may say, regard this country as the land of your birth. It is your Motherland. It is your own native land. Love of the country must get firmly rooted in our young persons. You have to take a firm resolve to protect your Motherland.

Be prepared to sacrifice yourselves for your Motherland

Once, Aurobindo asked a group of students in Calcutta: "For what purpose are you studying? If you are going to make use of your education for the benefit of the nation pursue your studies. Otherwise, you better burn your books. If you are studying only out of selfish motives, the education is of no value at all. If you are intent only on earning a living, you may as well beg from door to door. You must be prepared to sacrifice yourselves for your Motherland."

"Breathes there the man with soul so dead
who never to himself has said:
This is my Motherland; this is my mother-tongue.
To love my country is my religion."

A youth who is not prepared to sacrifice his life for his country is as good as dead. Service to the nation is the greatest thing one can think of. All religious practices are worthless without service to one's fellow-men. Without the spirit of service, holding any *udhyoga* (office or position) is meaningless. *Udhyoga* (official position) must stem from *Yoga* (realisation of the Divine).

True *Bhaaratheeya* culture consists in developing a spirit of service, with a feeling of all-embracing love. A man can get on without many things in life. But he cannot get on without love. Love is at the root of all action. This love is Divine. It is unchanging, pure and unsullied. It is unaffected by joy or sorrow, loss or gain. Feeling elated in a moment of joy and getting depressed in a moment of grief is the mark of worldly love.

Divine love is spiritual and is infinitely precious. It is not fickle and changing from moment to moment. One who is immersed in the ocean of Divine love will have no words to express its greatness and sweetness. He will speak in the language of silence. He will keep away from idle talk or debate. Those who experience the bliss of Divine love will be filled with an inner joy, whatever the external troubles they may encounter.

Eliminate pollution of air by *Naamasmarana*

It is only when we cultivate this kind of love that we can claim to have achieved real freedom. Today there is no unity in the country. In its absence, enmity has taken its place. Where there is enmity, there is no purity. Today, the air is polluted. Even the sound vibrations in the ether, air, fire, water and earth are polluted. How are they to be purified? Everyone should purify and sanctify the atmosphere by doing *Naamasmarana* (chanting the name of the Lord). Every sound emanating from man enters into the radio waves in the atmosphere and gets permanently recorded. If the sound waves in the world today are polluted, it is because of the unsacred words uttered by people. By chanting the name of the Lord, the sound waves in the atmosphere must be sanctified.

Thereby, these waves can bring about a great transformation. The world, it is said, can be destroyed by an atomic bomb. Sacred sound waves can achieve greater things for the world. They can create a new world.

The power of Consciousness is all-pervading

Man has to understand the power of three kinds of potencies: *Ichcha-Shakthi, Jnaana-Shakthi* and *Kriya-Shakthi. Ichcha Shakthi* (the power of the will) should combine with electrical energy. There is, for instance, an aura round My thumb. If this energy were not in the body, it cannot move at all. This is called *Chaithanya* (the power of Consciousness).

This Consciousness is all-pervading. From this Consciousness, every individual derives what is called Conscience. This Conscience, when it functions through the sense organs, brings about the conscious state. All actions belong to the conscious state. All functions of the mind are related to the Conscience. All that is done through *Buddhi* (intellect) is related to *Chaithanya* (Consciousness).

The Consciousness that is all-pervading is present in the human body from top to toe. In spite of the presence of this Consciousness, men are misusing it or making no use of it. Just as barely 2 percent of the energy coming from the sun is used by the world, hardly a minute fraction of the power of the Divine Consciousness in man is being properly used. Make use of it to help society. Do not live only for your own sake. When you use your energies in the service of society, the Divine power in you gets surcharged. It will not diminish to the slightest extent.

Consider every human being as the embodiment of the eternal Divine. The very name *Nara* for man means that his essence is imperishable. It also means he is the embodiment of the *Aathma*. Born as the immortal Spirit, if man leads the life of an animal, there can be nothing more disgraceful.

"Svathanthram" means freedom of the spirit

We celebrate what we call our *Svathanthram*—the freedom of the Spirit *(Svaa)*. *Svathanthram* relates to external freedom. *Svathanthram* is concerned with inner freedom. It is through the internal that we enjoy the external freedom. Hence, the first requisite is purity of the heart. If the heart is pure, all that you think and do will be pure, just as water from a tank filled with pure water will be pure in any tap. If your thoughts and actions are impure, you are the cause of their impurity because you have polluted your heart. You are the cause of your joy and sorrow. Do not blame others for your troubles. It is a sin. Blame yourself for your condition. Self-punishment is as important as Self-Realization. Through self-punishment you get self-satisfaction, which promotes self-sacrifice. That is the prelude to Self-Realization.

You must engage yourself in a constant process of self-enquiry into determine whether you are right or wrong. This is a spiritual exercise. It enables you to understand the true nature of freedom, namely, harmony in thought, word and action. Essentially freedom consists in maintaining complete accordance between thought, word and deed.

It is supremely important to have good feelings. One ends his life in a good way if he entertains always good feelings. Those who are racked by doubts and suspicions are ultimately a prey to their own doubts. It should be realised that death is more important than birth. The manner of one's death indicates the way he lived.

Therefore, fill your hearts and minds with good feelings and thoughts. What is good? It is love alone.

SATHYA SAI SPEAKS

Eschew hatred, envy and other vices. Fill your hearts
with love. Students today tend to fill their minds with
all sorts of stuff about the world. What is necessary
is to fill the heart with love and the head with wisdom.
Engage the hands in service. This alone will manifest
the significance of human existence.

Consider your body as a home

To lead a peaceful life, you should bear no ill-will
towards others. Cultivate unity as the key to peace in
the home or outside. Consider your body as a home.
The mind, the tongue and the limbs are like members
of a family. If they all function harmoniously, there will
be peace. But if the three are at variance with each
other, there can only be discord and disharmony. Therefore, in unity lies strength, peace and success.

This was the lesson that Dharmaja taught when
he declared that as against the rest of the world, they
were 105 (the five Paandava brothers and the 100
Kaurava brothers), but when they had internal differences, they were five against hundred. When the country is faced with an external threat, all parties should
come together. They should not divide the country. You
may fight among yourselves tooth and nail, but when
the nation is in peril, you should act as one. You must
protect the security and integrity of the nation. That
is the way to cherish our freedom. Unfortunately, today,
this unity is lacking. There is too much struggle for the
loaves and fishes of office. How can the nation progress
in this situation? The parties that have mushroomed
in the country are tearing the nation to pieces.

This is utterly wrong. You must all live in unity.
All are children of Bhaarath. All are equally entitled

to a share in the patrimony. You have to earn your right to this patrimony by your love for the country. Without earning the right, people are fighting over the spoils. They are not entitled to this right.

Pray for the welfare of the nation and the world

Dear students and devotees! Cultivate love and cherish divine feelings and pray for the welfare of the nation and the world. Bhaarath has always upheld the concept of universal well-being. All the five hundred odd crores of human beings in the world are the children of one God. Don't foster narrow regional loyalties. The world is one vast mansion. Countries like America, Russia, India are rooms in that mansion. The national barriers are like walls. Once the barriers are removed, humanity will be one family. National attachments should be got rid of. Differences of race and religion should go. Then alone will peace reign on earth. Therefore, develop love.

Discourse in the Sai Ramesh Mandap, Brindhaavan, on 15-8-1993.

My glory is spread daily through those who call themselves My Bhakthas. Your virtue, your self-control, your detachment, your faith and your steadfastness are the signs by which people read of My Glory.
—BABA

CHAPTER 29

A Righteous emperor and Virtuous subjects

Anapekshah Shuchir-Dhakshah
Udhaaseeno Gathavyathah
Sarvaarambha Parithyaagee
Yo Madhbhakthah Sa Me Priyah.

*A*NAPEKSHAH means one who is free from any kind of *Apeksha* (desire or expectation). Is it possible in this vast world for any man to be free from *Apeksha?* This is not possible. Some things may be attractive to some persons and some high aims may interest others. The objects that are desired are sensual pleasures and comforts and things of the world. The *Sreshtha* (higher aims) relate to the non-sensual, non-physical and ultramundane. Almost all desires fall into one or other of these two categories. How, then, is it possible to be rid of both kinds of desires? This is possible.

In the Bhagavath Geetha, the Lord has declared that he is present in all righteous actions. Therefore, those who perform righteous actions can develop *anapeksha* (desirelessness). This means that when a man performs all actions as offerings to the Lord, they become *anapeksha* (desireless actions). The Lord is one who, from within, makes a person act, speak, listen, see and do many other actions. He is the doer and the enjoyer. If a person performs all actions with the conviction that the Indwelling Lord is the real Doer, then his actions become desireless. Hence every *saadhak* should regard his actions as offerings to the Divine.

Shuchih: This means purity. This term does not merely refer to the external cleanliness of the physical body. *Saadhakas* need internal purity also. What are the implications of inner purity? All the actions a man does issue from internal impulses and not from external forces. They are a reflection of his inner being. It is only when man has pure feelings within him that his actions can be pure. When he is polluted within, all his actions will be impure.

How is purity in speech achieved?

How are the internal impulses to be purified? These relate to the mind, speech and the body. Of the three, speech is the most important. How is purity in speech to be achieved? *"Anudhvegakaram Vaakyam Sathyam priyahitham cha yath,"* says the Geetha. Every word you utter should be free from *Anudhvegakaram* (causing excitement or agitation). It should be *Sathyam* (true) and *priyam* (pleasing). There are four factors which account for the pollution of the tongue. One is, uttering falsehood; two, excessive talking; three, carrying tales against others; four, abuse or criticism of others. The tongue is prone to indulge in these four types of offences in speech. Unfortunately, in this *Kali* age, all these four are rampant. Untruth has become ubiquitous. People freely indulge in slandering others. Tale-bearing goes on. Indulgence in loquacity is widespread. It is only when one gets rid of these four evil tendencies can his speech become pure and unpolluted. Hence, the first task is to purify one's speech.

How to purify the mind and body

Next comes the mind. The mind is polluted by wrong thoughts and bad feelings. Man should strive to keep away all bad thoughts from invading his mind. When a man is ceaselessly filled with bad thoughts, he can only reap bad consequences. To purify the mind, all bad thoughts have to be expelled. No room should be given to them. Bad feelings should be banished from the mind. Only then the mind will get totally purified.

Then comes purity of the body. One must have a body that is free from the taint of *Himsa* (violence or harm). Men commit many acts of violence and many sinful acts with their hands. The body has been given to man primarily for practising *Dharma* (righteousness). Such a sacred gift should be used only for rendering service to others and doing Godly actions. This is the way to purify the body. Therefore, when speech, mind and the body are purified, internal purity is ensured. *Shuchi*, thus, calls for internal purity as well as external cleanliness.

Dhakshah: This means that one should have firm determination in performing actions. The determination should be confined to actions that are pure, helpful to others and sublimate man. No man can refrain from action of some kind or other even for a moment. In no circumstance should one engage himself in an impure act. This is the way to achieve purity through firm determination. Only such a person can be called a *Dhakshah* (a resolute person).

Udhaaseenah: This means freedom from attachment to anything. It means remaining serene and unruffled by fame or blame, peace or sorrow, loss or gain, pleasure or pain, not elated by prosperity or depressed by failure. One should not succumb to calumny. Nor should one exult over fame. Fame and censure are like passing clouds. One should look upon them as a mere witness. They should be treated with *Udhaaseenah* (equanimous feeling). To treat them seriously is to give rise to agitations in the mind, which may lead to demonic tendencies.

Be free from worries

Gathavyathah: Vyathah represents the greatest weakness in man today. Man ignores the duties he has to perform in the present. He broods over what has happened in the distant past. He is constantly speculating over what is likely to happen in the future. Why worry about the future or about dead past? The past is beyond recall or remedy. Forget the past. The future is uncertain. No one can be sure about what is likely to happen the next day. Don't think about the future, as you cannot be sure about it. Concern yourself with the present, which is the child of the past and the parent of the future. This attitude is represented by the term *Gathavyathah*. Brooding over the past and speculating about the future, man is failing in his duties in the present. This is the cause of his misery. Make right use of the present and a good future is assured. The aspirant should bear this truth in mind and concentrate his attention on the present. Mental worry about the past or the future is a *Raajasik* quality. It should be got rid of.

Sarvaarambha parithyaagi: This quality calls for the renunciation of *Ahamkaara* (egoism) in any form. The ego is rooted in the *Mamakaara* (possessive instinct). When egoism and possessiveness come together in a man, he is utterly ruined. Hence, one should be free from egoism and attachment.

The aforesaid six qualities are sacred virtues. The opening stanza declares that a devotee with these six qualities is dear to the Lord.

The six enemies of man

Apart from these six good qualities, man has six vices: *Kaama* (lust), *Krodha* (anger), *Lobha* (greed), *Moha* (delusion), *Madha* (conceit) and *Maathsarya* (envy). These six enemies of man have to be got rid of and the six good qualities should be cultivated. Only then human life can be made meaningful.

Emperor Bali was one who was endowed with these noble qualities. For this reason, the Lord came down to the earth and sought a gift from Bali. There are many philanthropists in the world. There are persons who make gifts of land, or of cows, or food, or clothes, or gold, but few can be found who are prepared to make an offering of themselves. Emperor Bali was one who was ready to give himself away as a gift. "I am offering to Thee, Oh Lord, everything that is mine, my wealth, and family. Only the *Aathma* remains. Save me, who is taking refuge in Thee," explains a *shloka*. "I gave my word to you. I am giving my kingdom to you. At this instant, I am offering my body to you." Declaring thus, Emperor Bali bowed before Vaamana.

In ancient times, there were many such noble and high-minded rulers. Bali was wedded to Truth. He cared only for the welfare of his people. He was a protector of Truth. He practised *Dharma*.

Such a ruler was reigning over Kerala at that time. He derived all his multifarious virtues from his grandfather, Prahlaadha. However, Bali's father, Virochana, was engaged in wicked thoughts and bad deeds like Hiranyakashipu, Prahlaadha's father. All three belonged to the same clan. Virochana attempted to make Bali pursue wrong paths. But, good and bad ways cannot be imposed on others. The marks of good behaviour of persons reflect their inherent goodness.

Prahlaadha was an impartial and fair judge

Once, there was a contest between Virochana, the son of Prahlaadha, and Sudhanva, the son of the Sage Angeerasa. It was agreed that whoever lost the contest should forfeit his life to the winner. Both of them prayed to Prahlaadha to act as the judge for the contest, being convinced that he would be totally impartial and fair. Prahlaadha agreed to act as judge because he was pledged to uphold truth, without any other consideration. After watching the contest, Prahlaadha declared Sudhanva as the winner and his own son, Virochana, as the loser.

Unable to control his joy over the verdict, Sudhanva embraced Prahlaadha and said: "Prahlaadha! It is because of unflinching upholders of Truth like you that the world shines in all its glory. If there were no meritorious people on earth, how can there be light in the world? Prahlaadha! Because of your adherence to truth you gave the verdict against your own son." Prahlaadha knew that whoever lost the contest should pay forfeit with his life. But that did not deter him from pronouncing the verdict against his son. There is no greater *Dharma* than Truth—"*Sathyaanaasthi Paro Dharmah.*" Prahlaadha was not swayed by any sense of paternal love. He shed no tears. He watched the outcome of his judgment with a sense of fulfillment.

Recognising the utter dedication of Prahlaadha to Truth and Righteousness, Sudhanva declared: "Prahlaadha! your devotion to Truth will restore the life of your son. I am not claiming his life as the reward for my victory. I am giving back your son's life to you."

Dharma protects its protector

"*Dharma eva Adharmo hanthi. Dharmo Rakshathi Rakshithah*" (*Dharma*   destroys the one who harms it. *Dharma* protects its protector). "Prahlaadha! You have stood by *Dharma*. Thereby you have saved your son." In this manner Sudhanva praised Prahlaadha.

Prahlaadha's life exemplified innumerable virtues and ideals. Because of such great and virtuous rulers in those days, the world was blessed with peace and prosperity. Today everywhere disorder, discontent, distrust, injustice, indifference to what is good and indulgence in what is bad, excessive attachment to sensuous pleasures, selfishness and self-centredness, are rampant among people. It is unfortunate that Bhaarath, which was once famous for its morality and righteousness, its dedication to Truth and *Dharma*, should have degenerated to this level today. This is a blot not only on the country but a matter of shame for the people of Bhaarath. If we have a look at the state of the society, we find that all activities in society are related to self-praise, abusing others and duplicity in speech. These triple vices are now ubiquitous. Bhaaratheeya society, which was once so glorious, is now plunged in darkness, enveloped in discord, agitation and pollution.

Pollution of heart is of great concern today

Man considers the air as polluted, water as impure and the sounds reaching him as intolerable. Even the food is polluted. The Government also considers the entire environment as polluted. Enormous sums are being spent on purifying the environment. It is not the environmental pollution about which we should be concerned. What is of concern is the pollution of *Hridhaya* (the heart). Man's mind is polluted. Man's heart is polluted. All his feelings are polluted. It is because of this basic pollution, all other things appear polluted.

The primary need today is to eradicate the pollution in the human mind. How is this to be accomplished? The mind today is immersed in worldly desires and pleasures. As a result, there is mental dissatisfaction as well as bitter frustration. The mind should be turned back to the source from which it came. A fish out of water has to be restored to the water for it to regain its life. Can it survive if it is placed on a couch and fed with coffee? It will regain peace and life only when it returns to its native home. Likewise, man's mind has to be restored to its original home in the Aathma (Self). Without doing this, how can peace be got? Thus, mental peace has to come from the Aathma. This calls for turning the mind towards the Aathma by the use of the conscience.

Follow the conscience with full self-confidence

Don't rely on the body. It is a water bubble. Don't rely on the mind, which is like a mad monkey. Follow the conscience. When you follow the conscience with full self-confidence, you can accomplish anything.

Emperor Bali was one who had such self-confidence. When his preceptor, Shukraachaarya, wanted to dissuade Bali from making the gift which Vaamana asked, pointing out that the young lad was no ordinary Brahmana but the incarnation of Vishnu Himself, Bali declared: "If the young lad is Vishnu Himself, as you say, that is all the more reason for me to stand by the offer I have made when the supplicant is the supreme Lord. Is it not my great good fortune to be in the position of a giver to the Lord? All human beings seek favours from the Lord. When such a Divine approaches me with a request for three foot-lengths of land, how fortunate am I? This opportunity has come to me because of my good deeds in previous lives. I am ready to go against the injunctions of the preceptor, but I will not transgress the commands of the Lord. The plighted word stands. You may see two objects with the two eyes and listen to two different things with the two ears. But the tongue is one. The word that is given must be honoured. I cannot go back on it. The man who does not fulfill his promise is dubbed a sinner. I am determined to keep my pledge. God is the Supreme person and Lord of all beings. I will abide only by His words."

Emperor Bali was such a resolute ruler. Thereby, he secured a glorious opportunity. However, Bali had one special attachment for his subjects. The subjects also were equally attached to the emperor. The people bore devotion towards the ruler. The ruler was attached to his subjects. Their mutual relationship was intimate and indivisible. It was because of such a ruler and such subjects that the country was happy and prosperous.

Significance of Onam day

Unwilling to forsake his subjects and at the same time, unable to go back on his promise to the Lord, Bali gave a pledge to the people that he would visit them once a year. This Onam day is the auspicious day of Bali's annual visit to the earth. It is the sacred day on which Emperor Bali returns to bless his people. In the month of Shravana, when the moon is nearest to the constellation Shravana, Bali said he would make his appearance. Today that auspicious combination is present. As Sri Eradi said in his speech earlier, this is the twenty fifth year in which the Onam festival is celebrated in Bhagavaan's presence. What is the lesson to be learnt from this Silver Jubilee of Onam? Over the past twenty four years you have been listening to Bhagavaan's discourses experiencing His presence and enjoying the celebration. How far are you practising Svaami's teachings? Every human being has a heart. This heart is filled with love. With how many are you sharing the love in your hearts? With none at all. What, then, is the use of that love if it is not shared? You must share with all the love in your hearts, not with humans alone, but with all beings in creation. Love, which is the gift of God, has to be shared with everyone in the world.

Share your love with one and all

All human troubles arise out of the failure to share this love with one and all because of selfishness. Everyone repeats the benediction: *"Lokaas-samasthaas-sukhino Bhavanthu!"* (Let all the people of the world be happy). To how many are you giving happiness? You are repeating the words mechanically, but are you praying from your hearts for the well-being of the world? No, not at all. You are concerned only with your selfish interests. The day you root out selfishness from within you, divinity will blossom in your heart.

People talk about *Saakshaathkaaram*. What is it? It is not something external. *Saakshaathkaara* is contemplation of the Divine at all times and in all states within one's self. *"Sarvadhaa, sarvakaaleshu sarvathra Hari Chinthanam"* (Thinking of God at all times, in all places continuously). People do recite the name of Raama incessantly. But will liberation be got by this repetition? To gain liberation, to win Rama's grace, it is not enough to repeat His name, you have to act upto Rama's principles. Raama sacrificed everything for the sake of *Dharma*. You have to make a similar sacrifice. Keep *Dharma* as your ideal. Engage yourself in righteous activities. Only then will Raama shower His grace on you. If, on the contrary, you perform no *Dhaarmik* acts but only repeat Rama's name, it is tantamount to abusing Raama.

Likewise, there is no meaning in repeating Krishna's name. What the devotee should do is to experience the ecstasy of Krishna Consciousness. Nor is that all. You should develop the equal-mindedness of Krishna. Krishna maintained the same serenity of mind whether he was in a *Yoga-Bhuumi*, or a *Yuddha-Bhuumi* (battle-field) or *Smashaaana-Bhuumi* (a cemetery). He was always in a state of bliss. You should aspire to experience such bliss. Only then can you be said to experience Krishna consciousness. Whatever deity you may worship, you should experience the lessons of the deity within you.

Experince Sai truths by filling yourselves with love

Svaami's main teaching is *Prema thathva* (the Love principle). You are all experiencing this love. With how many are you sharing it? All around there is only hatred. Only egoism is present all the time. Equally ostentation is displayed all the time. How then, can you be deemed to have experienced the Sai truths? Whoever has imbibed those truths must be filled with love. That is the true mark of devotion.

Emperor Bali was one who was filled with the sense of justice, with forbearance, compassion, Truth, *Dharma*, and devotion to the people. Are you cultivating atleast one of these good qualities? Bali gave his promise to the people to appear before them every year because his people had all these qualities. The people of today are different. How can anyone know whether Emperor Bali is appearing? People celebrate Bali's visit as a festival but Bali is not coming. Why? Because the qualities of the people of those days are not present today. Doubtless, Bali loves his people. But the people today must have the power to draw him to visit them.

They should be like a powerful magnet which can attract a heavy block of iron. They will then be able to move and melt the heart of the Divine. You are doubtless magnets. But you have to purify yourselves to increase your magnetic power. That purity consists in the triple purity of mind, speech and body.

Reasons for merger of the wicked in the Lord

Whatever anyone may do, there can be no deficiency in the Divine. Whether you praise or blame God, neither affects Him. In the Mahaabhaaratha once Dharmaja watched with anguish the abuses levelled against Krishna by Sishupaala and which Krishna tolerated for quite sometime. Then he hurled a plate at Sishupaala which severed his head. Dharmaja saw the blood from Sishupaala's body flowing towards Krishna and a divine flame from his body merging in Krishna.

Dharmaja asked Naaradha how the soul of a wicked person like Sishupaala could merge in Krishna. Narada explained that good and bad, fame and blame relate only to the body and not to the *Aathma*. The merger in the Divine of devotees who have worshipped the Lord in many ways takes place after a long period of trials and tribulations, but it lasts eternally. In the case of the wicked, who remember the Lord constantly out of hatred, the merger takes place quickly but remains only for a short spell. The merger of soul in the Divine takes place for different reasons. In the case of Kamsa it was fear of Krishna, which made him always remember Krishna, hatred in the case of Sishupaala and Dhanthavakra, maternal affection in the case of Yashodha, who merged in Krishna through love. The

Gopikas merged in the Lord through single-pointed devotion and Radha merged in the Lord owing to *Ekaathma bhaava* (sense of spiritual oneness). All attained merger. But in each case, it was upto a specific level.

Cultivate the spirit of sacrifice

Do not follow the body. Follow the mind and the *Aathma*. The one who follows the *Aathma* is the real spiritual seeker.

Contemplating on God with all your heart, chanting his name and surrendering to him, redeem your lives. The name and fame of God are not derived from outside. They are not the creations of newspapers and pamphlets. They do not change because of any circumstance. The Lord's name and fame grow out of their sacredness and love. Therefore, do not bother about anything. Develop your love. Promote your divine nature. Cultivate the spirit of sacrifice.

Discourse in the Sai Ramesh Mandap on 30-8-1993.

The tongue is liable to four big errors; uttering falsehood, scandalising, finding fault with others and excessive articulation. These have to be avoided if there has to be Shaanthi for the individual as well as for the society.

—BABA

CHAPTER 30

Role of the *Avathaar* in the cosmic play

Like oil in the thil seed
Like ghee in milk, fragrance in a flower,
Juice in a fruit, fire in wood,
Divinity is everywhere.

*E*MBODIMENTS *of the Divine Aathma!* From ancient times, the questions, "Where is God?" and "How does he appear?" have been agitating the minds of people. The answers have been sought by different ways of investigation, The believers, non-believers, those with doubts and others have not been able to get clear answers to these questions. To comprehend the truth, one should look within oneself. This cannot be learnt from text-books or from teachers. *Chaithanya*

(Consciousness) is there in the mind and pervades everywhere. The power of vision in the eye and of taste in the tongue are derived from this *Chaithanya.* People are using the sense organs but do not know the source of the power which activates them.

Chaithanya cannot be comprehended by the physical vision. It is within everyone in very close proximity. People undertake external exercises and spiritual practices in vain to find it. The entire Creation is a manifestation of the Divine Will. *Prakrithi* (Nature) is the manifestation of God. Man is also part of *Prakrithi* and thus has the Divine power in him.

Chaithanya is the seed of entire Universe

A seed germinates and grows into a plant and then into a tree with branches, leaves flowers, etc. The seed of the entire Universe is *Chaithanya* (Pure Consciousness). It is *Sath-chith-aanandha.* It grows in full bloom in the human being and blossoms into the flower of Awareness. Thus God incarnates in man. To understand this truth is the goal of human life. It is the mind that stands in the way of this realisation. The mind is perverted when it is centred on the ego (body consciousness) of a person but when it is directed towards the *Aathma,* it becomes sublime. One puffed up with ego forgets Divinity. Thinking on the physical plane and looking at the external world, man is not able to understand the Divinity within him.

It is wrong to think that spirituality has nothing to do with worldly matters. The physical world also reflects Divinity. There are two entities, *Svabhava* and *Prabhaava* the former emanating from the True Inner Self and the latter from worldly pursuits. Because man forgets his true Divine nature he is wallowing in troubles and tribulations. He is reflecting only animal qualities in his actions. Only when one enquires within, one has the chance of realising Divinity.

Today we are celebrating Ganesh *Jayanthi,* the birthday of Vighneshvara. Who is He? What is His greatness? What has He taught to the world? We celebrate the *jayanthi* but do not make any effort to understand the *thathvas* (principle) behind it. His supreme teaching by His own example is oneness of the Universe. When He was asked to go round the universe to get a prize from his parents, He just circumambulated His parents Lord Shiva and Paarvathi and claimed that He had completed the trip around the universe by going around them, as Lord Shiva and Paarvathi represented the Universe.

Unity in a family is the basis of unity in society

The vehicles of Shiva, Paarvathi, Ganesha, Subrahmanya and the objects worn on their bodies all get on harmoniously though they are in their original nature antagonistic to each other. Take the examples of the lion, the vehicle of Paarvathi, living in peace with the elephant, the form of Ganesha, and the bull, the vehicle of Shiva, the peacock, the vehicle of Subrahmanya, bearing no enmity towards the snake, the garland of Shiva.

Unity in a family is the basis of unity in society. Though there are lots of common features among mankind, people are not able to visualise their unity, but promote only their differences. The cause for the lack of peace in the world is the absence of harmony in thought, word and deed in each individual, which is reflected in the lack of unity among different individuals.

Spiritual values have been given up, resulting in the turmoil that we see today. Ganapathi taught that one should respect one's parents and thereby win their grace and secure bliss.

The form of Ganapathi cannot, by any human standards, be termed as handsome. He has a small head, big stomach and uncouth form. But still we are captivated by His form and like to see Him more and more and worship Him. Beauty does not lie in the *Aakaara*, the external form but can be experienced even in *Vikaara* (apparent uncouthness). Ganesha sacrificed his own tusk and used it as a pen to write down the Mahaabhaaratha to the dictation of Vyaasa, for the benefit of humanity. Man worships God only for selfish purposes. No one is prepared to sacrifice anything for getting Divine Bliss, while men are prepared to go to any length for worldly pleasures. Your mind and heart should be rendered pure to worship Divinity. You should see unity in diversity.

Role of the Divine in the cosmic drama

In the cosmic drama, the Divine has His own role to play. When one takes up a role in a drama, he should act according to the role and not according to his state in real life. Behind the screen he comes into his own. You should understand this truth clearly. A man may take up the role of Raama in a drama. Then he has to adhere to the principles of *Sathya, Dharma, Shaanthi* and *Prema* which governed all Raama's actions, though in actual life, the actor may not be righteous. Similarly God assumes a role in the drama of the world in human form. He has to behave as a human being only. This should be clearly understood by all.

Avathaar will not transgress rules and regulations

Krishna was *Paramaathma* (Supreme power) and *Sarvajna* (All-Knowing). Though He was very close to Dhraupadhi, at the time when she suffered humiliation in the court of Dhuryodhana, who ordered that she be disrobed, Krishna made an endless supply of saris to protect her honour. Some persons ask why Krishna did not punish Dhuryodhana on the spot when he was perpetrating such a heinous crime against a noble woman who was so devoted to Him. No doubt, Dhraupadhi was highly devoted to Krishna and Krishna had also the power to punish Dhuryodhana. But in this drama several more scenes had to be enacted. Dhuryodhana was predestined to be killed by Bhima in the war that was yet to come. So Krishna could not interfere.

Kamsa's life was in the hands of Krishna and Raavana's life was in the hands of Raama. Both Raama and Krishna are forms of Vishnu. But each had to play His specific role in His incarnation. For every incarnation there are certain rules and regulations which the *Avathaar* will not transgress. Mere mortals cannot understand the ways of the Divine.

In the Divine family of Lord Shiva, we should understand that Shiva represents Energy, Paarvathi represents *Prakrithi*. *Buddhi* (intellect) and *Siddhi* (fulfilment) are symbolic of Ganapathi and Subrahmanya, their sons. They are all one, though conceived in different forms. All the five fingers in the hands are not alike but different in size and shape. But when you do any work, they join together to give maximum effect. If all are of equal size, it will not be conducive to effective functioning. This is one of the secrets of God's creation.

Realise the wisdom of the Divine

There was a mathematician taking rest under a tree, who wondered why a pumpkin creeper bore such a huge fruit, while the huge banyan tree over his head bore only tiny fruits. He was doubting the sense of proportion of God. During his sleep some fruits from the banyan tree fell on his body. On waking up he realised that if the huge tree which attracted people to take shelter under its shade, had big fruits, like pumpkins, their fall would be harmful to those resting under it. This experience made him realise the wisdom of the Divine.

You should try to have complete knowledge of anything. Partial knowledge is dangerous. You should study the nature of the heart. God thinks of *Loka-Shreyas* (the welfare of the whole world). He has a broad vision, while human beings have a narrow selfish outlook.

You should also expand your heart—not the physical heart, which may call for surgery if it expands. I am speaking about the spiritual heart. It is called *Hridhaya*, meaning one which is filled with *dhaya* (compassion). It is all pervading. If you think of America, your heart goes there at once. The physical heart is like a machine with limited scope. The heart with *dhaya* (compassion) is *Dhaivam* (God). If one has no *dhaya* his nature is devilish. Compassion is the most essential quality of a human being. Without compassion, man is inhuman. A compassionate heart reflects divinity.

God has no birth or death. He remains an Eternal Witness. How to realise such an entity who is *Aprameya* and *Apramana* (beyond description and beyond proof)? He responds only to *Prema*. You should understand God through love and spend your life with love.

Discourse on 19-9-1993 at Sai Ramesh Hall at Brindhaavan.

You have been born for one purpose: to die. That is to say, to kill the "I". If Brahma dies, you become Brahmam, or rather, you know that you are Brahmam. All literature, all effort, all Yajna, all teaching is just to hold a mirror before you, so that you may see Yourself.

—BABA

CHAPTER 31

Glory of the Lord's lotus feet

Observance of right conducts has declined;
Dharma has been endangered;
Morality has nowhere to abide;
What can I say about human existence?
Morality and ethics are confined to books;
The heart has become a foul dust-bin.

EMBODIMENTS *of the Divine Aathma!* Wetness is the
natural trait of water. Hardness is the attribute of stone.
Sweetness is natural to sugar. Heat is the quality of
fire.

These are the *Dharma* (natural behaviour) of subs-
tances. For the individual, *Vaancha* (desire) is natural.
Because man is sustained by desire, it is considered
a *Dharma* (natural trait) of man. *"Dhaarayathi ithi
Dharmah"* (Dharma is that which sustains). Man is

sustained by desire. Man's primary duty is to offer all his desires to God.

This means that the practice of *Dharma* calls for the offering of all worldly desires to God and developing the inward vision. *"Sarvadharmaan pariththyajya maamekam sharanam Vraja"*—Renouncing all *Dharmas*, take refuge in Me alone—says Krishna in the Geetha. This implies that man must make it his primary aim to offer to God all external sensory, physical desires and cultivate spiritual thoughts centred on the eternal.

Purity of heart is essential for spiritual wisdom

To develop such a spiritual outlook and to inspire it in others, one has to possess *Chittha suddhi* (purity of heart). Spiritual wisdom can dawn only when there is purity of heart. Just as removal of weeds, tilling the land, sowing the seeds and watering them, are required before the crop can be harvested on a plot of land, the field of the human heart has to be cleared of bad thoughts and bad feelings, watered with love, tilled by spiritual practices and the seeds of the divine Name sown. Only then one is entitled to reap the harvest of *Jnaana* (Divine Wisdom).

Today the spiritual exercises are confined to listening to talks and not to practising the teachings. Listening has become a kind of disease. Merely after listening, men go about bragging that they know everything. This crazy boastfulness is deepening men's ignorance.

One should ruminate over what has been heard. After rumination, one should do *Nidhidhyaasa* (put into practice the lessons). Only then there is the triple purity of thought, word and deed. Today people are content with mere listening to discourses. This will not lead to Realisation.

Srinivasaraghavan referred to the practice of *"Naama Likhitha japam"* (repeated writing of the Lord's Name as a spiritual exercise). This practice promotes harmony in thought, word and deed (first thinking about ﹣the Name of the Lord, then uttering it and then writing it). All these three processes should be carried out with a pure heart.

"Sathyam" indicates the true form of man

Total purity is essential for all *Saadhanas* (spiritual disciplines). To achieve this purity one has to understand the difference between *Shreyas* (spiritual well-being) and *Preyas* (mundane happiness). True humanness consists in knowing the nature of the *Aathma* (the Indwelling Spirit). *Vaak* (speech), *Manas* (the mind) and *Praana* (the life-force) together constitute the *Aathma*. The three syllables contained in the Sanskrith word *Sathyam* indicate the true form of man. *Sath* represents food, *ee* represents water and *Yam* represents *Surya* (the Sun). The implied meaning of the term is that the Sun provides the water which helps man to grow food. When *Sathya* is interpreted in the reverse order, it means that the Reality is realised by the penance and control of the senses (*Sath* for Reality, *Tha* for *Tapas*—penance, and *Ya* for *Yama* and other forms of control over the senses).

Control of the senses and the desires arising from them is almost impossible. What can be done, however, is to turn all the desires towards the Divine. This will be rendered possible when one realises that all the sense organs—the eyes, the ears, the nose and the tongue— derive their functional capacities from the *Aathma* (Indwelling Spirit). It is the *Chaithanya* (the *aathmik* consciousness) that animates the sense organs and enables the eyes to see, the ears to hear and the tongue to taste. The role of consciousness is like that of the current, which enables a bulb to shed light. It is because this *Aathmik* consciousness is present in all beings, it has been described as *Brahman*.

Human body is an instrument to realise the Divine

Caught up in worldly desires, man does not realise his Divine nature. He identifies himself with the body, not realising that it is temporary and perishable. The human body is nothing but an instrument for realising one's inherent Divinity. Man tries to know all about the universe but makes no attempt to know who he is. Man is leading an artificial life because of his ignorance of his reality. Man's foremost endeavour must be to realise his divine nature. He is not a mere human being. He is truly Divine and has to realise this basic truth.

Man has to realise that all the limbs in his body function because of the divine power animating them. Too much importance should not be attached to these limbs intrinsically. Are not blind persons able to live without eyes? Are not deaf and dumb persons able to get on without the powers of hearing or speech? What matters is how these organs are used.

The saint Suurdhas wails in a soul-stirring song, 'Oh Lord! Inspite of being endowed with eyes, people are not able to see your beauty. Inspite of having ears they don't hear your melodious voice." Men hear only useless gossip. They do not listen to auspicious and sacred things. Having eyes, they look upon people with hatred and jealousy.

Monkeys, donkeys, dogs and pigs also have the same power of sight as humans. What is the difference between these animals and human beings? Animals eat, sleep and procreate. If men are also doing these things, what is the difference between them and human beings? Animals love their young ones, but that love is temporary but human love can last one's entire life.

How can one sanctify the body?

Man has to understand what it is without which he cannot exist. He can get on without eyes or ears or other organs, but not without *Praana* or *Aathma* (life). This is called *Praana prathishttha* (the installation of the divine Life-Force in man). In the mirror of the human body, the image of the Divine is reflected. Man foolishly considers the mirror as the *Chaithanya* (Reality). It is this consciousness that accounts for all that one is able to do and not the physical body.

How, then, is this body to be sanctified? By involving the body in actions related to the *Aathmik* consciousness. This lesson was taught to Vibheeshana by Hanumaan. Hanumaan told him that by mere repetition of Rama's name, the vision of Raama cannot be experienced. Only by dedicating himself to the service of Raama, together with chanting His name, can he (Vibheeshana) experience *Saayujyam* (oneness) with Raama.

Of what avail is it to recite all the 700 *shlokas* of the Geetha, if one does not practise even a single teaching of the Geetha? *"Adhveshtaa Sarva bhuuthaanam"* (Do not bear ill-will towards any living being), proclaims the Geetha. This is the primary injunction of the *Geetha* to mankind. This is based on the dictum that one *Aathma* (Divine) dwells in all beings as the *Antharaathma*

(Indweller). What use is there in reciting the Geetha if one has hatred towards others? You worship the Divine and hate the Divine in others. Your worship and your hatred cancel each other out and nothing remains to your credit.

Follow Lord Raama's injunctions

The Raamaayana is regularly read and Raama is worshipped by the vast majority of the people in Bhaarath. There is a Raama temple in every village. But how many are living up to Raama's commands? Raama chose to go to the forest to comply with His father's promise. How many today obey their fathers' injunctions? Raama sacrificed the Kingdom and all comforts for the sake of upholding Truth. He said his sole aim was to promote the people's welfare. He sought to serve the people in whom he saw the image of God.

No penance, no pilgrimages to sacred rivers,
No study of scriptures nor the recitation
Of the Lord's name will be of any use
For crossing the ocean of Samsaara
Without service to sajjana.

Sajjanam refers to those in whom *Sath*, the *Aathma*, dwells. As the *Aathma* dwells in all beings, *Sajjnana* refers to one and all. When you serve *Sath*, which is the Reality in every being, you get the Awareness of *Chith* (Consciousness). With this Awareness, the heart is filled with *Aanandha* (Bliss).

Annamaachaarya hailed the feet of the Lord as those which had been washed by Brahma himself which are of *Brahman* Itself, which bear the burdens of the entire universe, and the burden of all human bodies. How is this done. The Divine is *Puurna-Svaruupa* (All-encompassing form). Just as the feet of the individual bear the burden of the human body, the subtle body of the Divine bears on its feet the entire universe. Without the feet the body cannot move.

Significance of greatness conferred on Lord's feet

Recognizing that the macrocosm and microcosm are constituted by the same five basic elements, man should realise that the Divine is present in everything. Hence, man should chant the name of the Lord from the core of his heart and take refuge in the feet of the Lord. Annamaachaarya declared "Oh mind! Take refuge in the lotus feet of the Lord. They will relieve you of all your miseries and lead you to the Divine."

When Bharatha enthroned the *Paadhukas* (sandals) of Raama, Ayodhya was really protected by Raama's sandals. Bhadhraachala Raamadhas also sang in the same strain. "Oh Raama! I am holding on to your feet. I will not let you move even one step until you assure me your protection."

Thyaagaraaja, in a similar vein, declared that he would not allow himself to be tempted by the treasures offered by the Raaja of Tanjaavur and he preferred the lotus feet of Shri Raama to all the wealth of the world.

"Feet" do not mean sandals made in silver or gold. Feet refers to the Divine that sustains everything. Why is such greatness conferred on the feet? Viewing the matter from the point of view of science, it will be noted that blood flows from the feet upwards to all parts of the body. It is this blood which sustains the entire body. The feet that bear the burden of the entire body are essential for life itself. When you seek refuge in the Lord's feet, you can secure a vision of the Divine form.

Yashodha catches Krishna through His footprints

Here is a small example from the early life of Lord Krishna in Gokulam to show what the Lord's feet mean. Krishna was known as one who used to steal butter from all houses and feed his friends and playmates too. As there were a lot of complaints about this naughty child, Krishna's mother Yashodha caught hold of him one day as he was running away and asked him: "Why are you stealing butter from other houses while I offer you so much at home? Your mouth always smells of butter. Give up this habit. Otherwise, I will tie you to a mortar to restrict your movement. How do you do such things, being so small a child?" He smiled and ran away. Yashodha went from house to house in search of Krishna. He played a small trick. Yashodha could not move fast as she had a heavy body. She was in a fix how to trace him.

Krishna dipped his feet in milk in a house and ran from there, leaving behind the trail of his footprints caused by the milk. It was only with the help of Krishna's own footprints that she was able to catch him. In fact, because she was so eager to get at him, Krishna himself helped her to trace him. Yashodha was able to catch the Lord only through footprints of HIS Feet.

The Lord's feet are glorious in many ways. But they will confer blessings only if they are sought with real faith. The Lord's feet contain the Divine insignia of *Shankha* (Conch) and *Chakra* (Discus). *Shankha* symbolises *Shabdha Brahman* (the Cosmic

Divine sound). The discus represents the Wheel of Time. The Sound and Time together represent the different cosmic aspects of the Lord. The entire universe originated from sound vibrations. These vibrations are related to Time. Sound and Time are inseparable and interdependent.

It is a common practice among rural folk to advise anyone who has committed a wrong to hold the feet of the person whom he has wronged. Once a man holds the other's feet, it means that he has sought and secured the latter's forgiveness. Nowadays, with all the Courts and legal processes, no one attempts to hold the feet of anyone. In the old days in the villages, if a man fell at the feet of another, the latter had no options but to forgive the supplicant.

Seeking the Lord's feet is seeking forgiveness

The inner meaning of seeking the Lord's feet is that thereby the Lord will forgive the sins of the penitent. But mere holding of the feet is not enough. One must be genuinely repentant and declare that he will not commit similar offences again. Only then he will secure atonement.

Embodiments of the Divine Aathma! Different persons pursue different kinds of *Saadhana*. To realise the benefits of this *Saadhana,* they go to *Aashrams*. They adore elders and offer worship to them. As long as egoism remains in them, all these exercises are of no avail. Your egoism may even lead to your expulsion from the *Aashram*. Hence suppress the ego, bury the sense of possessiveness and develop attachment to the *Aathma* to realise your true humanness. Envy, hatred and anger are causing havoc among men. Even residents of the *Aashram* are filled with anger. Anger has been described as incense offered to sin. Therefore while you are worshipping the Lotus feet or writing the Lord's name, you have to get rid of these three evil traits.

Destroy the ego, do your duty and help mutually

At the outset, the ego has to be destroyed. Then anger will subside. Do your duty. Do not project your ego. Develop mutual helpfulness. Carry on your work with joy. Be friendly towards each other. It is only when you behave in this manner that you will realise the benefits of *Likhitha Japam* and worship of the *Paadhukas* (Lord's Sandals).

In the Sai organizations, the primary requisite is unity and mutual trust. Only with unity can you promote the well-being of the world. If there is discord within the organization, how can you serve others? Make forbearance your ornament. Through love, eliminate your bad traits. Leading members of the Sai organization, who undertake sacred activities such as *Naama Likhitha Japam* and *Paadhuka Seva* should develop sacred qualities.

In Tamil Nadu, in numerous villages devotees are engaged in *Naama Likhitha Japa* and offering worship to *Paadhukas.* Together with these they should also purify their hearts. Today in many parts of the world Nature is causing various disasters such as earthquakes, famines, floods and volcanic eruptions. What is the reason? The spiritual lapses of man account for these calamities. Disturbances in the heart (human heart) are reflected in earthquakes. Fill your minds with good thoughts and engage yourselves in good actions. Chant the Lord's name. When the ether is surcharged with the vibrations of the Divine name, the entire environment gets purified. Those who breathe this sanctified air will have pure thoughts. Purify the atmosphere, wh. h is now polluted.

Discourse in the Puurnachandhra Auditorium on 7-10-1993, the day of Paadhuka Prathishttha.

ॐ ‒‒‒‒‒‒‒‒‒‒‒‒‒‒‒‒‒‒‒‒‒‒‒‒‒‒ ॐ

Man should become the very embodiment of love. When he is filled with love the entire world will be transformed into a love-filled world. As long as he is filled with hate the world will appear as a hate-filled world. It is only when love is developed that the dualism of good and evil can be transcended and the joy of oneness with the Divine experienced.

—BABA

CHAPTER 32

Bhaarath's glorious *Vedhic* heritage

There is no greater eye than knowledge.
There is no greater penance than Truth.
There is no worse misery than greed.
There is no greater happiness than sacrifice.

KNOWLEDGE is the real eye. Truth is real penance. Penance does not consist in forsaking food and drink and roaming in a forest. Seeking the eternal Truth is real penance. Desire is the main cause of grief. Desire will go on multiplying. As and when one is fulfilled, it gives rise to another and this goes on endlessly. True Bliss consists in controlling desires. Sacrifice gives the greatest and lasting happiness. That is why the *Vedhas* have declared that it is not by work, progeny or wealth, but by sacrifice alone, one can get immortality.

Sacrifice is the life-force of a human being. The *Vedha* teaches *Thyaaga, Yoga* and *Bhoga* (sacrifice, spiritual practice and material pleasure). The word *Vedha* itself has many meanings. It means intelligence, knowledge, awareness, etc. To lead a meaningful life man has to follow certain *Niyamas* (regulations of discipline). It is also necessary to know one's own Inner Reality. Mere intelligence and acquisition of knowledge are not enough. Knowledge should foster wisdom leading to awareness. This is what the *Vedha* teaches. The word *Jnaana*, which is translated as wisdom, contains two syllables! *Jna* and *na.* That which is not true at all times—past present and future—cannot be termed *Jnaana.* *Adhvaitha Dharshanam* (Awareness of oneness) is the real *Jnaana.*

The Truth is one, it is infinite and it is *Brahmam.* "*Sathyam, Jnaanam, Anantham, Brahma,*" is the *Upanishathik* declaration.

Vedhas confer security on humanity

The *Vedha* should not be treated as mere *Manthra.* It helps to realise full knowledge and wisdom. The sages in ancient times had the inner vision and experience of the Divine and they gave expression to this revelation through the *Vedhas.* They are applicable to entire humanity for all times. They confer security on humanity and show the way to happiness and peace. The goal of human life is to sacrifice desires and realise the Divine.

Since the *Vedhas* are *Anantham* (infinitely vast), it is difficult to master them within the short life-span of human life. That is why Vedha Vyaasa divided them into four sections. He compiled the *Riks* into one part and called them *Rik Samhitha.* He put all the *Yajus* together and named the collection as *Yajus Samhitha.* All the *Saama* hymns were presented in the *Saama Samhitha.* Other *manthras* were complied in a fourth section termed *Atharvana Samhitha.* The *Yajus Samhitha* was further divided into *Shukla Yajur* and *Krishna Yajur Vedha,* bringing the actual number of *Vedha samhithas* to five.

The division of *Vedha Samhithas*

Each *Samhitha* was further divided into three parts, namely, *Brahmana, Aaranyaka* and *Upanishath.* The first part is full of *manthras* for rituals, and for doing acts of charity and other sastraic rites. *Manthra* has Life-Force in it and, when properly interpreted, every *manthra* is related to Divinity. The second part, *Aaranyaka,* relates to the chanting of *manthra* during *Vanaprasthaashrama,* when one finishes his *Grihastha-ashrama* (family life) and retires to the forest to lead a life of austerity.

The chanting of *manthras* should always be synchronised with practising of the prescribed *Karma.* By such practice one can realise the Divine. By merely listening to *manthras* and failing to practise, one can never get happiness or peace. In order to realise the Divine, you have to practise the precepts prescribed in the *Vedhas.* No doubt, even listening to the recitation of the *Vedhas* is itself capable of purifying your mind. It is *Shabdha Brahman.* Sound is the first attribute of God. *Vedha Shabdha* is all-pervasive.

Today a great deal of wickedness, troubles and turmoils are prevalent in the world because of the decline of the influence of the *Vedhas.* Water, air, food, noise are all tainted by pollution. We are forced to lead a polluted life. When the air we breathe is itself polluted, how are we to lead a pollution-free life? The environment and the elements should be pure to ensure purity of heart. The cause of this pollution lies nowhere else except in our own actions. Whatever words we utter, they spread to the entire atmosphere. We can purify the atmosphere of the world by chanting the *Vedhas* and singing the glory of God.

Cherish the *Vedhas* for sublimating your lives

The *Rishis* in ancient times used to move to forests and chant the powerful *Vedhic Manthras* to purify the atmosphere of the whole world. These *Vedhas* are neglected today. The people of this great country of Bhaarath have not understood the infinite potency of the *Vedhas*. It is a pity they have not tasted the sweetness of the *Vedhas*. The *Vedhas* should be cherished for sublimating life and not to earn a living.

The *Upanishaths*, which are termed as *Vedhaantha* or the concluding part of the *Vedhas*, detail the method of achieving the *Purushaarthas* (four fold goal of life), namely *Dharma, Artha, Kaama* and *Moksha*. These can be achieved by one's own efforts through *Vidhya* (acquisition of right knowledge), which is of two types— one is *Para Vidhya* (the Higher Knowledge) and the other *Apara Vidhya* (lower knowledge). *Para Vidhya* shows the way to *Moksha* (Liberation), while *Apara Vidhya* deals with worldly pursuits, which cause bondage.

For acquiring spiritual wisdom this worldly education is not necessary. *Sathyadhrishti* (the vision of Truth) is the only requisite for spiritual pursuits. Since

ancient times Bhaaratheeyas have taken to spiritual
pursuits as their goal in life.

Nine different appellations for the *Vedhas*

There are nine different appellations for the *Vedhas*.
They are: *Shruthi, Anusmara, Thrayee, Aamnaaya, Samaamnaaya, Chandhas, Svaadhyaaya, Nigama* and *Aagama*.

Shruthi: The *Vedhas* were taught by teacher to
disciple by oral recitation, adhering to the right *swara*
and tune. There were no gadgets such as tape recorders
or gramophone records in those ancient times. The
students used to learn the text only by constant
repetition with intense devotion day and night and get
manthras by heart. Even if the words are missed the
svara or tune of the chanting should be without the
slightest blemish, since *svara* is its basis. Hence it is
called *Shruthi* (that which is learnt by hearing).

Anusmara: Since the *Vedhas* were leant by memorising and constant chanting, they got the name of
Anusmara.

Thrayee: Originally there were only three *Vedhas*—
Rig, Yajur and *Saama,* which formed the basis of all
rituals, the *manthras* for *Yajna* and musical notes. Hence
they were termed as *Thrayee* (the three).

Aamnaaya: It means practice. The practice of
chanting and memorising was followed even in the
dream state and deep sleep state, apart from the waking
state. So it is called *Aamnaaya.*

Samaamnaaya: As the *Vedha* is preserved in the
heart of the students it is called *Samaamnaaya.*

Chandhas: The *Saama Vedha* lays down the basic
meter for the *Vedhic manthras,* meter which is *Chandhas.*
Hence the *Vedhas* are termed as *Chandhas.*

Svaadhyaaya: The *Vedhas* were learnt by son from father or disciple from teacher. Thus it was passed on from generation to generation, from grandfather to grandson. Since it is preserved only by constant self-study and practice after learning, it is called *Svaadhyaaya.*

Nigama **and** *Aagama:* As the study of the *Vedhas* is related to inhalation and exhalation, it is called *Nigama* and *Aagama.* For example, when one inhales the air the sound is "So..." While exhaling, the sound is "Ham..." With every breath this *Soham* meaning "I am He," is being repeated. This goes on 21,600 times per day. This is verily the practice of the *Mahaavaakyas* of the *Vedha*, "You are That"—*"Thath Thvam Asi."* This goes on all through life by every human being in the breathing process. When breathing stops life will be extinct.

Transcend body consciousness to realise Inner Self

Many sages and saints did penance for realising Divinity. They said, *"Vedaahametham Purusham Mahaantham"* (We have seen God Almighty). Where did they see Him? *"Aadhithya Varnam Thamasaah-Parasthaath"* (We have seen God beyond the darkness of ignorance). This darkness is the identification of oneself with the body and attachment to the senses. To realise the Inner Self, you have to transcend the body consciousness and attachment to sensual desires.

Vedha teaches many things with emphasis on unity and purity. Some say that the *Vedha* discriminates between people, declaring only some that are qualified to chant the *Vedha.* This is totally wrong. In the *Shanthi Shloka,* the *Vedha* says, *"Sahanaa Vavathu; Sahanau*

Bhunakthu Sahaveeryam karavaa Vahai, Thejasvinaavad-heethamasthu; Maa Vidhvishaavahai." What is the meaning of this? "Let us grow together; let us live together, let us study together, let us develop knowledge together, without conflict, with friendship, with broad-mindedness." While this is the teaching of the *Vedha* how can any one say that it discriminates against some? The *Vedha* teaches a subtle form of equality and equanimity.

Only a fraction of the *Vedhas* remains now

Each *Vedha* has many branches. The *Rig Vedha* has 28 branches, of which 26 have faded out of memory and only two remain now. The *Yajur Vedha* had 17 branches out of which only two are in vogue, while the *Saama Vedha* had 1000 branches of which 998 are lost. Even with this fraction of the original *Vedhas* existing now, the world is progressing at least to the present extent. Imagine how powerful this planet would have been if all the branches of the *Vedhas* were in vogue now!

This sacred land of Bhaarath, which was reputed to be the *Thyaaga Bhuumi* (land of Sacrifice) and *Yoga Bhuumi* (land of Spiritual communion), has now become a *Roga Bhuumi* (land of diseases). The reason is people are turning to *Bhoga* (worldly pleasure) forgetting *Yoga* and *Thyaaga*. People should learn to live in *Yoga*.

The *Vedhic* injunctions have infinite meaning. All may not be able to comprehend the inner meaning of the teachings. The truth that the earth has a gravitational force was there since the world was created. But it was discovered only by Newton after some experiments. Similarly, the truth hidden in the *Vedhas* was perceived by the *Rishis* after intensive penance and *Saadhana*. They have given to mankind the Eternal truth which was revealed to them. The vibrations of their spiritual *Saadhana* have spread throughout the Universe. They are not limited to Bhaarath or any particular place.

This can be practised anywhere in the world, whether in America or Australia. This is *Sathya Svaruupa* (Embodiment of Truth). It cannot change according to time or place. It is beyond time and space; that is why it is called the Transcendental Reality. Some people think lightly of the *Vedhas* and even make fun of them.

Learning the *Vedhas* give immense benefits

Embodiments of love! Even if you cannot chant the *Vedhas*, if only you listen to the sounds with devotion they will elevate you to a higher level. Though the child does not know the meaning of the lullaby sung by its mother, it is induced to sleep hearing the tune. Similarly, listening to the chanting of the *Vedha* with undivided attention will give you immense benefit. If you ruminate over it and practise it in your life, you can imagine the magnitude of the bliss you will attain. The hymns of the *Vedhas* constitute *NaadhaBrahman* (God in the form of sound), which is highly potent. Devotees who go to a temple ring the bell. The general belief is that it is intended to attract the attention of the Deity. Does it mean that God is asleep and you have to awaken Him by ringing the bell? God is always awake and is listening to the prayers of everyone. It is just like a visiting card which you present to any important person whom you want to meet any favour or help.

Ringing the bell is only to draw the attention of the Lord towards you. The sound of the *Vedha* is also like ringing the temple bell.

Omkaara is the correct address of the Lord

Sound emanates from the Primordial *Pranava,* which consists of the three syllables A, U And M. The correct address of the Lord is *Omkaaram.* The sound of the bell and the sound of the *Vedhas* also radiate *Omkaara naadha.* The uttering of *Omkaara* should be done in a sweet and smoothly progressive way starting with the sound of "A" which should come from the navel, and then the sound "U" from the throat, and finally conclude with "M" from the lips. It should resemble the sound of an aeroplane when it is far off, gradually increasing in volume as it approaches the aerodrome and finally subsiding after landing. (Svaami demonstrated the correct way of chanting the *Omkaara).* The *Vedha* teaches this very clearly.

The *Vedhas* lift the individual to higher levels. People are not realising this truth. Many *Vedhic* scholars send their wards to convent schools and seek to impart to them a secular education without caring to pass on to them the sacred legacy of the *Vedhas,* which will protect them. Because of lack of encouragement and proper propagation and promotion, knowledge of the *Vedhas* is declining day by day in this great country, which is the home of this sacred treasure.

Svaami expects the people to foster the *Vedhas* and is showing the way by making all the thousands of students of the Sai educational institutions, right from the primary school, to learn *Vedha* chanting. You have watched the children of the primary school, ranging from 5 to 8 years, chanting the *Vedhas* at the commencement of this meeting. There is actually no compulsion to learn the *Vedhas*. All the students willingly come forward on their own to learn *Vedha* chanting. There are *Vedha paathashaalas* (*Vedhic* schools) elsewhere where they impart this teaching, but the students discontinue the chanting later on. You should make the children learn the *Vedhas* with enthusiasm, without compulsion. They should be made to realise the greatness of the *Vedhas* by sweet persuasion.

The *Vedhas* have protected our country from ancient times. Since the Government has not cared to realise the beneficial influence of the *Vedhas* in contributing to the welfare of the nation, the country is facing a lot of troubles. The propagation of *Vedhas* should be taken up by the people.

The essence of the *Upanishaths* is given in the *Bhagavath Geetha* and the *Brahmasuuthra*. Several saints have related stories to explain clearly the import of the *Upanishathic* truths. The *Eeshavaasyopanishath* is the first among the *Upanishaths.* It declares that God pervades the whole universe. Because people have neglected the study of Sanskrith they are unable to enjoy the treasures of knowledge contained in the *Upanishaths.*

Inaugural Discourse in the Puurna Chandhra Auditorium on 18-10-1993 at the Vedha Purusha Sapthaaha Jnaana Yajna which was revived after three years.

CHAPTER 33

The message of the Upanishaths

The Dashara celebrations in October, during which
Bhagavaan revived the Vedha Purusha Sapthaaha
Jnaana Yajna after a break of three years were
made immensely significant for spiritual aspirants
as well as Sai devotees in general by the series
of discourses on the Upanishaths which He gave
for seven days at the Puurnachandhra Auditorium.
The discourses from 19-10-1993 to 23-10-1993
are given below in a condensed form.

ONE may study all the scriptures, perform all types
of sacrifices, go on extensive pilgrimages, master
the eight types of knowledge, but it is not easy to
control the senses and the mind, direct one's vision
inward and maintain equanimity of temper. In ancient
times, the sages and seers maintained purity in

thought, truth in words and righteousness in deeds. But in this *Kali* Age to-day, people have forgotten human values and exhibit animal qualities such as lust, anger, greed and hatred. Purity of heart and selflessness are the hall-marks of the human life which one gets after passing through several births. Foolishness, pride, covetousness and other such qualities are a hang-over from their previous lives as sheep, buffalo or cat. One who is in the habit of attacking and harming others out of hatred reveals the tendencies in his previous birth as a dog. One who lacks steadiness of mind and constantly jumps from one thing to another, reflects the quality of the monkey from which he has evolved. It is to get rid of such bad qualities that *Yajnas* (Sacrifices) are undertaken.

Mind is the altar of the *Yajna*

In *Thretha Yuga*, Vishvaamithra took the help of Raama to ensure the conduct of the *Yajna* without hindrance from the demonic forces. His *Aashram* was called *Siddhaashrama*. Actually the heart of every human being is a *Siddhaashrama*. The moment evil thoughts or bad feelings arise in man, that is the beginning of all sins. When the heart is polluted with such sinful thoughts, one should seek the help of *Aathma Raama*, just as Vishvaamithra sought the help of Raama to put an end to the ogress Thaataki. If you think of God and pray to Him with sincere devotion, every deed done by you will be a *Yajna*. The mind is the altar of this *Yajna*. You must offer all the evil qualities at the altar of the mind. That is the ideal internal *Yajna* to be performed by every person as distinct from the external *Yajna* done ritualistically.

The Raamaayana as allegory

The allegorical meaning of the Raamayana story should be properly understood. Raama stands for *Yajur Vedha,* as he was the embodiment of *Dharma.* Lakshmana esteemed Raama's words as law and followed him. He was always chanting the name of Raama. He represents *Rig Vedha.* Bharatha represents *Saama Vedha,* as he was always singing the glory of Raama. Shathrughna represents *Atharva Vedha.* Thus the four sons of Emperor Dhasharatha of Ayodhya represent the four *Vedhas.* Dhasharatha's capital, Ayodhya, symbolises a place where no enemy can enter. Dhasharatha symbolises the *karmendhriyas* (five organs of action) and the *Jnaanendhriyas* (five organs of cognition). The three queens of Dhasharatha—Kaushalya, Sumithra and Kaikeyi—represent the *Saathvik, Raajasik* and *Thaamasik Gunas* (qualities of Goodness, Passion and Inertia). If the inner significance of the Raamayana is properly understood, it will serve as a manual of ideal living for all mankind.

If the principle underlying the *Yajna* is understood, it will be realised that the Divinity pervading everywhere is within you too. *"Antharbahischa thath sarvam vyaapya Naaraayanasthithah."* Through the conduct of a *Yajna* one can understand the immutable permanent Reality in a fast-changing world.

Fire has an important role in the *Yajna.* Fire for the *Yajna* is created by churning two wooden sticks placed together. The top stick is the mother and the bottom piece is the father of *Agni* (Fire). Immediately after birth, *Agni* devours both father and mother. Fire is the presiding priest or *Brahma* (for the *Yajna*). He takes the offerings and acts as a courier to convey them to the

Gods. *Yajna* has, moreover, many significant inner meanings. Those who do not know them make fun of it or deride it.

Since people have forgotten the real significance of such holy rituals performed for promoting the welfare of mankind, humanity is suffering from all sorts of tribulations and miseries. In the ethical, physical, scientific and all other fields today man has given up his *Svabhaava* (true nature) and is keen only to earn *Prabhaava* (fame). Fame is like passing cloud. Today one may be a Prime Minister, full of fame and power. But when he steps down from that post no one will care for him.

Upanishaths proclaim the real nature of man

What is the true nature of man? A term for man in Sanskrith is *Nara*. *Nara* means *Aathma* (the Self). The five elements have come from *Aathma*. They are called *Naaramu*. The term Naaraayana has come from this. *Nara* does not refer to the physical form of a human being. He is the *Aathma* and should behave in keeping with his reality. A man without human qualities is like a flower without smell, a fruit without juice and a cow that cannot give milk.

The *Upanishaths* explain this truth. They stress the importance of man knowing his own Reality, transcending the body, the senses, the mind and the intellect. They proclaim that the real nature of man is love, compassion and selflessness. But people have forgotten their original nature and are nourishing unnatural qualities. How can *Dharma* be sustained in such circumstances? People are mainly engaged in selfish pursuits. They use their sense organs in wrong directions, instead of seeing good, hearing good, speaking good and doing good, which is the godward path. When there is no trace of any good quality in human beings, how can one expect purity of heart?

Power of the Divine

Yajnas with sacrifice as the basis provide the royal road to Self-Realisation as opposed to the perilous path of self-destruction, in which people are engaging themselves now. *Yajnas* are designed to invoke the power of the Divine for the welfare of mankind. Divine power is limitless and beyond the comprehension of the limited intellect of man, who is labouring under the delusion that he is all-powerful and can achieve anything. Even the great saint musician and composer Thyaagaraaja once doubted the power of God when he was subject to great misery and suffering, but recovered his faith immediately after he recollected how, without the power of the Divine, a monkey (Hanumaan) could cross the ocean or Lakshmana do service at Raama's feet or Bharatha worship His sandals or Lakshmi, the Goddess of wealth, serve at His Lotus Feet. He blamed himself for doubting the power of the Lord and regretted the lapse in his devotion.

The significance of the offerings made in the holy fire of a *Yajna* is that whatever is offered is converted into *Amruth* (Divine Ambrosia) and conveyed to the gods. When man sacrifices his bad qualities, he is transformed into the Divine. With this in view, the *Upanishaths* declare: "Lead me from untruth to Truth, from ignorance to Knowledge, from death to Immortality." Thus the *Yajna* helps man to progress to the summit of eternal bliss.

The *Yajna* is not for passing time. The cosmic energy issuing from the *Manthras* will go up in the fire from the *Yajna* hearth and spread all over the world and purify the atmosphere. Some agnostics may criticise this as wasting food, ghee and other valuable articles by throwing them into the fire. This is as foolish as the criticism of an ignorant person that a farmer wastes good quality seeds by casting them on his farm. He does not realise that one small measure of the seed will yield several bags of grain as harvest. The *Yajna* is done not for selfish purposes but for the welfare of the entire world. It reflects the noble ideal of service and sacrifice before self.

Excerpts from Discourse on 19-10-1993.

The quest for happiness

There is no penance other than *Shaanthi* (stillness of the mind). It is the ornament adorned by saints and it is what every one yearns for in his heart. Saint Thyaagaraaja sang that there is no comfort or happiness without peace—*"Saaanthamu leka soukhyamu ledhu."*

Sukham (the state of enjoyment of happniess) is like heaven. The pleasures derived by the senses from worldly objects are transient, while real happiness lies in experiencing the bliss from the Inner Self. People are unhappy because of *Thrishna,* or the insatiable thirst for worldly pleasures. Desires are always multiplying endlessly. The only way to overcome misery or grief is to put a curb on desires.

Dhaya (compassion) is inherent in every human being. But few are prepared to share this with their fellow-beings. Man is deluded by the trivial pleasures from mundane things and is filled with greed and lust. This is the main obstacle in the spiritual path.

Basis of *adhvaithik* principle is *Ekaathma bhaava*

The *Vedhas* deal with rituals and worship, which imply a dualism between the worshipper and the object worshipped. *Vedhaantha* spells out the principle of *Adhvaitha* (non-duality). It is interpreted in different ways, but the real basis of the *Adhvaithik* principle is *Ekaathma bhaava,* that is the feeling that there is only one *Aathma* pervading everywhere and none else. *"Adhvaitha Dharshanam Jnaanam"* (Wisdom lies in the perception of oneness). The *Upanishaths* preach this oneness, based on the concept of unity in diversity. *Upa* means "near," *ni* represents *"nishtha"* and *shath* means "sit". *Upanishath* means that one should sit near the preceptor to acquire the Supreme Spiritual Wisdom.

The *Upanishaths* originated during different periods of time. That is why we find that the teachings of the different *Upanishaths* are not based on the circumstances obtaining at one particular time, but they are applicable universally at all times as they teach only what is vital for the welfare of humanity.

"Eeshaavaasyam Idham Sarvam" says the *Eeshopanishath.* There is no place in the universe where God is not present. Just as air is everywhere even though we cannot see it with our eyes, Divinity is all-pervasive. But for this Divinity, the Sun and the Moon cannot shine, rivers will not flow, crops will not grow. The Divine governs the whole universe. All things in creation are for the use of the entire world. No one can claim exclusive right over these gifts of Nature.

The *Eeshaavaasya Upanishath* teaches man how to combine *Bhoga* with *Thyaaga* (enjoy the world with an attitude of sacrifice). One imbued with the feelings of *Thyaaga* (sacrifice) will not revel in mundane pleasures. Sacrifice and sensual pleasures cannot co-exist just as water and fire cannot co-exist. What, then, is the inner significance of this directive that man should enjoy *Bhoga* (pleasurable experiences) with *Thyaaga* (renunciation)?

It means that though one is not interested in mundane things, he has to do his duty. He cannot escape doing *karma*. He should shed his ego while doing his work and should not consider himself as the doer. He should do his duty without any desire for the fruits thereof. Because man is filled with ego and is not interested in experiencing the real bliss, he suffers from *Roga* (disease). When work is done with a selfless attitude there is no difference between *bhoga* and *thyaaga*. We find today in the world only *rogis* (persons afflicted with disease) and not *bhogis* or *thyaagis*. You should give up attachment to worldly things and direct your attachment to the Divine only. Sage Yaajnavalkya taught his wife Maithreyi this principle of oneness. The same *Parabrahman* (Supreme Self) is present in everyone in the form of Awareness.

Desireless action leads you away from misery

The *Eeshaavaasya Upanishath* teaches that this *Sathyam* (Truth) is changeless. It is the basis of the *Sanathana Dharma* that has been followed in Bhaarath. Man cannot live without *Karma* (action). But he should do it without the feeling of ego and desire for reward. When the seed is sown, the tree will grow and yield fruit wheth-

er you like it or not. The desire for fruit is the cause
of misery. The *Upanishaths* teach the way of getting
rid of the ego.

Prakrithi is like a mirror which reflects whatever
object is placed before it. When you look into the mirror
there are three entities—yourself, the mirror and the
reflection. But if you remove the mirror, there is only
one left and that is 'you.' The reflection is gone. Because
of worldly feelings, you look at the reflection. Remove
the worldly feelings, you see your Inner Self which
is the Reality. When you get rid of the feelings of I
and Mine everything becomes one.

The *Upanishaths* taught the difference between
pleasure and pain. If you shed your ego and experience
Divinity you will get rid of your pain and enjoy lasting
bliss. The *Upanishaths* teach through stories the subtlest
truths. You should understand their inner significance
and taste the nectarine sweetness. This is possible only
when there is *Bhaava-Shuddhi* (inner purity). Purity of
heart leads to *Siddhi*—Self realisation.

Qualities that are Nature's gift to man

It is unnatural for man to behave like animals with
selfishness, anger and jealousy. A compassionate heart
is Nature's gift to man. It is a pity that man does not
make any effort to realise that the Divine is closer to
him than his own parents. One should search within,
and not in the external, for God.

Love, Compassion, Self-Confidence and Sacrifice
are the real human qualities. You are *Amrithaputhra*
(Son of Immortality). Purity in thought, word and
deed is a basic requisite for man. Under any circumstances, man should not allow this threefold purity

to be affected. Patience is another ideal quality one should develop. Whatever troubles or obstacles one may meet with while doing his proper duty, he should bear with them. One should not get depressed when others blame or abuse him but should stick to the path of truth. The third quality is perseverance which is indeed a prime need for any one in any field but more so in the spiritual path.

Once you have taken up a vow to do a good thing, you should not go back on it under any circumstance. You should fulfill it even at the cost of your life. This is the hallmark of a true devotee. In ancient times, people had this determination and became good souls. The Paandavas had to spend their lives in forests feeding on leaves and fruits. Still they never gave up their adherence to the plighted word. In the *Kali Yuga* devotees have to face a lot of trials and challenges, but they should not waver even a wee bit in their devotion to God.

Just as gold has to be heated, hammered and subjected to many processes before it can be made into a jewel, devotees have to pass through ordeals ordained by the Divine.

The divinity in man

With *Premabhaava* (feeling of pure love) you can realise your oneness with the world. Every object has five attributes, namely *Asthi, Bhaathi, Priyam,* Name and Form. The first three—Existence, Cognisability and Uitlity—are permanent and changeless, while Name and Form are subject to change. Human beings with different names and forms are just like waves on the ocean of *Sath-chith-aanandha.* They are also the same *Sath-chith-aanandha*. The essence is the same in all names and forms. The realisation of this truth is spirituality. This is the message of the Upanishaths. It does not matter if you cannot understand every word of the Upanishaths. It is enough if you realise the truth that you are embodiments of the Divine.

When you get some troubles, you cry in a state of despair and even blame God. There is no need for you to feel aggrieved at all. All troubles are passing clouds. The clouds cannot hide for long the effulgence of the Sun which is permanent. Similarly the *Aathma* cannot be affected by anything. If you identify yourself with this Reality you will have no cause for grief at all as you will be embodiments of bliss.

Excerpts from Discourse on 20-10-1993.

Descent of the Divine

The same Supreme Being who saved Prahlaadha by appearing from the pillar and punishing his demonic father, the same Supreme Being who came to the rescue of Kuchela, the same Being who descended from Vaikuntha to save Gajendhra, the Lord of the elephants, has now come to the world as *Sath-chith-aanandhamurthi*, presiding over the hearts of all as *Puttaparthi Chakravarthi*.

You should realise that I have come to remind you of your Reality, that in fact, everyone of you is an embodiment of *Sath-chith-aanandha*.

Excerpts from Discourse on 21-10-1993.

Unity in diversity

Though the *Upanishaths* are termed as *Vedhaantha* (the end of the *Vedhas)* they are actually the *Siras* (head) of the *Vedhas.* The *Eeshaavaasya Upanishath* emphasises that man is bound by action and purity of heart is the basis for right action—"*Chitthasya Shuddhyaye Dharmah."* Right action has to be done for achieving purity of heart. When you get rid of bad feelings, evil thoughts and evil deeds, you can experience your Inner Self.

As long as one is puffed up with the pride of education, wealth, status and position one cannot comprehend the *Aathma.* You must turn your mind away from all these transient mundane pursuits and redirect it towards the Inner Self to realise the *Aathmabhaava,* which is eternal and changeless. This is the basis for all the changing phenomena of the mundane world. (At this stage, Bhagavaan materialised a gold chain by a wave of His hand and went on to explain that the basis for all gold jewellery is gold). The gold chain can be melted and turned into solid gold from which other ornaments can be made bearing different names and forms. Similarly, the basis for all the different forms and names of beings in the world is Divine.

The *Eeshaavaasya Upanishath* stresses the unity in diversity. It teaches that the mind and the body will change but the *Aathma* is the unifying, changeless and permanent entity. Man, in his ignorance, considers all changing objects as true and does not look into the common basis which is changeless.

Excerpts from Discourse on 22-10-1993.

Man and the Divine

The *Vedhic* invocation says "*Puurnamadhah Puurnamidham,*" meaning "That is whole and this is whole." This implies that Divinity and humanity are not different. The same constituents are there in both. In fact there is only one Supreme Power which manifests itself in multitudes of forms.

If you take the *Gaayathri Manthra*, it starts with "*Bhur Bhuvah Suvah,*" in which *Bhur* is the *Bhuuloka* (this world where we live), *Buhvah* is the other world and *Suvah* is the world of Radiation. All the worlds are within every human being. Man is an embodiment of the three phases of time (past, present and future) and the three powers of creation, preservation and dissolution. He is thus the embodiment of the *Prajna* (principle of the Supreme Consciousness).

The five vital airs, *Praana, Apaana, Udaana, Samaana* and *Vyaana* are the constituent elements of *Naadha* (the primordial sound). *Bindhu* represents steadiness of our body, mind and intellect. *Kala* represents the *Aathma*. The *Eeshaavaasya Upanishath* deals with the different aspects of *Naadha, Bindhu* and *Kala*. It says that these three are like a triangle with the Self as the apex and the body and mind as the two points at the base. The body is gross, while the Self is subtle and the mind is a combination of the two. Just as *Naadha, Bindhu* and *Kala* are everywhere, the mind is also all-pervasive as stated in the *Eeshaavaasya Upanishath*. The mind is the cause of pain and pleasure, happiness and misery, bondage and liberation. It should be properly directed towards *Prajna* (Awareness). The body is inert matter and cannot function without the *Prajna* principle, which is radiation. *Praana* (vibration) animates the whole body. All the three are constituents of *Sath-Chith-Aanandha*. Man experiences *Aanandha* in the deep sleep state—*Swapna-Avastha* and perceives worldly things in the waking state—*Jaagratha-Avastha*.

The body houses the immovable *Aathma*

The *Upanishaths* point out that there are three entities: the *Kshara*, *Akshara* and *Kshraakshrara* (Immovable, movable and movable-immovable). The movable body houses the immovable *Aathma*. One who understands this principle of *Akshara* will have nothing to do with the world. The body is given only for knowing the *Aathma* principle, but man is using it for other purposes and thus abusing it.

The human body consists of eyes, ears, nose, tongue, etc. These are but instruments that help one to make the journey of life. There are three elements in all actions: the *Kartha* (doer), *Karma* (action) and the *Kaarana* (purpose of the action). The *Upanishaths* declare that if all the three are in harmony one will achieve success. All the limbs and sense organs in a man can function only when the life force is there. That is *Chaithanya Shakthi*. It comes from the Self, which is *Prajna, Aathma Shakthi* or Radiation. Even scientists are aware that matter cannot move on its own without energy. But they are not able to recognise the *Aathmashakthi* which was recognised by the ancient *Rishis*. The moment one becomes aware of this truth he can be considered to be free from the bondage of the phenomenal world.

Socrates told his disciples that the Universe is governed by truth, goodness and beauty. These are the same as *Sathyam, Shivam Sundaram*, the terms used by the *Bhaaratheeyas* to describe Divinity from time immemorial. The truth that transcends the categories of time is the Real Truth. Man is an embodiment of this Truth. But people have forgotten this today. People relish only untruth. Truth is not palatable to them, while untruth seems sweet, though it is poisonous. "Speak the truth, do righteous acts" is the motto of Bhaarath, as declared in the *Vedhas*. But people today kill truth and jettison *Dharma*. How then can they have peace?

The *Kenopanishad* proclaims that the basis of every action should be Truth which is Divine. The *Rishis* did not compile the *Upanishaths* as a pastime. They gave this valuable treasure for the welfare of mankind.

Devotees' failure to know what Svaami wants

Several persons holding high positions come here to get Svaami's blessings for achieving higher positions or for other personal benefits. Big businessmen and traders come here to take Svaami's blessings and return. Those in the teaching, legal and other professions come here. Theists come here, participate in *Bhajans* etc., and go away. All of them come to Svaami to get their desires fulfilled. No one comes to know what Svaami wants. How many strive for Svaami's sake? Everyone comes only with selfish motives. I want to point out that enjoying benefits and failing to show gratitude is grievously wrong. In ancient days the devotees of the Lord sacrificed their lives by engaging themselves this divine quality of selflessness. It is only by sacrifice you can achieve immortality. You should love all without distinction and serve society.

"Sacrifice and share Divinity with every one" is the message of the Upanishaths. You should not bother about your close relations alone, as these relationships are only temporary. You should develop *Vishva Prema* (Universal Love).

You may wonder why I am telling this repeatedly. Though I have been telling you all this for several years no one seems to change for the better. So I have to emphasise the need for your getting rid of too much attachment to your kith and kin. Love your children but do not get excessively attached to them. You must make use of your body for doing your duty, but do not get too much attached to it.

Act according to your role in life

Every person has to play his role in life. How this should be done is illustrated by a story. Once an actor went to the court of Bhoja Raja to exhibit his talents and get a reward. First he went in the role of a renunciant wearing saffron robes. When the king offered him some gold he declined to accept it. When questioned whether what he gave was not enough, the actor replied he would come again the next day.

The next day he came in the guise of a dancing girl and gave a fine performance which pleased everyone. When he was offered some gold coins in a plate by the king, the actor said what was offered was not enough. When the king questioned him as to why he had refused to take anything on the previous day, but was asking for more that day, the actor replied that he had to behave in a manner befitting the role he took. The previous day he had come as a renunciant and had to decline the gold offered to him. But on that day he was in the role of a dancing girl and so could demand more money. The moral of the story is: Students should behave as students and devotees as devotees only. Every person in any field has to uphold certain values appropriate to the role he has taken up. When I say devotees should do selfless service to humanity as a way of serving God, it is only in your interest and for your spiritual uplift. Discriminate between what is permanent and what is temporary and pursue the path leading to permanent bliss. Do not hanker after trivial transient pleasures. Speaking the truth, do your duty. This is the message of all the Upanishaths.

Excerpts from Discourse on 23-10-1993.

Love is the vital force. Love is the governing principle. It is only when the precious diamond of love is shining in one's heart that sacred and divine thoughts about God will arise in the mind.

—BABA

CHAPTER 34

Significance of *Yajnas*

Neither Charity, nor the performance of sacrifices,
Neither penance, nor the highest knowledge,
Nor any other thing can be equal
To the power of control of the senses,
Whatever enquiry or investigation one may make.

FEW men in the world are able to recognise what
is the primary goal of life. Many are not even
worried about this inability.

What is life? What is its highest goal? Man has
to enquire into these basic questions. Man's highest aim,
however, appears to be to obtain food, clothing, shelter
and progeny. All these are, no doubt, necessary to some
extent. But these are related to mere living and have
no relation to the supreme goal of life. Along with
leading one's ordinary life, one has to take note of

the great aim of life. Man must recognise the immense preciousness of human life. Every householder has to consider not only his duties as a householder living in the Grihasthaaranyam (forest of family life) but also about Brihadhaaranyam (the message of the Upanishath of that name). Those living in the jungle of the family, need to know about the life envisaged in Brihadhaaranyaka.

Brihadhaaranyaka Upanishath

What is this Brihadhaaranya? It is the Immense (Brihath) hermitage. This aashram is the combined expression of the mind, speech, and life. Thejas (effulgence), symbolises vaak (speech). Mind is represented by food— Annamaya. Praana (the Life-Principle) is Rasamaya (essential sweetness). The effulgent speech, in association with the mind as food becomes the essence of the Life-Principle. This truth was proclaimed by the sages in the Upanishathik declaration: "Raso vai Sah" (He, the Divine, is all sweetness)— the form of Brahman.

The Rasa principle is present only in Praana (the Life Principle). The cosmos is based on life. There is, however, the aathma, which transcends the Life Principle.

The Brihadhaaranyaka Upanishath is the unified form of Vaak, Manas and Prajna. As the sages in the forest contemplated on this form and realised the bliss of experiencing the Divine, this got the appellation Aaranyaka (Forest). As fire arises in forests, Agni (Fire) got the name Aaranya. Man's life originates in fire, grows on fire and ends in Agni. Born from the warm womb of the mother, sustained by the fire of his digestive organ, man ultimately ends on the funeral pyre. Fire is thus the basic cause of human birth and death.

Agni is an embodiment of the Divine. Fire is effulgent. It nourishes the whole world. But it needs to be kept under control. "There is nothing great without restraint."

Rationale behind sacrifices

The ancients started performing *Yajnas* and *Yaagas* (sacrifices) to propitiate the Divine in the form of Fire. The sacrifices were performed not to secure personal benefits or to get desires fulfilled, or to get over difficulties. They embarked on sacrifices only to secure *Aathmaanandham* the (Bliss of the Spirit).

Once, Emperor Janaka performed a big *Yajna*. Many scholars participated in the sacrifice, including scholarly women. Among such women were Maithreyi, Gargi and others. At that *Yajna* a *pandith* called Ashvala started putting questions to the sage Yaajnavalkya. "How many deities are there?" he asked. Yaajnavalkya, being a very shrewd person, took the cue from the word "here." He answered "There are 3306." The entire assembly was taken by surprise at this figure. They wondered whether there could be 3306 deities present at the *Yajna*.

What lay behind Yaajnavalkya's reply? He considered everyone present at the *Yajna* as divine. "God appears in human form." Hence, in those days, men were not regarded as mere human beings at *Yajnas* and *Yaagas*. Every individual was considered as a manifestation of the Divine.

Ashvala then posed another question to Yaajnavalkya. He asked: "Is it possible to reduce this number of deities?" "Yes, it is possible," said Yaajnavalkya. There was no mention of "here" in the second question. Yaajnavalkya answered: "Thirty three deities." Asked whether he could state who these deities were, Yaajnavalkya said: "There are eight *Vasus,* eleven *Rudhras,* twelve *Aaadhithyas, Indhra* and *Prajaapathi.* All these together make 33."

Yaajnavalkya reduces the number of deities to one

The assembly was satisfied with the answer. Then, Gargi got up and asked: "Venerable sage! Is it possible to reduce this number further?" "Certainly yes," declared Yaajnavalkya. "There are six! *Agni* (Fire), *Bhuumi* (earth), *Vaayu* (the Wind-God), *Aadhithya* (the Sun God) *Amarathvam* (Immortality), and *Adhvara.*" These six are the true deities, he said.

Ashvala got up and asked whether the number could be reduced further. Yaajnavalkya said the number could be reduced to three: The Past, the Present, and the Future. The answer was accepted by the assembly.

In answer to further questions whether the number could be further reduced to the most important deities, Yaajnavalkya said: "They are two: Food and *Praana* (Life)."

Asked whether the number could be further reduced, he said that it could be reduced to one-and-a-half and he explained that the all-pervasive *Vaayu* (the Wind God) is known as *Adhyartha* (one and a half). Asked whether a further reduction was possible he said it could be reduced to one, namely, *Praana* (Life).

When enquiries from the scientific, the spiritual and other points of view are carried out to find out the ultimate divine entity, *Praana,* the presiding deity of Life, emerged as the only one.

Where does this Life Principle dwell? The answer is: it has no specific place or time. It is everywhere.

The purpose of the *Yajna* is to propitiate this all-pervading Life-Force.

Yajna means acquiring the highest wisdom

What is *Yajna*? It is not merely offering oblations to the sacred fire, *homam*. *Yajna* means acquiring the highest wisdom by *Yama* and *Niyama* (control of the senses and practice of spiritual discipline). This wisdom is not related to worldly knowledge. All the knowledge acquired through the intellect is illusory. It is based on dualism and is tantamount to ignorance. It may serve to score debating points; such debates also promote discord.

The knowledge that transcends all controversies and is related to the eternal verities is the *Aathma-Jnaanam* (Knowledge of the Self). It is for acquiring this supreme knowledge that the ancient *Rishis* performed *Yajnas* and *Yaagas*.

Practices like reciting the *Lalitha Sahasranaama* cannot be considered *Yajna* in the true sense. Only when one embarks on the internal quest for the realisation of the Self within can he acquire *Aathma Jnaana* (Knowledge of the Self).

For this purpose there is no need to study any books. Only by direct experience and one's own spiritual *Saadhana* can this awareness of the Self be realised. Man has to understand that he is the cause of his own happiness or misery and that all that he seeks or loves are not for their sake, but for his own sake. Hence, he has to understand his own true nature. Realising the ephemerality of all worldly objects, man should recognise that enduring happiness can be got only by developing love for God.

A great sage like Yaajnavalkya declared that the whole cosmos is a manifestation of the Divine. The Divine is omnipresent. This awareness of the Divine has to be experienced by everyone.

Sense of oneness is the message of *Pranava*

The *Brihadhaarnyaka Upanishath* pointed out that this oneness is proclaimed by the all-pervading sacred *Pranava* "OM". This pervasiveness can be experienced in a myriad ways, above all, in the sound that can be heard when one is alone and closes his ears. Man has to realise the redemptive power of *Pranava Manthra*. It is the means to overcome the vicissitudes of life and realise union with the Divine. The body is like a water bubble that originates in water, grows in water and merges in water. The body is the water bubble and Naaraayana is the water. It has come from Naaraayana and has to merge in Him.

The *Yajnas* and *Yaagas* are designed to teach such spiritual truths. But human beings, caught up in the coils of worldly life, are a prey to all kinds of troubles and tribulations. Some of them are always prone to doing harm to others. They convert even the good to evil. For such persons there is no end but utter destruction. Everyone, therefore, has to know something about human life and the Divine life. There are many who cannot see anything good, but see only what is bad. There are others who always see what is bad, but consider it as good. Both these ways of looking at things are false. The man with a godly outlook sees the good always.

In human life, one should not have any kind of bad thoughts. Even when someone reviles you, you should practise self-restraint and remain calm. There is no power equal to such self-restraint. Everyone should develop such tranquillity (or peace). The more peaceful you are, the greater your longevity. People today easily lose their peace. They get enraged on the slightest provocation. There are four types of men who view the good and the bad in different ways. Of these, worse than demons are those who deride all that is good and picture it as evil. These perversions are a reflection of the bad times confronting mankind. Such attitudes are indications of impending disaster.

Portents of the *Kali* age even before its dawn

Once Krishna and Balaraama were engaged in a lively conversation. Balaraama asked Krishna: "How is it many untoward things are happening today? Apart from the differences between the Paandavas and the Kauravas, discord is rearing its head even among our own Yaadhavas. There are growing conflicts amongst them. Bitterness is rampant. Enmity is growing." Krishna smilingly replied: "This is a manifestation of the power of *Kali*. The *Kali* Age is dawning. These are its portents. These evil tendencies are an indication of the disasters to come."

All the evil tendencies that are manifest today are indication of the impending disasters. The future is in your hands. To avert disaster, all evil thoughts have to be eschewed. You have to develop always peaceful thoughts. When any thought of doing harm to somebody arises in your mind, examine whether it is right or wrong. If you wish to make any public statement examine whether it is true or false. Don't broadcast any kind of bazaar gossip. Investigate the truth. Do not be in a hurry. Wait till you have got all the facts. To draw conclusions in haste on the basis of imperfect information is a sign of stupidity.

A lesson to be learnt from the Mahaabhaaratha

Why do untoward events happen? Only to promote what is good. They have a cleaning effect. Rise and fall are natural events. When any such thing takes place in relation to the Divine, it must be regarded as the prelude to something elevating and sublime.

Here is an illustration from the Mahaabhaaratha. The battle between the Paandavas and Kauravas had gone on for nine days. On all the nine days, the Paandavas were the losers. Yudhishtira and Arjuna were dejected.

At that time Krishna told them: "Why are you getting so impatient? Unrighteousness score some victories in the beginning. Gradually, it declines and the forces of righteousness, peace and truth gain the upper hand. Therefore, do not have any worry. Get up, Dhananjaya (Arjuna). *Dharma* is bound to win. Selfishness will be destroyed. Alas! the parents of a hundred sons will ultimately have not even one to perform their obsequies. What a fate! What is the reason? It is the result of the crooked stratagems of evil-minded men. They are full of low cunning. They have the worst traits in men. Such persons bring ruin on great royal dynasties. Only a rain of arrows can bring about peace." Krishna thus roused the drooping spirits of Dharmaja and Arjuna.

The Kauravas were unable to tolerate the popularity and good name of the Paandavas. The Paandavas were the very embodiments of Righteousness. They were totally wedded to truth. Were it otherwise, would valiant heroes like Bheema and Arjuna remain inactive when Dhraupadhi was sought to be disrobed? They allowed events to take their inevitable course.

Hence, mishaps in life should be regarded as happenings which serve to further one's spiritual progress.

Uniqueness of Sai Seva activities

Today when the Sai Seva organisations are rendering glorious service all over the world, there are some persons who, like the Kauravas, are consumed by envy. They have their abettors and accomplices like Shakuni, Dhuryodhana's uncle. Such men cannot be considered as educated or intelligent persons, If they were really educated, they would not indulge in such mean tactics. But what is the outcome of all this? The maligners will be defeated by their own weapons.

Very soon the glory of Sai will spread to every part of the world. It will increase a thousand-fold. The reason is the essential goodness of the Sai Mission. It is totally free from any taint. Every act is done out of the purest of motives. Everything that is said is based on truth. All activities are conducted without depending on any outsider. Hence, there is no room for fear.

After the harvest when the sheaves of grains are winnowed, the wind blows away all the chaff, leaving only the grains behind. Through this process, the true devotees will remain steadfast. The wavering puppets will drift away. This is the process of winnowing.

Hence, adhere firmly to the truth of your convictions. Be prepared to meet any challenges. Life is a challenge, meet it. Be ready to face any situation. How is this

to be done? Not by tit-for-tat or blow-for-blow. You
have always to be truthful. Do not accuse anyone. You
have no need to harm anyone. Adhere to the truth
and esteem it as the life-breath of a true devotee. Strengthen your faith in God. Envious people invent all
kinds of stories. They feed the flame of hatred in others.
All these belong to the evil breed of Shakuni. And
where do they find their moorings? In the company
of evil-minded men like Dhuryodhana and Dhussasana.
They will never go near righteous men like Dharmaja
(the eldest of the Paandavas). There is only a bad end
for such persons. The good will never come to grief.
Good causes are bound to flourish. Hence establish your
life in truth.

Carry on the good work

Embodiments of love! Good opportunities come rarely.
Once lost, they may not recur. Making good use of
the present opportunity, see that the Sai organisations
grow from day to day. Every street must reverberate
with the name of Sai. Every heart should be purified.
Every mind should be full of happiness. Love even
your enemies. Treat even the one who hates you as
friend. Then, there will be no need to accuse anyone.
When you adhere to your truth and live upto it, you
are bound to be successful. Truth is one. That is the
truth which should be the sheet-anchor of your life.

As many are gathered here, I wish to inform you
that the programme for the Seventieth Birthday is
being drawn up. Whatever may happen, these
celebrations will go on. Sai's resolve will be fulfilled.
Even if the heavens fall, Sai's resolve will not alter.
We do not speak about these resolves, nor are they

broadcast among the public. In the world only goods that are not easily sold, are advertised. Goods that have a ready market are not advertised.

Important events for Seventieth Birthday

During the next two years, many important events are going to happen. Programmes are afoot to help the poor and the needy. On November 18th, 70 marriages will be performed. People often talk about mass marriages. They are rather simple affairs. The marriages we intend to perform will be different. The weddings will be such that the married couples will say: "We never imagined that such a thing could happen in our lives!" Each bride will be given a wedding medallion (*bottu*) in a gold chain. The bridegroom will receive a gold ring. A set of cooking utensils will be presented along with some provisions. The brides will be given valuable Kanjeevaram saris. The couples will also be given houses in due course.

It is also intended to provide sewing machines to women who are confined to their houses and cannot support themselves by working outside.

All are our people. The Divine is in all. But owing to their past actions, and their misfortunes, some of them entertain silly ideas. They are transient and not lasting. Even Dhuryodhana and Dhussasana praised Krishna in the end. Therefore, do not have ill-will towards anyone. Love everyone and pray for everybody's well-being. To the extent possible, take part in the work of Sai Organisations. Today there is no nobler work in the world.

I shall not speak about the numerous other organisations in the world. But the purity that obtains in the Sai Organisations cannot be found anywhere else. Gossip mongers may talk as they please. But so far as our organisations are concerned their watchword always is "Help! Help! Help! Serve! Serve! Serve!" This is their primary aim.

I do not have any differences based on race, caste, or creed. The weddings will be performed without regard to any of these considerations. Every couple will be blessed with happiness and inducted into the right code of conduct for householders. Those seeking to get married should abide by the laws of the country.

Valedictory Discourse at the Vedha Purusha Sapthaaha Jnaana Yajna, on Vijayadhashami Day, in the Puurnachandhra Auditorium on 24-10-1993.

Ό―――――――――――――Ώ

Those who seek to know God, must steel themselves to bear insult, injury and torture, with a smile.

—*BABA*

CHAPTER 35

Education should develop human values

Education confers beauty on man;
It is his secret treasure;
It confers pleasure, fame and happiness;
It is the teacher of teachers;
It is one's kinsman when abroad;
It confers supreme vision;
In a royal assembly it is learning alone,
Not wealth, that counts;
A man without learning is an animal.

STUDENTS and teachers! Today neither students nor teachers are aware of the true meaning of education. Education should foster morality, righteousness and character. Man today has acquired prodigious knowledge in the fields of science and technology. But this serves only to promote a material civilisation and teaches only knowledge of the external worlds to students. What man truly needs today is not this external knowledge. He needs refinement of the heart. This can be got only by internal culture.

It is not enough today to make a man a mere human being. He has to be transformed into an ideal human being. Education makes a man compassionate. That is the fulfilment of the purpose of education. Education should not be equated with book knowledge or the acquisition of skills for leading one's life in the world. The modern student is unable to determine what is the basis of his life and what is important in it. Hence, he loses confidence in himself. Because they lack the patriotism, born out of love for the country, and the devotion to God, which instills a spirit of sacrifice, students today have lost all self-confidence.

Loss of self-confidence is the cause of all troubles

Most of the troubles tormenting the world today stem from loss of *Aathma-Vishvaasa* (self-confidence).

Devoid of the fear of sin and love for God,
Mankind today is plunged in a grave crisis.

The eternal verities proclaimed in the scriptures have assumed bizarre forms. Sacred nature is divorced from humanity. The ancient wisdom is in eclipse. Perverted knowledge is growing. In such a situation, how can ethical and spiritual values appeal to youth?

The entire educational system should be changed. The true purpose of education should be understood.

Reading and writing cannot make a man educated.
Are those acquiring degrees scholars?
Without right knowledge and proper conduct,
Can one be deemed educated?
If learning for earning a living is esteemed as education,
Are not birds and beasts able to live without learning?

Education is the life-breath of human beings

Education should be the life-breath of human beings. By converting education into a means of earning a livelihood, people are forgetting the meaning of life. Character determines life. It is pure and holy. Without character how can man lead a worthwhile and sacred life? For this reason, from ancient times, Bhaaratheeyas fostered a life-style based on ethics. Students are forgetting this ancient culture of Bhaarath. Pursuing worldly, ephemeral knowledge, they do not understand the nature of life.

Man should recognise the cosmic basis of education. Education today is based on mechanical skills. Students should strive to promote blossoming of the heart together with development of the intellect. Intellectual knowledge alone cannot suffice for the conduct of life on right lines.

It is true that Bhaarath is lagging behind in the economic sphere. But what harm does this do to the world? There is a greater danger from another source. This arises from the fact that people are immersed in material pursuits, ignoring moral and spiritual values. Unless this process is reversed, education cannot make headway.

Two hundred years ago, scientists in other countries started exploring the powers of nature and experimented with control of the five basic elements (ether, air, fire, water and earth). They invented dreadful bombs and envisaged terrible wars. This is a wholly misguided effort.

Role of science in promoting human welfare

The arrogant claim that they have achieved scientific progress is utterly unwarranted because this is not true science at all. Does knowledge of how to cause mass destruction merit the name of science? Cannot their scientific investigations be devoted to causes which promote human welfare and betterment?

All the scientific discoveries of today were excelled by the achievements of Hiranyakasipu. The powers obtained from them are prone to be misused. Deluded by their scientific and technological progress, the nations are losing their wisdom. What is the purpose served by these discoveries? While they promote temporary pleasures, they virtually destroy the sources of inner strength. The education that we must aim at is one which will direct the children towards the right path and promote the well-being of the nation. Only when mankind realises this need will world peace be a reality.

Man needs today a mind free from attachment and hatred, speech that is untainted by falsehood, and a body that is totally free from violence. Of these, truthful speech is most essential. Unfortunately, man is not free from these taints. Hence, students should receive an education that produces purity of mind, speech and body.

Of what use is man's conquest of the external world if he cannot realise his own true nature? Scientists are only helping to satisfy man's selfish desires. They are keen on securing accolades for themselves, but are not concerned about the welfare of society or the goals of life. How glorious will be their achievements if their discoveries are useful to the people and promote the prosperity and welfare of nations?

Today every step of man is marked by unrighteousness. Every word is tainted by untruth. His thoughts are not free from evil. All his desires are rooted in selfishness. Caste and religious conflicts are rampant. Parochialism is growing. In short, humanness has reached its nadir. How then, can man be called a human being, when there is no harmony in thought, word and deed?

Bad example set by elders make students go astray

Moreover, there are no ideal leaders today. Even exemplary parents are not to be found. Nor are there ideal teachers. In olden days, the leaders, the parents and the teachers led exemplary lives. It is because such persons are absent today that students are without ideal examples to follow. There is a Thelugu saying that the calf follows the cow. Because the elders set a bad example, the students also are going astray.

The students are not to blame. They are inherently good hearted and good natured. But they take to bad ways because of the elders. Therefore, the first requisite is for the national leaders and the parents to understand how the educational system should function. They should realise that education should aim at developing good qualities in the children and should not be regarded as a means to acquire wealth. Character is based on good conduct. Only a young man with good qualities can become a good leader. He must take part in social service as a preparation for leadership. Everyone should realise that his happiness is bound up with the happiness of society as a whole. Parents and teachers should develop such attitudes in the students.

Despite all his achievement in the physical world, how far has man been able to develop his human qualities? This is the question facing the world today. If people study the ancient history of Bhaarath, they will realise the importance which the ancients attached to Truth.

Need for unity to protect national interests

There may be differences at the individual level, but when national interests are involved, these differences should be forgotten and all should act in unity. This was the attitude of Dharmaja in respect of his Kaurava cousins. At the individual level, Dharmaja said that the five Paandava brothers might be ranged against the hundred Kauravas. "But if the nation is in peril, we are 105 against the rest. It is our duty to protect the nation."

Unfortunately, today, each party is ranged against the other and there is discord among the people. This should go. All should bear in mind the interests of the people.

Education today is not inculcating in the students the spirit of compassion and kindness. Once Gandhiji told a foreigner that he was feeling sad because education was making students heartless and lacking in fellow-feeling. Students do not show any sweetness in speech. They have no sense of gratitude. Of what avail is such an education? The foremost quality students should have is humility. They must be free from conceit. They must be unselfish. Without these a student lacks lustre. Students today lack these qualities. They have little concern for the plight of their parents. But, there are also parents who pamper their children like Dhritharaashtra, the father of the Kauravas. If parents do not correct their children, who will correct them? How can parents cherish children who misbehave and earn a bad name?

The birthday that should be celebrated is the day when good qualities are born in one. You must become ideal students. Students must work hard. They have to be grateful to their parents for all that they have received from the latter. Children who cannot please their parents, how will they serve the nation?

The five life-breaths for a student

Every human body is sustained by the five life-breaths—*Praana, Apaana, Vyaana, Udhaana* and *Samaana*. What are the five life-breaths for a student? They are: Truth, Righteousness, Peace, Love and Non-violence. All these five principles have to be rigorously observed to sublimate one's life. Each one should cultivate the qualities of compassion, patience and oneness. These qualities will promote the unity of mankind. These are based on the love-principle. Without love, there is no life. Love gives rise to truth. Love begets peace. When you have love, you practise non-violence. Love is the under-current in all these.

Education has to be reformed. But Ministers are only trifling with changes. Reports of Committees are gathering dust in shelves. Educational reforms should be related to the five basic human values, without which education has no meaning and life itself is devoid of purpose. A student today has no conception of the value of *Thyaaga* (sacrifice). He has to learn to do his duty without expectation of any reward. This is a form of *Yoga* (Spiritual discipline).

Knowledge is to wisdom as lightning is to cloud

Dear students! Giving up the craze for going abroad after the completion of your studies, take a resolve to dedicate yourselves to the service of your village, your state and your nation. Act according to your conscience. In your heart shines *Aathma-Vidhya* (the knowledge of the Spirit). Knowledge should beget wisdom like the lightning in a cloud.

Everyone of our students should stand forth as a shining example to others. The light of their example should spread all over the world and bring about spiritual unity among mankind.

All changes in the educational syllabi or other changes in the economic and political spheres are of little value. There should be change in the mental attitude of the people, as the prelude to a change in the national scene. Transform yourself first and then preach to others.

True science should foster the well-being of the people and promote unity amongst them. Unity will lead to purity and both will lead to Divinity. Today there is none of these. We have only Community (caste). It is this communal feeling that is the cause of conflict. Giving up all differences based on caste or creed, people should regard themselves as the children of one human family. There is only one religion, the religion of humanity. Students should develop this spirit of unity.

Truth and Righteousness are inter-related

Students! The future of the country, for good or ill, depends on you. The older generation cannot reform the nation. Only a disciplined and well educated younger generation can serve the nation well, as future leaders. Treat the whole world as a vast mansion. Strive for the well-being of all nations equally with Bhaarath.

The Sri Sathya Sai Institute has been established to promote sacred ideals among students. Adhere to your principles and beliefs regardless of what others may say. Have the example of the *Gopikas* in mind. Their devotion to Krishna was firm and unwavering. Consider truth as your life-breath. If you speak the truth and practise righteousness, you will attain the highest state.

Truth and Righteousness are inter-related. Together they constitute humanness. Bear in mind the glorious example of Harishchandhra, who sacrificed everything for the sake of truth.

Adhere to truth in earning a living or in experiencing anything in life. Ill-gotten wealth will be lost in the same way. Engage yourselves in some kind of socially useful activity in the educational, medical or other fields. Sacrifice is more important than earning money. Students imbued with this spirit of service may go to any country. Do not use your diplomas as begging bowls for jobs. Make proper use of your education to render service to the nation and to lead noble lives. This is my benediction to all of you.

Address to the Convocation of Sri Sathya Sai Institute held in the Vidhyagiri Stadium on 22-11-1993.

CHAPTER 36

Purity, patience, perseverance : steps to Divinity

In this sacred land of Bhaarath
Forbearance is our best wealth;
Of all forms of rituals, the highest
Is the observance of Truth and Morality;
Of sweetness of disposition
The greatest is maternal love;
Jettisoning the national ideal
That honour is greater than life itself,
What a pity people have
Fallen a prey to exotic practices!
What can I say about
The plight of Bhaarath!
Like the elephant unaware of its strength
Bhaaratheeyas have become docile today.

WHEN the heart is filled with compassion, the hands are dedicated to the service of others, the body is engaged in constant help to others, the life of such a person is sacred, purposeful and noble.

The entire Cosmos is based on the bedrock of Truth. Wealth and Welfare and all comforts and pleasures are dependent on Truth. Wherever you turn, Truth shines effulgently. The Goddess of Wealth, Lakshmi, dwells in the abode of Truth. The world cannot exist without Truth, just as the rays cannot exist without the sun. Truth is the Cosmos and the Cosmos is Truth.

The entire Cosmos is permeated by the Divine— *Eeshaavaasyam idham Jagath.* It is foolish to imagine that the natural, physical and mundane is unreal and there is something else that sustains it. The Cosmos is Vishnu and Vishnu (the Supreme) is the Cosmos. The Cosmos is a manifestation of the Divine.

The Universe is a Divine manifestation

Considering this universe, composed of the five basic elements, as a Divine manifestation, the ancient sages embarked on a spiritual enquiry and realised the Truth. It is because this profound and eternal Truth has been forgotten by man that the world is a prey to all kinds of troubles and difficulties.

Among the five elements, the primary one is the earth. It is all-pervasive. All the mountains, rivers, villages, towns, etc., are based on the earth. The scientists found that the earth is revolving round itself. In that case, all the objects on the earth should also be revolving. But that is not so. The earth has a divine power of attraction. This power of attraction holds all the objects together. Hence, the earth alone cannot be regarded as the basis for all the objects. If we enquire more deeply, it will be found that even the earth is supported by something else. The earth is based on a higher power, the Divine power.

The Divine remains steady and unchanging

Thus, the Divine is firm, pure and changeless. Without this Divine power, nature and the physical world cannot function well. If, for instance, the rails on which a locomotive runs, were also to move along with the train, the results would be disastrous. Likewise, if the road were also to move along with the car running on it, there will be accidents. It is the car that moves and not the earth. In this manner, many objects are in motion in the universe, but the Divine remains steady and unchanging.

The next is the water element which is present everywhere. Whether we perceive it or not, Life is impossible without water.

The next one is Fire. This fire element is present in every living being including humans, as *Jatharaagni* (the digestive fire). This fire is not only on the earth, but is even in space. When clouds clash against each other, fire is generated in the form of lightning. When two inert flint-stones are struck against each other, fire emanates from them. Likewise when two sticks are rubbed against each other, fire emerges. Thus, fire also is an all-pervading power.

Then, there is *Aakaasha* (space or ether). It pervades everything. There is *Vaayu* (air). There can be no life without air. You experience the presence of air during a storm or a whirlwind. But air is present all the time everywhere.

When the five elements have such immense power, you can imagine what must be the potency of the Divine which sustains them. The five elements are *Paramaathmasvaruupa* (manifestations of the Supreme Omniself). No one can deny Its existence, whether one is a theist, an atheist or an agnostic. Today, these five elements are not being properly used. Instead, they are very much misused. Their misuse is the root cause of all the travails of the world. As the five elements are based on Truth, the ancient *rishis* observed restraint in speech so that they may adhere to truth. Restraint in speech nourishes truth. Excessive speech is the cause of great unrest. It is essential, therefore, for everyone to recognise the basic role of the five elements and live in consonance with that awareness.

Religion is the reflection of belief

The mind demonstrates the nature of the five elements. *Mathi* (belief) has emerged from the mind. *Matham* (religion) is reflection of belief. Religion is not what it is normally understood to be. There are many engaged in destruction of religion. If religion is destroyed, belief or faith will be destroyed and then the mind itself will be destroyed. Religious hatred has to be got rid of, not religion as such. Adherents of all faiths recognise the power of the five elements and worship them.

Bhaaratheeyas have upheld unity in thought, word and deed by their conduct. The *Vedhas* have proclaimed that the Divine is present in all five elements. This truth is accepted by the adherents of all faiths. But while professing belief in this truth and proclaiming it, they are not acting upto it in practice. Only the

Bhaaratheeyas practised this truth and experienced the bliss derived from it. Bhaaratheeyas adored hills, birds and trees. Adherents of other faiths ridiculed such practices. This is due to thoughtlessness and is not a sign of sanity. All people say that God is in all beings and all things. But to deride Bhaaratheeyas, who act on that saying, is sheer folly. How can one, who acts according to his words, be regarded as a fool? Should not the one who does not live up to his words be treated as a fool? Let the wise determine the right answer.

The Supreme Reality is one, which is God

Bhaaratheeyas are known to act upto their words. People of other faiths may profess one thing and practise differently. We need not criticize any religion.

All religions teach only what is good.
People should lead their lives on this basis.
If the minds are pure,
How can religion do any harm?

People are spoiling their minds. Religion is not at fault. Today what is needed is transformation of minds and not of men. When the minds are reformed, men will automatically change for the better. Men's lives are based on how their mind thinks. Today men should develop mental purity and sacred feelings.

The Supreme Reality is one. It is God. Men of all faiths—whether they are Hindhus, Christians, Muslims, Paarsis or others—have recognized that God is one. It is only when men develop feelings of forbearance, compassion and unity, that men will have fraternal feelings towards each other and foster equality and justice. It is only when men develop *Ekaathmabhaava* (oneness in Spirit) that bitterness and discord will cease. Men must act on the conviction that the same Divine dwells in all beings.

From the body to the Omni Self

The Cosmos is an organism with multifarious limbs. A human being has eyes, ears, mouth, etc. All these organs are limbs of the human body. The body is a limb of society. Society is a limb of humanity. Humanity is a limb of *Prakrithi*. *Prakrithi* is a limb of the *Paramaathma* (Omni Self). This shows the relationship between the sense organs in man and the Divine. Therefore, one should make proper use of the senses, comprehend the nature of the Divine that sustains them and lead a meaningful life.

There is the body. There is the world. There are forests, trees and many other things. In referring to all these, we use the word "is"—that it exists. This term "is," signifying existence, proclaims the fundamental fact about man. There is only one thing that exists. But man forgets this Divine Reality because of his selfishness and self-centredness. The latter reflect his egoism and ostentatiousness. It is only when the last two are extinguished, will man's inner Divinity manifest itself.

The bad traits which are found in man are the result of his food and other habits and do not arise from his *Aathma*. Vices like lust, anger, envy and pride are the outcome of bad food and improper associations and are products of external factors. They do not arise from within. Qualities like love, compassion, consideration for others arise from within one's self. These are human values. Forgetting these values, following animal qualities, men are leading an animal existence. This is wrong. Men should lead lives based on their human estate.

Divine love is permanent and imperishable

Wealth may come and go. Strength may grow or decay. All things in the world may pass away. But there is one thing that is imperishable and unchanging. That is permanent Divine Love. All other forms of love are not real love at all. They are temporary, worldly attachments, based on physical, communal or other desires.

True love is related solely to the *Hridhaya* (heart). Man today is not cherishing such an unchanging and enduring love. He is wasting his life, pursuing temporary allurements. Wandering about aimlessly in the pursuit of evanescent and trivial pleasures, man is immersed in all kinds of troubles. He can discover his true path only by seeking spiritual illumination. Spirituality does not mean performance of ritual worship. It calls for the removal of the animal traits in man. Only then sacred feelings will arise in him. That is real spirituality. Regard all beings as children of God. Bear no ill-will towards anyone. It is because of hatred and ill-will that mankind is plunged in violence and bloodshed. Man's blood is inherently pure, divine and unsullied. To misuse that blood in wrong ways is a sign of animal or demonic nature.

Bhaarath today is in a crisis created by a myriad difficult problems. But not Bhaarath alone, all other countries are also facing similar crises. What is the reason? It is the total failure to remember the spiritual oneness of mankind. Only the sense of spiritual unity will generate universal love. That love alone will bind men together in unity. This love principle should emanate from the heart. Only then true unity will emerge.

Embodiments of Love! Do not be deluded by the belief that life has been given to you for eating and drinking and enjoying other physical pleasures. This is not the reason for human birth, which is rare blessing. What is the difference between a human being and the animals? It is qualities like kindness, compassion, forbearance and sympathy which differentiate human beings from animals. But man tends to forget these inherent qualities out of absorption in selfish, mundane desires. Those wearing the glass of selfishness can only see selfishness all around them. A defective vision produces an apparent defect in creation. There is nothing wrong with *srishti* (creation). Every defect is related to the defective *dhrishti* (vision).

Perform duties but do not claim any rights

Men must realise that true humanness will be achieved only when the five elements in the universe are properly used. The earth is a sacred base of the Supreme. The other four elements are super-imposed on it. Without the base, the other elements will be functionless. Hence all human beings living on earth should cooperate with each other, engage themselves in socially helpful activities and redeem their lives. Every man has duties to perform, but can claim no rights. Today people tend to assert their rights without regard to their responsibilities (or duties). Duties and rights go together. Today men tend to assert their rights but have no regard for their responsibilities. Absolute unconcern for responsibilities has become a kind of epidemic in all spheres of life today. When you discharge your responsibilities, your rights will be automatically ensured.

In Bhaarath today everybody is clamouring about rights. What is the meaning of "right"? It is that to which you are entitled. How do you get it? Can you get the fruit without sowing the seed? Without a tree can there be a fruit? But you aspire for the fruit without sowing the seed or rearing the tree? What folly is this? No one has any inherent claim to any right. He has only responsibility. Do your duty. Duty is God. Work is worship.

When you perform your duties, you will be acquiring the title to your rights. Every man should discharge his duties. Performance of duty is your *yoga*. It is your enjoyment. It is your sacrifice. Discharge of duty is the basis for everything.

Have respect for the faiths of others also

If duties are performed according to one's respective role—as householder, student, renunciant or ascetic— the world will not suffer from lack of peace or prosperity. People are not attending to their respective functions. They are not carrying out the duties properly. Ignoring their duties, they interest themselves in the activities of others.

This attitude is prevalent in the religious sphere also. Members of one faith consider it supreme and deride the faiths of others. No one is qualified to make such a claim. Even as you prize your faith, you must realize that others are equally entitled to prize their faiths. You may esteem your religion greatly. Adhere to it accordingly. But do not criticize or despise the religions of other people. Unfortunately men have lost this sense of respect for other faiths. If all people recognise this truth, there will be no room in the world for conflicts and discord.

Man strives for peace in many ways. Where is peace to be found? It is not in the external world. Peace must be found within. Outside you have only pieces. You must seek to manifest the peace within you. There are millions in the world who preach and propagate what is good. But not one in a hundred practises the good teachings. The world will pay no heed to those who do not practise what they preach.

It is the liar who is haunted by fear

Whether others esteem or not, you must be content to act according to your conscience. The inner conviction that you are acting righteously is your best witness. There is no greater *Dharma* than adherence to Truth. You need have no fear as long as you adhere to truth. It is the liar who is haunted by fear.

Therefore, go forward to render social service with faith and fortitude. Eschew religious hatred, which is the cause of conflict. Respect every religion.

People today talk about protecting the nation. The nation does not need protection. If you protect and foster truth and righteousness the nation will be automatically protected. In the name of protecting the country, arms and bombs are piled up which are ruining the nation.

At the root of all troubles is human selfishness. Some amount of concern for selfish interests is justified. But when anything is carried to excess, it proves calamitous. Man is endowed with the discriminating power to control his desires. This power must be used to decide whether any action is right or wrong.

"Be," "do" and "speak" what is good

All of you are embodiments of the *Aathma* (Spirit). You are all the manifestations of the Divine. The Indwelling Spirit is one and the same in all beings irrespective of their external differences, like the current that illumines bulbs of different wattage and colour. Fill your hearts with love. Then you can experience real bliss. With a narrow mind and heart, if you indulge in magniloquent words, no one will care to listen to you. First of all "Be"—be good yourself. Then you "Do"—act likewise. Then "Speak"—tell others about what is good. Only thus you will be setting an ideal example.

Do not entertain bad feelings about anyone. They do you more harm than to others. As the saying in a Thelugu poem goes: "One's own anger is one's enemy and one's peace is one's friend and kinsfolk. One's happiness is heaven and one's sorrow is hell." Develop sacred and pure feelings. We claim to celebrate the birthdays of people. But the birthday is truly celebrated when there is the birth of pure ideas in one.

You celebrate the birthday of Bhagavaan. But do you follow the teachings? You will experience the fruits of celebrating the birthday only when you follow the teachings. Jesus said: "Love everyone." Christmas is celebrated, but how far does one practise love? None at all.

There is love in everyone's heart. Share it at least with ten persons every day. This is seldom done. People are more keen on receiving than on giving. They are willing to give away only things which they do not relish. There is no sacrifice in this.

This was the message given by Vyaasa in his eighteen *puraanas*. "It is meritorious to help others. It is sinful to inflict harm on them."

You should not be concerned with how many have come for Svaami's birthday but how many are following Svaami's teachings. If every devotee is able to influence two persons, soon the whole world will be reformed.

Pray for the welfare of all countries

Embodiments of love! There is only one thing you have to offer to Me today. Pray that people in all countries, may the entire humanity, should be happy and at peace. "*Lokaas samasthaas-sukhino bhavanthu*" (Let all the worlds be happy). Then alone there will be real unity. Do not wish merely for the peace and prosperity of India alone. Pray for the welfare of all countries. All are our brothers, whether they are in Pakistan or America or elsewhere.

Whether you believe it or not, realise that I am able to attract people from so many countries because of my all-embracing love.

If every person observes three things, he will be one with Svaami. You will experience the Divine in you. As the following three are in Me, I can declare firmly about them. They are three P's: Purity, Patience and Perseverance. These three are in Me and around Me. Anyone with these three qualities will be unafraid wherever he may be.

The most important quality is purity. Today everything is polluted. Water, air and all the five elements are polluted. As a result the mind of man is also polluted. How is purity to be achieved? Fill your minds with thoughts of God, dedicate all your actions to God and consider God as the inner motivator. Contemplation of God is not a matter for derision. You need have no fear on that account. You must have full faith in God, who is the universal sustainer. He is the protector, but not the punisher. The punishment you get is the consequence of your own actions.

Therefore, chanting the name of God, doing *bhajans* and performing good deeds, engage yourselves in service of your fellow-beings. Nourish love in your hearts. Love will drive away all bad thoughts. It will promote the spirit of forgiveness.

> *Birthday discourse in the Puurnachandhra
> Auditorium on 23-11-93.*

ೞ ─────────────────────── ೱ

When the sun rises, all the buds of lotus in the lake do not open out in full bloom. Only those which are full grown can blossom; so the rest have to bide their time and grow.

—BABA

CHAPTER 37

Let love prevail

Whom the Mohammedans adore as Allah,
The Christians as Jehovah,
The Vaishnavites as the Lotus-eyed Lord,
The Shaivites as Sambhu,
That God, who confers on all
Long life, health and prosperity,
Is one only—have this conviction.
The Lord is all love;
Love is His Divine form;
That Love is the redeeming Manthra
For all beings in this world.
Without experiencing a fragment
Of that Love how can you experience
The Divine, Oh man?

*E*MBODIMENTS *of Divine love!* If one object has to combine with another, or one individual has

to associate with another, love is the basis for the affinity.
The entire world is filled with love. The world is Love
and Love is the world.

In every human being love is present as an
effulgence which shines in his feelings. Love is life and
life is love. Even as the power to burn is natural for
fire, and the power to cool is natural for water, love
is a natural trait for man. Without it he ceases to be
human.

Love and life are inter-related

Love is an inborn quality in man. It is his life-
breath. We nourish a sapling with great love. When
the sapling grows and later becomes a dry plant, we
cast it away without any concern. How much love did
we lavish on the sapling? We cherished it as long as
it had life. After it became dry and lifeless, we had
no love for it. From infancy we bear love for the mother
who has borne us and reared us. But when she passes
away, the dead body is burnt without any attachment.
What is it that was loved earlier? The living being was
loved. Hence life and love are mutually inter-related.

Men today tend to forget the love-life relationship.
Love today is mingled with self-interest. In the tree
of every man's life there is the fruit of love. To enjoy
this fruit, the rind that covers it has to be removed
at the outset. The seeds in the fruit have also to be
removed. The sweet juice in the fruit can be enjoyed
only after the rind and the seeds have been removed.
In the fruit of the tree of life, the rind is *Ahamkaara*
(egoism). The seeds in that fruit are the selfish interests
of man. Only when the ego and selfishness are
eliminated, the sweet juice of love can be experienced.

The *Upanishaths* described this love as "the sweet juice that is *amritham* (nectarine) and the Supreme *Brahman*." This means that the juice (of love) is nectar itself, is verily the *Brahman* (Divine). It is life itself. It is the Divine Effulgence—*Thejas*.

This juice of love is equal to *Brahman*. It confers immortality on man and fills him with Divine bliss. Men today are unable to grasp the meaning of this Love Principle. It is essentially Divine in its nature. Hence, "Love is God; live in Love."

Most people, however, in their fascination for sensuous pleasures and worldly objects, are deeming the attachments to these as love. Immersed in selfish pursuits and interests, men seek everything for only selfish reasons and have no regard for the transcendental. Everything is desired for self-enjoyment and not out of love for the sake of love. We should love for the sake of the Divine, to realise the eternal. Love should be for experiencing the effulgence of *Jnaana*.

The martyrdom of Jesus

Love is thus, an amalgam of sweetness, effulgence and wisdom. Compassion is the reflection of love. Jesus is the embodiment of compassion. He looked with compassion at the poor and the miserable and gave them succour. In those days, people used to treat birds and animals without pity in the temple in Jerusalem. Jesus sought to put an end to these cruel practices.

From those times to the present, those who care for the well-being of all living beings and humanity were subjected to many trials and tribulations. Good people are always pursued by difficulties and troubles. The messiahs, the prophets, saints and God-men have always suffered from troubles and ordeals of various kinds. You should not bother about them. Have faith in God. When you live up to the truths you believe in, you will be indifferent to what others think.

Jesus was unaffected by the persecution to which he was subjected on a charge of treason. Moreover, whatever attempts may be made to suppress good people, their goodness cannot be extinguished.

> *A fine diamond even if it is in a heap of garbage*
> *will not lose its brilliance or its value.*
> *A pumpkin, even if it is grown beside a hedge,*
> *will not lose its sweetness.*
> *A peahen's egg, even if it is hatched in a crow's nest,*
> *will not lose its colours.*

Love is an expression of the Divine effulgence

Likewise, the glory and greatness of good men will suffer no diminution in whatever circumstances or situation they may be placed. Such Divine effulgence is shining in every human being. Love is an expression of this effulgence. To manifest this love, men must be prepared to bear every kind of suffering.

> *Can the sweet juice of the*
> *sugar be had for*
> *Making sugar without the*
> *cane being crushed?*

The human body is like the sugarcane filled with the juice of love. It is only when the body is subjected to hardship that the divine, sweet juice of love can flow from it. Without trouble to the body, pains to the mind, and control of the feelings, how can you expect to experience the Divine? Men today aspire for liberation without suffering from their part. God's love is not to be secured so easily. The precious gem of love can be got only in the bazaar of *Thyaaga* (sacrifice). It is valued only in the Kingdom of Love. How can it be got in the market of cheap wares?

Devotee should first give up selfishness

Man's devotion these days is suffused with selfishness. Everything he does stems from self-interest. The first requisite is the giving up of selfishness. There must be a curb on egoistic conceit and possessiveness. The mind must be submerged in pure love.

You may have heard about the life of St. Paul. In the beginning he was bitterly opposed to Jesus. He was ceaselessly criticizing Jesus. One day Jesus appeared in his dream and said: "Saul, are you not a human being? Is it proper for you to revile one who has done you no harm, has entertained no evil thoughts about you and has not led you to wrong ways? What harm have I done to you? Why are you abusing me? This is sheer folly. You are thereby demeaning yourself. Beware, beware!" After uttering this warning, Jesus vanished. On waking up in the morning Saul (as Paul was known before his transformation) lamented that he had been false to this human nature by deriding and condemning fellow beings. He felt that Jesus was doing many good deeds. He was one who could not bear the sight of others' sufferings. He was showering love on everyone. Saul felt that it was a sin to revile such a person. From that date Saul became a devotee of Jesus and came to be known as St. Paul.

In this manner, in the lives of many *Avathaars* one finds that despite all the love and blessings they

receive and the benefits they derive from the *Avathaars,*
some devotees turn against the Divine when their selfish
desires are not fulfilled.

Three types of traducers of God

There are three types of traducers of God. In the
first category are those who have no belief in God and
always indulge in abuse of God. Without faith, how
can there be any devotion? And without devotion, how
can there be love? Without love, how can he be termed
human? The words of such a person are worthless.

The second category of persons are those who adore
God when their desires are fulfilled and deride God
when their wishes are not satisfied. They imagine that
they have a right to receive favours from God. Such
petty-minded persons revile God. Their desires are sky-
high. But their deserts are minimal. Their spiritual efforts
are insignificant. Nevertheless, they criticise God when
their insatiable desires are not satisfied.

The third category of persons are those who turn
against God out of jealousy. They cannot bear the
prosperity or position of others towards whom they
think, God is partial. There is a remedy for almost
every malady, but none at all for the disease of Jealousy.
The envious indulge in calumny against God.

It is because of the ubiquitous presence of these
three categories of anti-God men that spirituality and
the divine feeling of love have become rare commodities
today.

There is a *Vedhic* saying: "The knower of *Brahman*
becomes *Brahman* himself." You are aware of the Godly
man, Moses, described in the Bible. He was one who
was ceaselessly praying to the Lord. He was a fervent

lover of God. His intense devotion and love ultimately transformed his face and filled it with a divine radiance.

Likewise, the *Gopikas,* through their intense devotion to Krishna, became the living images of Krishna. Rathnaakara, who was a highwayman in his early years, acquired the radiance of Raama by continually chanting the name of Raama.

Develop the sense of oneness with God

Whatever the God you worship, adore Him with *Thadhaathmabhaava* (a sense of oneness). Bodies may be two, but the heart is one. This is the feeling with which God should be worshipped. Only then you reach the state when you can declare: "You and I are one."

How this state is to be realised is illustrated by a biblical episode. Once St. John, while walking along, saw an angel reading a book. He asked who she was and what she was reading. She replied that she was an angel and that she was reading a book dealing with the doctrine of love. He asked for the book and the angel gave it to him, but said: "You must eat this book. When you are consuming the book, its taste will be bitter. But after you have eaten and digested it, it will become very sweet." "Eating the book" means absorbing the contents of the book, practising them and experiencing the bliss derived therefrom.

While reading and digesting "the book" the experience was bitter as declared by the angel. But, in due course, there was great transformation in St. John. His speech acquired a unique sweetness. His looks were sweet. Everything about him became sweet. What does this mean? It signifies the truth that you should completely identity yourself with the Divine love, which you seek from God. This love is not a purchasable commodity.

Today, devotion is treated as an exercise in shareholding, a kind of business partnership. But this is not right. The devotees should feel: "Everything is Thine." It is only when there is such a feeling of total surrender that the nature of Divine love can be comprehended.

Activities of "Messengers of Sathya Sai"

There is nothing more easy in the world than the spiritual path. It has to be followed in the form of *Seva* (loving service). To demonstrate to the world the beauty, the sweetness and the glory of selfless and loving service, the association called Messengers of Sathya Sai was formed (from among the old students of the Sathya Sai College for Women at Ananthapur). These girls, regardless of the families into which they got married and the countries where they had to live, pledged themselves to carry on their service activities. What this vow means should be properly understood. Men have greater freedom to act as they please. Married women have less freedom. They come under the sway of their husbands and in-laws. Despite these constraints, these former students have not only carried on their service activities but also interested their husbands in them.

The service activities of the "Messengers of Sathya Sai" are beyond praise. There are boy students amongst us. Of what use are they? They enjoy freedom, but are making no good use of it. They take no part in service activities. They are self-centred. But the girl students are not like that. They are not concerned about publicising themselves. To mention some of their service activities: In many small hamlets, these girls are building the roofs for the villagers' houses, working like men. They go to the foreign countries where their husbands are employed.

The annual report of the Messengers of Sathya Sai mentions that their members are rendering service in different countries like Kuwait, Australia, and New Zealand. Their varied service activities are highly commendable. I am confident that very soon their activities will cover the entire world and promote the welfare of every country. Whatever work they take up, they carry it out with firm resolve.

For instance, there are numerous primary schools in which men and women teachers work. But men teachers do not work with the same zeal and earnestness as women teachers. For one thing, women are by nature accustomed to rearing and teaching the young. The record of performance of the students is much better in schools taught by women teachers than in schools with male teachers.

Follow the women's example

For the past sixteen years, these ex-students of the Women's College have been rendering great service. For the past one week the old students present in Prashaanthi Nilayam have been eager to train themselves for security duties in the Nilayam. Male students have shown no such eagerness. It is unbecoming of men students to be indifferent to service activities. It is a pity that they have not been impelled to action although they have been listening to the reports of the services of the girls year after year.

There was an officer by name Raammohan Rao. He used to sport an impressive moustache. One day when he was going to his office, he passed by a man who was lying on the road, injured in an accident. He went on without rendering any help to the injured man, while some women rushed to his aid. In the office he reflected over his conduct and felt ashamed that he had failed to go to the help of an injured man while some women had gone to help him. Feeling that he had behaved in an unmanly way, he removed his moustache. When he went to the officers' club the next day, the members noticed the change in his face and asked him what accounted for it. He confessed that he had failed to act as a true human being and had forfeited the right to call himself a man. From that day, he dedicated his life to social service.

Service should be your watchword

All those who are in high positions will acquit themselves as true human beings only when they render selfless service to their fellow-men. Plunge yourselves in society and take part in service activities. When women are doing such splendid services, why should men lag behind? If men and women together render service, Bhaarath will be a gloriously prosperous nation. Not in Bhaarath alone, but in every country men and women should render service to those in need. Many overseas devotees here are found eating and strolling about without doing any useful work. They should shed their laziness and take part in some worthwhile activity.

Service should be your watchword. The spirit of sacrifice is essential. To speak about devotion without a spirit of sacrifice is meaningless.

Many of the women carry on their service activities inspite of the troubles which they face from their husbands. This shows their spirit of sacrifice. The Messengers of Sathya Sai are doing signal service. They need not confine themselves to their own members. They should try to draw other women into service activities and strive to improve the living conditions of the poor people in rural areas.

Follow the message of Sai

If the name of Jesus is glorified all over the world today, it is because of His boundless love. He served the lowly and the lost, and in the end, offered his life itself as a sacrifice. How many of those, who call themselves devotees of Jesus, are following His teachings? Those who claim to worship Raama, how far are they following His example? How many professed devotees of Krishna are living up to His teachings? There are many who claim to be Sai devotees. How many of them are following the message of Sai? If everyone seeks the answer within himself, he will see that it is a zero. Anyone who claims to be a Sai devotee should dedicate his life to Sai ideals. That is true devotion and real penance. That is the hall-mark of humanness. It will be reflected in love, which will find expression in compassion that generates real *Aanandha.*

The greatest quality in every man is love. When love is absent, evil qualities like hatred and jealousy rear their heads. Make love the breath of your life.

Christmas Day Discourse in the
Puurnachandhra Auditorium on 25-12-1993.

Glossary

Meanings of *Sanskrith* words used in discussing religious
and philosophical topics, more particularly used in the
discourses by Sri Sathya Sai Baba, reproduced in this
volume, are given in this glossary. While the English
equivalents for the *Sanskrith* words have been given in
the text with reference to the context, this glossary attempts
to provide comprehensive meanings and detailed
explanations of the more important *Sanskrith* words, for the
benefit of lay readers who are interested in Hindhu religion
and philosophy.

Aakaasa — Space; ether; the subtlest form of matter.

Aanandha — Divine bliss. The Self is unalloyed, eternal
bliss. Pleasures are but its faint and impermanent
shadows.

Aaraadhana — Divine service; propitiation.

Aashrama Dharma — The life of a Hindu consists of four
stages. *Aashrama Dharma* is the code of disciplines laid
down for the blossoming of spiritual consciousness

during the four stages *Brahmachaari* (the student celibate), *Grihastha* (householder), *Vaanaprastha* (the recluse in the (forest) and the *Sanyaasin* (the ascetic or the monk).

Aasthika — One who believes in God, scriptures and the *Guru.*

Aathma — Self; Soul. Self with limitations, is *jiva* (the indi-vidual soul). Self, with no limitations, is *Brahman* (the Supreme Reality).

Aathma Jnaana — Knowledge of the Self which is held out as the Supreme goal of human endeavour.

Aathmaswaruupam — Self embodied; of the nature of Self. The real man in us is the Self which is pure consciousness!

Aathma thathva — Principle of the Self; the truth or essential nature of the Self.

Abhayaswaruupam — Fearlessness embodied; of the nature of fearlessness. *Brahman* is fearless.

Adhvaitha — Non-dualism. The philosophy of absolute oneness of God, soul and Universe.

Aham Brahmaaasmi — "I am *Brahman.*" This is one of the great *Vedhic* dicta (*Mahaa Vaakyaas*).

Ahamkaara — Egotism resulting from the identification of one's self with the body. It causes the sense of "I do" and "I experience."

Ajnaana — Ignorance (which prevents perception of the Reality).

Annamaya kosha — Material or gross sheath of the soul; the physical body.

Antharyaamin — Inner Motivator or Controller. (God is thus described because He resides in all beings and controls them from within).

Archana — Ritual worship of a deity, making offerings with recitation of mantras and holy names.

Avathaar — Incarnation of God. Whenever there is a decline of *Dharma*, God comes down to the world assuming bodily form to protect the good, punish the wicked and re-establish *Dharma*. An *Avathaar* is born and lives free and is ever conscious of His mission. By His precept and example, He opens up new paths in spirituality, shedding His grace on all.

Bhaagavatham — A sacred book composed by Sage Vyaasa dealing with Vishnu and His incarnations, specially Shri Krishna.

Bhaagavath thathvam — The truth or essential nature of the Lord.

Bhajan — Congregational chant, group worship by devotees with devotional music in which repetition of holy names predominates.

Bhaktha — Principle of God head. A devotee who has intense selfless love for God.

Bhakthi — Devotion to God; intense selfless love for God.

Bhavasaagaram — Ocean of worldly life. The worldly life of a being is considered to be the ocean which he has to be cross and reach the other side of liberation from the cycle of birth and death.

Bhoga — Enjoyment; experience; the antithesis of *yoga*.

Bodha — Perception; knowledge; consciouness.

Buddhi — Intellect; intelligence; faculty of discrimination.

Brahma — The Creator; the First of Hindu Trinity.

Brahmaandam — The Cosmic egg; the Universe.

Brahmachaari — A celibate student who lives with and learns from his spiritual guide.

Brahman — The Supreme Being; the Absolute reality; Impersonal God with no form or attributes. The uncaused cause of the Universe; Existence-Consciousness-Bliss Absolute (*Sath-Chith-Aanandha*); The Eternal Changeless Reality, not conditioned by time, space and causation.

Dhama — Selfcontrol; restraining the sense organs which run after sense objects seeking pleasure. This is an important discipline for an aspirant practising *yoga*.

Dharma — Righteousness; religion; code of duties; duty; essential nature of a being or thing. It holds together the entire Universe. Man is exhorted to practise *Dharma* to achieve material and spiritual welfare. The *Vedhas* contain the roots of *Dharma*. God is naturally interested in the reigns of *Dharma*.

Dhyaana — Meditation; an unbroken flow of thought towards the object of concentration. It steadies and stills the mind and makes it fit for realisation in course of time.

Dhvaitha — Dualism; the doctrine that the individual and the Supreme Soul are two distinct principles.

Gayathri manthra — The very sacred *Vedhic* prayer for self -enlightenment repeated piously at dawn, noon and twilight devotions.

Guna — Quality; property; trait; one of the three constituents of Nature (*Sathva, Rajas and Thamas*). They bind the soul to the body. Man's supreme goal in life is to transcend the gunas and attain liberation from the cycle of birth and death.

Guru — Spiritual guide; a knower of *Brahman*, who is calm, merciful and ever ready to help and guide the spiritual aspirants who approach him.

Hirdhayaakaasha — Space in the (spiritual) heart in which the Self is imagined in meditation and prayer.

Ishta Dhevatha — The chosen deity through which a devotee contemplates on God.

Eeshvara — The Supreme Ruler; the Personal God; He is *Brahman* associated with *Maaya* but has it under His control unlike the *jeeva* who is *Maaya's* slave. He has a lovely form, auspicious attributes and infinite power to create, sustain and destroy. He dwells in the heart of every being, controlling it from within. He responds positively to true devotion and sincere prayer.

Japam — Pious repetition of holy name or sacred *manthra*, practised as a spiritual discipline.

Jeeva/Jeevaathma — The individual soul in a state of non-realisation   of its identity with *Brahman*. It is the self-deluded, bound spirit unaware of its own true nature. It is subjected to sensations of pain and pleasure, birth and death, etc.

Jnaana — Sacred knowledge; knowledge of the spirit, pursued as a means to Self-realisation. It is direct experience of God, as the Soul of the souls. *Jnaanam* makes a man omniscient, free, fearless and immortal.

Jnaani — A sage possessing *Jnaanam* (unitive spiritual knowledge and experience).

Kaarana shareeram — Casual body which carries the impressions and tendencies in seed state. It is the sheath of bliss; the innermost of the five sheaths of the soul.

Karma — Action; deed; work; religious rite; the totality of innate tendencies formed as a consequence of acts done in previous lives. Every *karma* produces a lasting impression on the mind of the doer, apart from affecting others. Repetition of a particular *karma* produces a tendency (*vaasana*) in the mind. *Karma* is of three kinds: (i) *Praarabdha* : which is being exhausted in present life, (ii) *Aagami* : which is being accumulated in the present life and (iii) *Samchitha*: which is being stored to be experienced in future lives. *Akarma* is an action done without any intention to gain the consequences; *Vikarma* is the action that is intentionally done.

Koshas — The five sheaths enclosing the soul— sheaths of bliss, intelligence, mind, vital energy and physical matter.

Kshathriya — A member of the warrior caste, one of the four social groups (*varnas*) of the Hindhu community.

Kshethra — Field; the body in which the *jieea* reaps the harvest of his *karma*.

Kshethrajna — The Knower of the field; the Spirit; the individual knowing Self.

Leela — Sport; play; the Universe is viewed as Divine sport or play.

Lingam — Sign; symbol.

Linga shareeram — The subtle body with its vital principles, subtle organs, mind, intellect and ego. When the gross body dies, the self departs, clothed in the subtle body.

Loka — Any of the 14 worlds (visible and invisible) inhabited by living beings.

Maaya — The mysterious, creative and delusive power of *Brahman* through which God projects the appearance of the Universe. *Maaya* is the material cause and *Brahman* is the efficient cause of the Universe. *Brahman* and *Maaya* are inexcritably associated with each other like fire and its power to heat. *Maaya* deludes the *Jeevas* in egoism, making them forget their true spiritual nature.

Mahaabhaaratha — The Hindhu epic composed by sage Vyaasa which deals with the deeds and fortunes of the cousins (the Kauravas and the Paandavas) of the Lunar race, with Lord Krishna playing a significant and decisive role in shaping the events. The Bhagavath Geetha and Vishnu Sahasranaama occur in this great epic. It is considered to be the fifth *Vedha* by the devout Hindhus. Of this great epic, it is claimed that "what is not in it is nowhere."

Manas — Mind, the inner organ which has four aspects: (i) *Manas* (Mind) which deliberates, desires and feels; (ii) *Buddhi* (intellect) that understands, reasons and decides; (iii) *Ahamkaara* ('I' sense) and (iv) *Chittha* (memory). The Mind with all its desires and brood, conceals the divinity within man. Purification of the Mind is essential for realisation of the Self.

Maanava — Man, descendent of *Manu*, the law-giver.

Manomaya kosha — Mental sheath. One of the five sheaths enclosing the soul. It consists of the mind and the five subtle sensory organs. It is endowed with the power of will.

Manthra — A sacred formula, music syllable or word symbol uttered during the performance of the rituals or meditation. They represent the spiritual truths directly revealed to the *Rishis* (seers). The section of the *Vedha* which contains this hymns (*manthras*) is called *Samhitha*.

Moksha/Mukthi — Liberation from all kinds of bondage, especially one to the cycle of birth and death. It is a state of absolute freedom, peace and bliss, attained through Self-realisation. This is the supreme goal of human endeavour, the other three being, *dharma* (righteousness), *artha* (wealth and power) and *kaama* (sense pleasure).

Naamasmarana — Remembering God through His name; one of the important steps of spiritual discipline (*saadhana*) to obtain God's grace and to make progress in the spiritual journey.

Nidhidhyaasana — Concentration of the truth about the Self after hearing it (*sravana*) from the *guru* and reflecting on it (*manana*). It is thus the third step on the path of knowledge (*Jnaana Yoga*).

Nivritthi Maarga — The path of renunciation that demands giving up desires and concentrating on god. The *Upanishaths* which form the *Jnaana Kaanda* (the section dealing with unitive spiritual knowledge) of the *Vedhas*, deal with this path. This path is opposed to the *pravritthi maarga* (the path of desire) which worldly men pursue, seeking the good things here and hereafter.

Praanamaya kosha — Sheath of vital energy. It consists of five vital principles and five subtle organs of action. It is endowned with the power of action.

Prakrithi — Nature; the Divine Power of Becoming; also known as *Maaya, Avidhya* and *Shakthi*; the world of matter and mind as opposed to the Spirit. *Prakrithi* has three dispositions or *gunas (sathva, rajas and thamas)* that go into the makeup of all living and nonliving beings in the Universe, in varying proportions leading to the appearance of infinite multiplicity in form, nature and behaviour.

Pranava — *Om*; the sacred seed sound and symbol of *Brahman*; "the most exalted syllable in *Vedhas*." It is used in meditation on God. It is uttered first before a *Vedic* mantra is chanted.

Prema — Ecstatic love of God; (the divine love of the most intense kind).

Puuja — Ritual worship in which a deity is invoked in an idol or picture and propitiated as a Royal guest with offerings of flowers, fruits and other eatables along with recitation of appropriate manthras and show of relevant signs.

Puraanas — The Hindu *Shasthras* (scriptures) in which *Vedhic* truths are illustrated through tales of divine incarnations and heroes. Sage Vyaasa is believed to have written them. Of the 18 *Puraanas*, Srimath *Bhaagavatha* is best known.

Raamaayana — This sacred Hindhu epic composed by sage Vaalmeeki deals with the incarnation of Vishnu as Shri Raama who strove all his life to reestablish the reign of *Dharma* in the world. The *Raamaayana* has played a very important role in influencing and shaping the Hindu ethos over the centuries.

Rajas/Rajo Guna — One of the three *gunas* (qualities or dispositions) of *Maaya* or *Prakrithi*. *Rajas* is the quality of passion, energy, restlessness, attachment and extroversion. It results in pain.

Saadhana — Spiritual discipline or effort aimed at God realisa-tion. The *saadhaka* (aspirant) uses the spiritual discipline to attain the goal of realisation.

Samaadhi — It is the superconscious state transcending the body, mind and intellect, attained through rigorous and protracted *Saadhana*. In that state of consciousness, the objective world and the ego vanish and the Reality is perceived or communed with, in utter peace and bliss. When in this state the aspirant realises his oneness with God, it is called *Nirvikalpa Samaadhi.*

Samsaara — Worldly life; life of the *jeeva* through repeated births and deaths. Liberation means getting freed from this cycle.

Sanaathana Dharma — Eternal religion. A descriptive term to what has come to be called Hindhuism. It has no single founder or text of its own. It is more a commonwealth of religious faiths and a way of life.

Saamanya Dharma — Code of conduct common to all persons in any one social group.

Shaasthras — The Hindhu scriptures containing the teach-ings of the *Rishis*. The *Vedhas*, the *Upanishaths* and the *Itihaasas* (epics), the *Puraanas* and the *Smrithis* (codes of conduct), etc, form the *Shaastrhas* of the Hindhus. They teach us how to live wisely and well with all the tenderness and concern of the Mother.

Sathva — One of the three *gunas* (qualities and dispositions) of *Maaya* or *Prakrithi*. It is the quality of purity, brightness, peace and harmony. It leads to knowledge. Man is exhorted to overcome *thamas* by *rajas*, and *rajas* by *sathva* and finally to go beyond *sathva* itself to attain liberation.

Sthitha prajna — A man of realisation with a steady, tranquil and cheerful mind ever dwelling on God. He is a man of selfcontrol, evenminded in all circumstances and totally free from all selfish desires. After death he attains freedom from *Samsaara.*

Svadharma — One's *dharma* or duty that accords with one's nature. This is an important concept in the Geetha.

Thaapam — Pain, misery; distress caused by three types of agencies (*thaapathrayam*). The agencies are *aadhyaathmika* (diseases and disturbances of body and mind); *aadhi bhowthika* (other beungs); and *aadhi* *dheiveekam* (supernatural agencies like storm, floods, earthquakes, planets, etc).

Thamas — One of the *gunas* (qualities or dispositions) of *Maaya* or *Prakrithi*. It is the quality of dulness, inertia, darkness and tendency to evil. It results in ignorance.

Upaasana — Worship or contemplation of God.

Upanishath — The very sacred portion of the *Vedhas* that deal with God, man and universe, their nature and interrelationships. Spiritual knowledge (*jnaana*) is their content. So they form the *Jnaana Kanda* of the *Vedhas*.

Vairaagya — Detachment; desire and ability to give up all transitory enjoyments.

Varna Dharma — The Hindu community is divided into four *varnas* (social groups), based on gunas and vocations. *Brahmana* (the custodian of spiritual and moral role), *Kshathriya* (the warrior group which rules and defends the land), *Vaishya* (the group dealing with commerce, business and trade, *Shudhra* (the group devoted to labour and service to the community). Each *varna* has its own *dharma* (*varna dharma*), restrictions and regulations which strive to canalise his impulses and instinct into fields that are special to his place in society, controls pertaining to the duties cast upon.

Vedha — The oldest and the holiest of the Hindhu scriptures, the primary source of authority in the Hindhu religion and philosophy. They are four in number—the *Rig Vedha, Saama Vedha, Yajur Vedha* and *Atharva Vedha*.

Vedhaantha — Means the "end of the *Vedhas*." It is the essence of the *Vedhas* enshrined in the *Upanishaths*. The philosophy of non-dualism, or qualified non-dualism, or dualism based on the *Upanishathik* teachings, is denoted by this term.

Vishesha Dharma — Code of conduct to be observed in special situations; obligations to be discharged on special occasions, or when faced with special situations.

Vijnaanamaya kosha — One of the five *koshas* (sheaths) of the soul. It consists of intellect and the five subtle sense organs. It is endowed with the power to know. The "I" or subject of experience or action is seated here.

Viveka — Discrimination; the reasoning by which one realises what is real and permanent and what is non-real and impermanent.

Vriththi Dharma — The moral code that regulates and enriches a person's profession.

Yajna — A *Vedhic* rite or sacrifice. Any self-denying act of service in the name of God.

Yoga — Union with God, as also the path by which this union of the soul with God is achieved. The four important parts of *Yoga* are that of knowledge, action, meditation and devotion.

SRI SATHYA SAI BOOKS AND PUBLICATIONS TRUST

PRASHAANTHI NILAYAM PIN: 515134,
ANANTAPUR DISTRICT, ANDHRA PRADESH, INDIA
IMPORTER/EXPORTER CODE NO. 0990001032
RESERVE BANK OF INDIA EXPORTER CODE NO.HS–2001198

OUR CLASSICS IN ENGLISH

THE VAAHINI SERIES: *(Books written by Bhagavan Sri Sathya Sai Baba)*
Bhagavatha Vaahini *(The Story of the Glory of the Lord)* 25-00
Dharma Vaahini *(The Path of Virtue and Morality)* 12-00
Dhyana Vaahini *(The Practice of Meditation)* 12-00
Geetha Vaahini *(The Divine Gospel)* 22-00
Jnana Vaahini *(The Stream of Eternal Wisdom)* 12-00
Leela Kaivalya Vaahini *(The Cosmic Play of God)* 12-50
Prashaanthi Vaahini *(The Bliss of the Supreme Peace)* 12-00
Prasnothara Vaahini *(Answers to Spiritual Questions)* 15-00
Prema Vaahini *(The Stream of Divine Love)* 17-00
Rama Katha Rasa Vaahini–Part I 38-00
    (The Sweet Story of Rama's Glory)
Rama Katha Rasa Vaahini–Part II 28-00
    The Sweet Story of Rama's Glory)
Sandeha Nivarini *(Clearance of Spiritual Doubts)* 16-00
Sathya Sai Vaahini *(Spiritual Message of Sri Sathya Sai)* 26-00
Sutra Vaahini *(Analytical Aphorism on Supreme Reality)* 16-00
Upanishad Vaahini *(Essence of Vedic Knowledge)* 17-50
Vidya Vaahini *(Flow of Spiritual Education)* 11-00

SATHYA SAI SPEAKS SERIES: *(Discourses by Bhagavan Sri Sathya Sai Baba) (Revised and Enlarged Editions).*

Sathya Sai Speaks Vol. I	Years 1953 to 1960	30-00
Sathya Sai Speaks Vol. II	Years 1961 to 1962	38-00
Sathya Sai Speaks Vol. III	Year 1963	35-00
Sathya Sai Speaks Vol. IV	Year 1964	34-50
Sathya Sai Speaks Vol. V	Year 1965	43-00
Sathya Sai Speaks Vol. VI	Year 1966	45-00
Sathya Sai Speaks Vol. VII	Year 1967	47-00
Sathya Sai Speaks Vol. VIII	Year 1968	26-00
Sathya Sai Speaks Vol. IX	Year 1969	28-50
Sathya Sai Speaks Vol. X	Year 1970	36-50
Sathya Sai Speaks Vol. XI	Years 1971 to 1972	51-00
Sathya Sai Speaks Vol. XII	Years 1973 to 1974	36-00

SATHYAM SIVAM SUNDARAM SERIES:
(Life Story of Bhagavan Sri Sathya Sai Baba)

SUMMER SHOWER SERIES: *(Discourses on Indian Culture and Spirituality by Bhagavan Sri Sathya Sai Baba)*

CHILDREN'S BOOKS:

OUR OTHER PUBLICATIONS:

INLAND/OVERSEAS BOOK ORDERS & SUBSCRIPTION FOR MONTHLY MAGAZINE SANATHANA SARATHI

Books are despatched by Regd. Book Post only subject to availability. Indents and remittences within India should be received by Money Order/Indian Postal Order/Account Payee Cheques/Bank Drafts.

REMITTANCES

Remittances from Overseas towards Book Orders/Sanathana Sarathi Subscriptions (English & Telugu) can be sent by A/C payee Cheque/

Demand Draft/International Money Order in **FOREIGN CURRENCY ONLY AND NOT IN INDIAN RUPEES.** Sending Cash Currency is liable to be confiscated by Government.

All remittances should be in favour of **THE CONVENOR, SRI SATHYA SAI BOOKS & PUBLICATIONS TRUST, PRASHAANTHI NILAYAM, ANANTHAPUR DISTRICT, ANDHRA PRADESH, INDIA, PIN CODE - 515 134,** payable at State Bank of India, Prashaanthi Nilayam (Branch Code No. 2786) mentioning full address in capitals with Area Pin Code. Zip Code No., where the books are to be despatched.

POSTAGE (INLAND)

At the rate of 50 paise per 100grams plus Registration Charges Rs.10/. For an order of 1 kg parcel, postage Rs.5/- (+) Regn. Charges Rs.10/- ; total Rs.15/-. For 2 kgs parcel Rs.20/- ; For 3 kgs parcels Rs. 25/-; For 4 kgs parcel Rs.30/- and for 5 kgs parcel Rs. 35/-.

While remitting, Please calculate cost of the Books indented (+) postage (+) Registration charges.

POSTAGE (OVERSEAS)

1 Kg Parcel Rs. 60/-

2 Kg Parcel Rs. 78/-

3 Kg Parcel Rs. 110/-

4 Kg Parcel Rs. 140/-

5 Kg Parcel Rs. 172/-

* Packing & Forwarding charges Rs. 20/- extra.

***

NOTES

NOTES

NOTES

NOTES

NOTES

NOTES

NOTES